38.80

Alamance Community College
Library
P.O. Box 8000
Graham, NC 27253

D1432699

Alamance Community College
Library
P.O. Box 8000
Graham, NC 27253

About Island Press

Since 1984, the nonprofit Island Press has been stimulating, shaping, and communicating the ideas that are essential for solving environmental problems worldwide. With more than 800 titles in print and some 40 new releases each year, we are the nation's leading publisher on environmental issues. We identify innovative thinkers and emerging trends in the environmental field. We work with world-renowned experts and authors to develop cross-disciplinary solutions to environmental challenges.

Island Press designs and implements coordinated book publication campaigns in order to communicate our critical messages in print, in person, and online using the latest technologies, programs, and the media. Our goal: to reach targeted audiences—scientists, policymakers, environmental advocates, the media, and concerned citizens—who can and will take action to protect the plants and animals that enrich our world, the ecosystems we need to survive, the water we drink, and the air we breathe.

Island Press gratefully acknowledges the support of its work by the Agua Fund, Inc., The Margaret A. Cargill Foundation, Betsy and Jesse Fink Foundation, The William and Flora Hewlett Foundation, The Kresge Foundation, The Forrest and Frances Lattner Foundation, The Andrew W. Mellon Foundation, The Curtis and Edith Munson Foundation, The Overbrook Foundation, The David and Lucile Packard Foundation, The Summit Foundation, Trust for Architectural Easements, The Winslow Foundation, and other generous donors.

The opinions expressed in this book are those of the author(s) and do not necessarily reflect the views of our donors.

Alamance Community College
Library
P.O. Box 8000
Graham, NC 27253

FUNDAMENTALS OF SUSTAINABLE DWELLINGS

FUNDAMENTALS OF SUSTAINABLE DWELLINGS

AVI FRIEDMAN

ISLANDPRESS

WASHINGTON | COVELO | LONDON

© 2012 Avi Friedman

All rights reserved under International and Pan-American Copyright Conventions.
No part of this book may be reproduced in any form or by any means
without permission in writing from the publisher:
Island Press, Suite 300, 1718 Connecticut Ave., NW, Washington, DC 20009.

ISLAND PRESS is a trademark of the Center for Resource Economics.

Library of Congress Cataloging-in-Publication Data

Friedman, Avi, 1952-
    Fundamentals of sustainable dwellings / Avi Friedman.
        p. cm.
    Includes bibliographical references and index.
    ISBN-13: 978-1-59726-807-3 (cloth : alk. paper)
    ISBN-10: 1-59726-807-0 (cloth : alk. paper)
    ISBN-13: 978-1-59726-808-0 (pbk. : alk. paper)
    ISBN-10: 1-59726-808-9 (pbk. : alk. paper) 1. Ecological houses-
-Design and construction. I. Title.
    TH4860.F679 2012
    690'.8047--dc23

                                                        2011038481

Printed using Eldora Text and ITC Officina Sans

Text design by Joan Wolbier
Typesetting by Joan Wolbier
Printed on recycled, acid-free paper

Manufactured in the United States of America
10 9 8 7 6 5 4 3 2 1

Keywords: aging in place, climate change, cradle-to-cradle design, daylighting, edible landscapes, energy
conservation, energy-efficient windows, geothermal energy, green roofs, green building, greywater harvesting
and recycling, indoor air quality (IAQ), insulation, LEED, life cycle assessment, live-work dwellings, low-
emissivity glass, modular design, multi-generational living, prefabrication, radiant heating/cooling, solar energy,
sustainable design, USGBC, waste management, water conservation, Xeriscaping

CONTENTS

PREFACE

Current modes of dwelling design face challenges of both philosophy and form. Over the past half century, homes and communities have been built with disregard for nature while exhausting resources during construction and occupancy. Society also faces mounting economic challenges, forcing the need for solutions with smaller price tags. Demographic and cultural transformations led by a large elderly population require designers to conceive of housing prototypes that respond innovatively to new users and fluctuating trends.

Sustainable is a term that best captures these new sought-after directions. The thrust of sustainable thinking in its most rudimentary form is that one needs to regard the future consequences of present actions. We can no longer assume that wealth, be it monetary or natural, will last forever. Polluting air, water, or soil will have lasting consequences and can drive flora and fauna to extinction.

A call to adopt sustainable practices is not new. Background theories and principles have been articulated over the past decades. Yet, their application has been slow in coming, in spite of the urgent need for change. Policy makers and practitioners are wrapping their minds around the fact that society has passed a point of no return. Old ways are beginning to give way to new approaches.

The building profession is no exception. In North America, during construction the built environment consumes some 40 percent of all natural resources used, and when occupied, 30 percent of all energy consumed. Since residential construction traditionally accounts for about 35 percent of all building activity, it is evident that homes make significant contributions to the consumption of resources and energy. It has, therefore, become clear that the design of tomorrow's dwellings must employ a new thought process, and their construction, a different practice. The level of resources consumed in the building and use of a structure must be considered at every stage of its conception and construction. It also needs to be designed to accommodate transformation once the useful life of its components comes to an end. In addition, a new partnership must be forged between homes and their surrounding natural environment. Topography, water streams, flora, and fauna should be preserved once the decision to build has been made. Designers and developers are recognizing that building with nature can be an asset rather than a hindrance.

This book takes part in charting a new course in residential design. It considers the delicate relationship between the home and the natural environment and provides the basic knowledge necessary to create a livable, sustainable, healthy home. The options for choosing materials, location, and design can be daunting. For example, certain materials, like aluminum, consume large amounts of energy in their manufacturing and processing, yet their use requires little maintenance throughout their life cycles. This book will help you navigate the increasingly complex world of residential green building. It combines successful existing principles with new ones and highlights commonsense ideas that have too often been overlooked. Offering ideas cannot be complete without illustrating them with applications. Each chapter features a contemporary project whose designers strove to achieve sustainability while adhering to real-world constraints.

The chapters have been arranged to walk the reader systematically through the design and construction stages.

Chapter 1 describes basic principles of sustainability, available resources, and common green-building certification methods.

Chapter 2 discusses key planning considerations in siting a home, including climate, passive solar gain, wind direction, and preservation of flora, fauna, and topography.

Prior to delving into the more technical aspects of home design, chapter 3 stresses that sustainable solutions are not necessarily only technological. The chapter illustrates several concepts that focus on social, economic, and cultural aspects, such as "aging in place" and "multigenerational living."

Chapter 4 discusses unit-planning principles of a general nature. Shape, overall size, height, and relation to other units and interior spatial organization are elaborated.

In chapter 5, the design of an improved building envelope is discussed, as well as efficient framing, construction details, and prefabrication.

In chapter 6, an examination of building materials shows how to evaluate their sustainability through a step-by-step process.

Chapter 7 focuses on energy-efficient windows to provide a guideline for their selection and installation.

Chapter 8 reviews various heating and cooling systems to point out their efficiency and constraints.

Chapter 9 examines aspects related to indoor air quality and suggests alternative design strategies and products that can reduce harmful emissions while improving comfort.

Chapter 10 looks into water efficiency. It examines sources of water consumption and suggests various strategies for their management.

Designing green roofs is the topic of chapter 11. It offers classifications and examines their benefits, construction principles, and applications.

Chapter 12 examines alternative landscaping methods. Edible landscapes and xeriscaping are the topics of study here, along with principles and applications.

Finally, chapter 13 discusses sustainable waste management and disposal to point out methods of composting and recycling, among others.

Sustainability in the residential environment is likely to be achieved when a comprehensive approach to design that includes many of the above-noted subjects is taken. Yet, considering and applying all of these aspects may not be feasible for all projects. Applying some of these aspects will no doubt stand to make a difference as well.

ACKNOWLEDGEMENTS

The study of the subjects outlined in the book and their application spans several years and involves many people who have contributed to generating and articulating these ideas. My thanks to them all and apologies to those whose names I accidentally omitted.

A report called *"Greening" the Grow Home*, which was funded by the Canada Mortgage and Housing Corporation, planted the seed and laid the foundation for the writing of this book. The research team included Vince Cammalleri, Jim Nicell, Francois Dufaux, Joanne Green, Susan Fisher, Aud Koht, Kevin Lee, Aryan Lirange, Denis Palin, Mark Somers, Nicola Bullock, and Michelle Takoff.

Additional background research and contribution to the information and the writing assembled here were made by Thi Ngoc Diem Nguyen and Linda Zhang, whose dedication and hard work are truly appreciated. Stephanie Huss researched and contributed to the Sustainable Residential Design Concepts chapter and its figures. Nancy Serag-Eldin offered highly valued constructive criticism, proofreading, verification and updating of the accuracy of the data, and ideas for the figures. Rainier Silva contributed to the research and conception of the figures in the Healthy Indoor Environments chapter, and Maria Garcia to the Building Materials chapter.

Ji (Cayte) Yeon Kim coordinated the case-studies part of each chapter. She obtained information, organized it meticulously, and redrew some of the drawings displayed here. Her attention to accuracy and quality is much appreciated.

Special thanks to Elisa Costa, who patiently and with utmost dedication drew most of the figures in the book. Elisa's work complemented work done by Jeff Jerome.

Special thanks is extended to Nyd Garavito-Bruhn. Nyd's hard work and dedication in organizing the data and providing editorial comments and touching up all the figures were vital to the production of this volume.

To all the architectural firms who graciously agreed to let us use their work and to the photographers who took the photos, thank you. Their names are listed at the end of the book.

To the Faculty of Engineering at McGill University and the Summer Undergraduate Research in Engineering (SURE) grant program who, for two years, supported the work of some of the research team members—many thanks. Also, much appreciation to the McGill School of Architecture for offering an environment where many of the thoughts expressed here have been developed and articulated.

To Heather Boyer, a senior editor at Island Press, who saw the value in having such a book, and Courtney Lix and Sharis Simonian who shepherded this book to publication, many thanks.

This vote of thanks will not be complete without embracing my family, Sorel Friedman, PhD, Paloma, who proofread the text, and Ben. Endless thanks for your love and understanding.

CHAPTER 1

Principles of Sustainable Dwellings

The limits of our environment, and how we have pushed those limits, are perhaps more apparent today than they ever have been. A growing awareness of the finite nature of energy and other resources has led more people to think of sustainability as a plus. The desire for environmental sustainability, along with today's economic climate, has homeowners looking for alternatives to large, expensive, and expensive-to-maintain dwellings. Prior to introducing key components below, this chapter deals with overarching issues. Causes of global and local trends are discussed, sustainability principles illustrated, various resources categorized, and certification methods listed.

GLOBAL AND LOCAL TRENDS

New design practices have emerged in reaction to local and global trends. Understanding these trends is vital to the selection of appropriate strategies and solutions. Some of the most acute issues affecting the built residential environment, and principles to help in addressing them, are elaborated in the sections that follow.

Population Growth and Energy Consumption

In 2007, the Intergovernmental Panel on Climate Change (IPCC) published a report that addressed the role of humans in climate change. Among other things, they found that "global GHG emissions due to human activities have grown since pre-industrial times, with an increase of 70% between 1970 and 2004" (International Energy Agency 2008). The residential sector in the developed world is known to be the third-largest contributor to greenhouse gas (GHG) emissions, preceded by the industrial and transportation sectors. In 2005, for example, the residential sector of the Organization for Economic Cooperation and Development (OECD) countries contributed 21 percent of the total direct and indirect carbon dioxide emissions, totaling 23.1 gigatons (21 gigatonnes), as shown in figure 1.1 (International Energy Agency 2008).

Demand for energy is also growing rapidly. Between 1990 and 2005, consumption in OECD countries increased by 23 percent and electricity use by 54 percent (In-

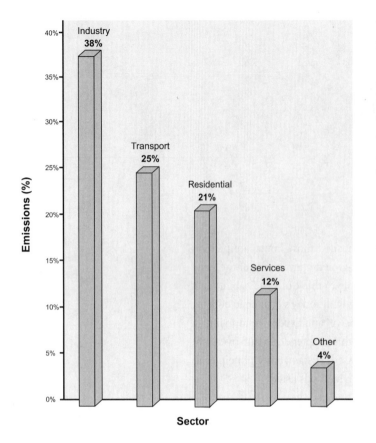

FIGURE 1.1 Carbon dioxide emissions by sector for OECD countries in 2005.

ternational Energy Agency 2008). In 2008, the residential sector of the United States consumed 21,635 trillion Btu (2.2826×10^{13} kJ), a staggering growth from the 14,930 trillion Btu (1.5751×10^{13} kJ) consumed in 1973 (US EIA 2009). Although efforts are being put forth to increase efficiency in energy creation, delivery, and use, it has become abundantly clear that further steps will have to be taken to encourage residential concepts that conserve natural resources and energy.

The global energy consumption increase can be attributed to several factors, including population growth and expanding home size. The US population grew by 30 percent to reach 300 million in 2005, up from 228 million in 1980 (US DOE 2009). The increase led to growth in the number of families and individuals seeking a shelter, which expanded the number of homes and, consequently, energy demand. In addition, the average household size shrank. There are simply more single-occupancy homes and apartments consuming energy. The number of households grew by 40 percent between 1980 and 2005, rising to 113 million from 80 million, which is significantly greater than the 30 percent population increase for the same period (US DOE 2009) (fig. 1.2). The average size of a North American home also grew along with the population and number of households. Increasing home size is regarded as the leading factor affecting the need for space heating, the

FIGURE 1.2 Population and household increase in the United States illustrating greater growth in dwelling units than population over the same period.

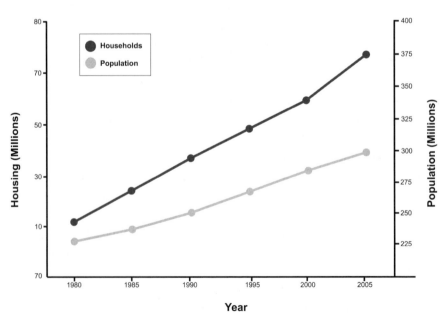

largest energy consumer in the residential sector, as shown in figure 1.3.

Another rapidly growing energy consumer is household appliances. Because of their growing use, they are considered the second-largest household consumer, surpassing water heating. From 1990 to 2005 the energy consumption of appliances grew by 57 percent because of an increased number of large appliances per household and a variety of new smaller ones, as illustrated in figure 1.4 (International Energy Agency 2008). The use of Energy Star–certified appliances helped lower consumption, yet these savings were offset by the introduction of new gadgets such as high-energy-consuming LCD flat-screen TVs.

Wood-Frame Construction

Energy consumption is not the only environmental concern related to the development of homes and communities. Ubiquitous low-rise single-family wood-frame construction consumes a large amount of solid sawn lumber and therefore puts an increasing strain on forests and the environment. This dwelling type is addressed in this book since it constitutes some 65 percent of all residences built in North America. An acre (0.4 hectares) of forest is consumed to manufacture lumber for the construction of a single 1,700 sq ft (153 m^2) dwell-

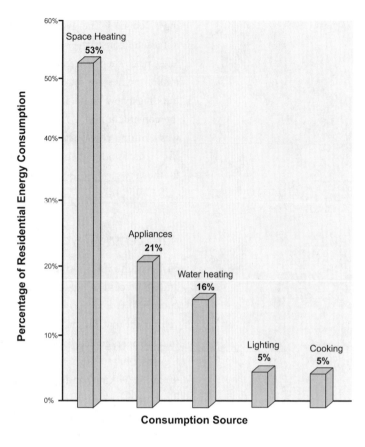

FIGURE 1.3 Residential energy consumption in the United States by source.

FIGURE 1.4 Growth of residential equipment and appliances in the United States by type.

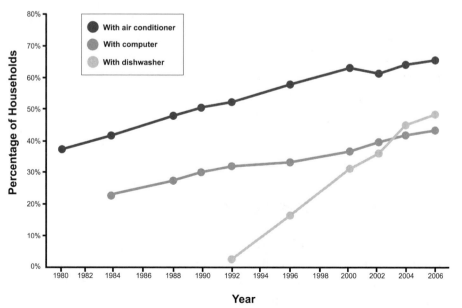

ing (Nebraska Energy Office 2006). Since approximately 2 million new wood-frame homes are constructed annually, 2 million acres (0.8 million hectares) of deforestation takes place each year in the United States and Canada alone (US DOE 2009). Also, 27 million homes are retrofitted each year. While renovation consumes less lumber than building a new home, it still greatly contributes to extensive use of lumber. Additionally, the construction of a 2,000 sq ft (180 m^2) house will produce 8,000 lb (3.6 tonnes) of waste during construction alone. Of this waste, 25 percent is solid sawn lumber while 15 percent is other manufactured wood products. Furthermore, if demolition is required for the very same house, the amount of waste increases to 127 tons (115 tonnes) per home (US DOE 2009; US EPA 1997).

Auto-Centric Development

In 2005, the transportation sector contributed 26 percent of the total energy demand and 25 percent of the total direct and indirect carbon dioxide emissions of the OECD countries. A large portion of this consumption can be attributed to low-density development that requires extensive use of private cars. The US Census Bureau found that the average daily commute time to and from work in 2003 was 48.6 minutes (US Census Bureau 2009). Assuming that the vehicle is traveling at an average speed of 40 mph (64 kmh) and gets 20 mpg (8.45 km/L) of gasoline, the vehicle would travel 32.4 mi (52.1 km) daily, consuming 1.62 gallons (6.13 L) and emitting 31.69 lb (14.37 kg) of carbon dioxide per day. When a dwelling is sited within walking distance of amenities or when public transit is used, emissions are significantly reduced. In the Chicago metropolitan region, for example, households that live within a half mile of public transportation emit 43 percent less auto-related GHGs than those that reside farther away. Residents who live downtown, with the highest concentration of transit, jobs, housing, retail, and services, have 78 percent lower emissions. Furthermore, if sprawl continues to expand at the present rate, by 2030 its associated 60 percent rise of vehicle miles driven will completely negate progress made from efficient cars and low-carbon fuels (Hodges 2010).

In addition, a 2010 report by the US Department of Transportation has, upon rigorous examination of transit-related research, identified that public transportation can reduce GHGs in three principal ways: providing low-emission alternatives to driving; facilitating compact land use, which reduces the need for longer trips; and minimizing the carbon footprint of transit operations and construction (Hodges 2010).

PRINCIPLES OF SUSTAINABLE SYSTEMS

There are several perspectives on sustainability, each with its own importance to the environment, society, culture, and the economy. From an environmental perspective, for instance, every decision should be based on concerns for nature. In the private sector, meanwhile, decisions may be based on preventing the transfer of costs resulting from today's bad decisions to future generations. The author's perspective, however, is that the four fundamental aspects need to be given equal weight.

A sustainable built environment will result from overlapping these four issues, as shown in figure 1.5. The purpose of this book is to provoke and suggest new approaches to designing and building dwellings that are more sustainable and affordable.

The current, mainstream practices of dwelling design and construction need, in the author's view, to be reconsidered. The three general principles that are shown in figure 1.6 can illustrate the process. When followed, they can guide the building of sustainable homes and communities.

The Path of Least Negative Impact

Development should follow the principle of *the path of least negative impact*. This principle argues for the least short- and long-term damage to the environment, society, and the economy.

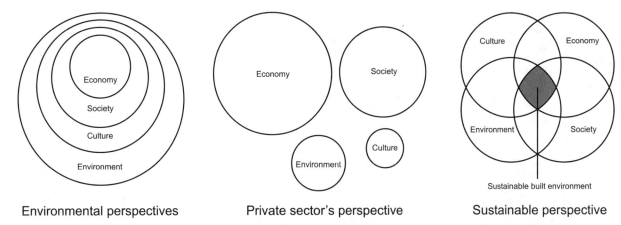

FIGURE 1.5 The various perspectives of sustainability. The built environment is the outcome of equal consideration of all four issues.

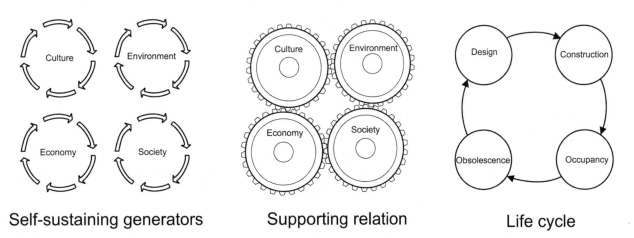

FIGURE 1.6 Principles of sustainable systems.

Self-Sustaining Process

Ideally a dwelling will be part of a *self-sustaining process* and will not need to draw extensively from external sources. Energy needs can, for instance, be supplied by photovoltaic panels, which can power appliances, and by solar collectors that can heat water. Additionally, if excess energy is produced, it can be used for communal needs and to power streetlights. Similarly, a self-sustaining water source can be obtained through the collection and purification of rainwater and the integration of a gray-water recycling system. This will help reduce the amount of energy used on public water purification.

Supporting Relationship

If one component of sustainability can positively affect another, then a *supporting relationship* will be formed. As more relationships emerge, a network will begin to develop. A dwelling that uses low-cost recycled materials, for example, not only helps the environment but becomes affordable to a wider range of consumers, leading to societal equity—a fundamental pillar of sustainability. Its "green" image may also turn out to be a marketing draw, as demonstrated in figure 1.7.

FIGURE 1.7 The integration of environmentally friendly features in the design of the EcoResidence housing in Lancaster University, UK, that was designed by the firm GWP attracted students to the institution.

A Life-Cycle Approach

A dwelling is constantly evolving to accommodate the needs of its occupants. A dwelling that can be refurbished to extend its life is more sustainable than one that has a finite life. The home's design concept, therefore, ought to include adaptability to emerging circumstances. If a home is well built, the owner will save on maintenance and operational expenses during occupancy. These savings can be invested in new eco-friendly technologies. Additionally, the home can be designed to be adaptable to the needs of various occupants and be retrofitted rather than demolished.

RESOURCES

The proper management of resources is a key to sustainability. New eco-friendly technologies and products that rely on renewable resources are becoming common in initial construction and renovation.

Resources can be categorized in three groups: renewable, nonrenewable that can be recycled, and nonrenewable that cannot be recycled. *Renewable resources* are those that have the ability to replenish themselves through naturally occurring processes. Examples are water, air, and organic matter such as food and timber. Examples of *renewable energy* sources include tidal energy, geothermal systems, solar power, biomass, wind energy, and hydroelectric power (fig. 1.8). The natural replenishment of renewable resources may take centuries for some materials and millennia for others. Some can, however, be collected after use and recycled, which will be elaborated below.

Nonrenewable resources that *cannot* be recycled include all fossil fuels, such as coal, oil, and natural gas, which are not replenished by nature over a millennium. In 1993, Buchholz suggested that the quantity of fossil fuels used annually would take nature a million years to replenish. Moreover, when fossil fuels are used, they are burned and cannot be collected for recycling, creating significant pollution. Nonrenewable resources that *can* be recycled are all pure metals and metal alloys (e.g., aluminum, steel, copper) and petroleum-based products such as plastics.

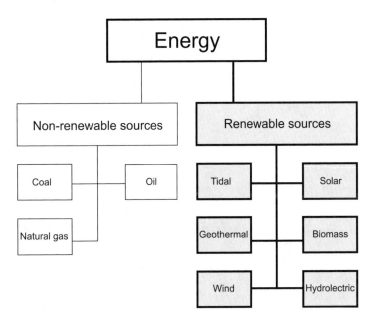

FIGURE 1.8 Non-renewable and renewable energy sources.

CERTIFICATIONS OF SUSTAINABLE PRACTICES

In recent decades, governments, construction associations, and nongovernmental organizations around the world have set standards for sustainable building practices. Green building movements are thriving in many countries, with significant effect on education and construction practices. Innovative approaches to residential design, such as passive and net-zero homes, are recasting the way design is conceived, with the intention to reduce to minimum the environmental footprint of dwellings. In addition to national building codes, which established minimum requirements for energy performance, the new standards address other criteria for a higher level of efficiency. In recent decades agencies and rating systems have been established to foster greater environmental awareness and streamline evaluation criteria. Some of the more established ones are BREEAM (originally from building research establishment environmental assessment method) in the United Kingdom, the HQE (Haute Qualité Environnementale) standard in France, and Green Star from the Green Building Council in Australia. Other notable institutions include the Passivhaus Institut in Germany and the World Green Building Council, which is a union of national councils.

The US Green Building Council (USGBC) is the nation's leader in the promotion of environmental responsibility. The agency established the Leadership in Energy and Environmental Design (LEED) Green Building Rating System, which became a nationally accepted benchmark for the design, construction, and operation of high-performance green buildings. The method has also been extended to Canada. It includes ratings for new construction, existing buildings, interiors, and schools, as well as homes and neighborhoods, which will be outlined below. The LEED standard is divided into several categories with prerequisites and additional credits. Points are accumulated for each satisfied requirement, and certification is given once a minimum specified number of points are acquired. Depending on how many points the building is awarded, it can be considered LEED platinum, gold, silver, or certified.

LEED for Homes

The LEED for Homes (LEED-H) standard initially focused on construction of new single-family homes but eventually expanded to include low-rise multifamily housing. Both types of housing are addressed in this book. Categories and credits were adapted to the residential sphere and are similar to those for LEED for New Construction. They concern construction, design, and site aspects specific to the house (USGBC 2007).

The *location and linkages* category recommends that the home be sited in a community that fulfills requirements similar to those of a LEED neighborhood. The location should be served by existing or adjacent infrastructure, developments should be compact and efficient, and the community should be equipped with services such as banks, convenience stores, post offices, pharmacies, and schools, to encourage walking.

The goal of the *sustainable sites* category is to encourage responsible site development that minimizes ecological impacts as well as the effects on the environment as a whole. Landscape features that reduce the need for irrigation and synthetic chemicals should be used, and paved areas such as sidewalks, driveways, and patios can be shaded with trees and shrubs. To reduce unnecessary consumption of potable water, rainwater collection and gray-water reuse are recommended. Where irrigation is necessary, highly efficient systems are a must. In terms of indoor water use, low-flow faucets and shower-heads are recommended, as are dual-flush toilets.

For desired *indoor air quality*, LEED-H recommends the use of the Energy Star Indoor Air Package, which includes ventilation systems, source control, and air removal. Other equivalent systems may also be used to regulate indoor humidity levels, air distribution, and air filtering. The USGBC also offers recommendations for local exhaust systems for kitchens and bathrooms.

The *materials and resources* section of LEED-H recommends the use of recycled and local materials and "environmentally friendly" products. It goes a step further by providing guidelines for appropriate sizing of homes. Based on the number of bedrooms, usually a good indicator of the number of residents in a home, square-footage recommendations are provided for the home's floor area.

In the *energy and atmosphere* section, once again the Energy Star package is recommended. The house should be well insulated, with efficient windows, minimal air leakage from ducts, highly efficient space heating and cooling, and an efficient water heating and distribution system. Outdoor lighting fixtures should have motion sensors to minimize use, and indoor lighting, as well as appliances, should be highly efficient. Installing renewable energy sources such as wind generators and photovoltaic panels is encouraged, and points are allocated for each 10 percent of annual electrical load met by the system. Finally, homeowners should receive a user manual and a 60-minute walk-through of their new home to provide them with the necessary information for proper operation. For the design of a green home to be effective, its features must be used correctly and efficiently.

These subjects will be further explained and elaborated in the following chapters.

LEED-ND: Neighborhood Development

LEED for Neighborhood Development (LEED-ND) seeks to create environmentally responsible communities that protect and enhance overall health, natural environment, and quality of life. LEED-ND seeks to aid in the design of neighborhoods that promote efficient use of energy and water (USGBC 2007). Some of its components are listed below.

The *location efficiency* category examines the relationship between a site and its surroundings. The first prerequisite is access to efficient modes of transportation that promote pedestrian activity and use of public transit. Neighborhoods should be well connected to reduce reliance on cars. The second prerequisite is proximity to existing water and storm-water sources necessary to conserve resources and minimize new infrastructure. Additional points are allotted for projects that plan to rectify contaminated land and/or infill projects.

Several prerequisites stipulate that public parkland and farmland must be preserved. The siting of a project may not be such that it poses a threat to animals on the endangered species list or threatens the presence of existing bodies of water or wetlands. Finally, an erosion and sedimentation control plan to protect existing soil, bodies of water, and air needs to be carried out. The main goal of this category is to minimize disturbance to the site.

The *complete, compact, and connected neighborhoods* category borrows from the principals of New Urbanism. Established in the 1980s, the movement seeks to create denser communities based on traditional town design and advocates narrow streets, mixed-land uses, walkability, and public transit. Projects therefore must foster a sense of place, conserve land, be transportation efficient, and attract diverse uses.

Projects that incorporate LEED-certified green structures or other eco-friendly buildings that provide energy and/or water efficiency can also accumulate points. Plans should include designs that shade paved surfaces, use light-colored materials to diminish the urban heat island effect, provide underground parking, and/or use green roofs. Infrastructure such as street and traffic lights should be energy efficient, and additional points can be allotted where on-site power generation or renewable energy sources are installed.

CHAPTER 2

Siting a Home

The site chosen for a home and its location and orientation on the site can significantly detract from or enhance its sustainability. It is necessary to recognize the implications of siting decisions early on in the design process to ensure a successful integration of site and dwelling. This chapter discusses key planning considerations, including climate, passive solar gain, wind direction, preservation of flora and fauna, and topography.

SITE SELECTION

As noted earlier, criteria for site selection form part of LEED for Homes. Consulting those criteria is, therefore, a recommended step in the design process. When selecting a site, it is necessary to recognize the relationship between the home and its built and natural surroundings. In general, a dwelling needs to complement the site's existing natural conditions, and one should thoroughly examine the site early on to understand its full potential. In addition, some locations may include buildings or infrastructure to which the new dwelling should relate. Properly integrating homes with their physical conditions will not only create a sustainable environment but also foster a sense of place.

The natural characteristics of a site that affect the dwelling include patterns of water flow, wind direction, sun exposure, soil composition, topography, animal paths, plant material, and climate. The water flow, for example, may affect not only the dwelling's location but also how it should be designed. A home is likely to be built away from a water course, and the construction method used will vary depending on the level of the water table. For example, building near a lake, where the water table is high, may require use of piles or avoidance of a basement.

The site conditions also influence the dwelling. For instance, the existence of roadways and other infrastructure not only should influence the site location but also can reduce building costs, and if a home is planned near existing transit or pedestrian and bicycle infrastructure, that can reduce transportation expenses and emissions from travel. It is preferable to select a location that will reduce dependence on private vehicles by giving priority to pedestrians and cyclists and by having proximity to public transit. Incorporating existing commercial establishments and social amenities such as schools and medical

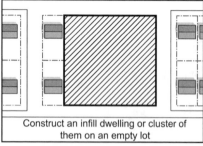

Add to or subdivide an existing home

Construct an infill dwelling or cluster of them on an empty lot

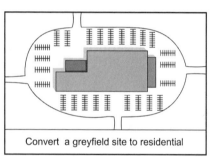

Convert a greyfield site to residential

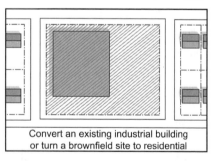

Convert an existing industrial building or turn a brownfield site to residential

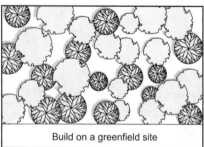

Build on a greenfield site

Decreasing priority

FIGURE 2.1 Preferred development sites will be those that avoid construction on greenfield.

clinics will contribute greatly to the sustainability of a community. While it is important during site selection to know that amenities exist nearby, it is equally important to integrate them through paths and roadways.

The following section classifies sites into four categories—greenfield, grayfield, infill, and brownfield—and discusses the merits and drawbacks associated with each. It is important to note that these categories are not mutually exclusive. For example, a brownfield site can also be infill.

A *greenfield* site is undeveloped virgin land to which new roads and services must be built. Although greenfield sites might be cheaper to develop, more readily available in large areas, and restricted by fewer regulations, their use contributes to urban sprawl, eats up valuable farmland and habitat, and requires the construction of new infrastructure. Development on greenfield sites should be avoided.

Sites that have or had built infrastructure but that have suffered from disinvestment and are underutilized or abandoned are known as *grayfield* sites. They are most often areas where a large regional mall, office park, or other commercial establishment had been viable. Building on grayfield sites can be cost effective given the presence of existing infrastructure such as sewage systems, roadways, and public transportation.

Infill sites are plots of land within an already developed area. They are likely to be in close proximity to existing amenities and are more likely to be walkable and accessible to transit, and development on them can help to rebuild social and urban fabrics. With so many advantages, in a strong market it is not likely that an infill plot will remain available for long unless it has serious drawbacks such as soil contamination or an irregular shape.

The name *brownfield* is given to sites that formerly had facilities of an industrial nature. Toxic substances may have seeped into the ground, and therefore these sites must be carefully tested to determine appropriate cleanup methods. While soil tests and cleaning can be expensive and can increase construction costs, many programs are available to help defray the cost of cleanup. Although infill and grayfield sites are preferred, as recommended in figure 2.1, the potential challenges associated with each must be carefully assessed prior to their selection.

Three fundamental strategies can help foster a sustainable design: mixing land use, building at higher densities, and offering a range of housing types. *Mixing land use* places amenities and dwellings within walking distance of each other. *Higher densities* promote construction of more dwellings per unit area, narrower roads, and alternative parking solutions and will help limit urban sprawl. Finally, a *range of housing types* will encourage social diversity through the mixing of household types and incomes. Assuring a mix of housing types can be done through inclusionary zoning. Creating *inclusionary zoning* assures that land uses of various types can be combined. For example, commercial establishments can exist next to dwellings, which will encourage residents to walk to them rather than use their cars and drive to a farther location.

ZONING

Once a site is selected, the planner will consider the relevant zoning and either adhere to existing regulations or apply for a variance. The first case often occurs on infill sites where the ordinances are similar to those for neighboring buildings. Because the zoning dictates a wide range of aspects, from parking to building density and dwelling type, it must be studied prior to design and followed, since applying for a variance is a time-consuming process. Direct control or planned unit development commonly occurs in greenfield sites where zoning ordinances have yet to be established. The designer needs to develop and submit zoning ordinances along with dwelling design. The plan must then be approved by the municipality and may be modified. In *direct control* the municipality puts in place zoning that determines what can be built on the site, to which the developer and the designer have to adhere. In *planned unit development* no specific zoning has been pre-scribed. Designers are therefore free to suggest theirs, which may be accepted, rejected, or modified by the authority. Another ordinance of note is the SmartCode, which is a form-based zoning document largely based on environmental analysis. The intention is to create walkable communities and foster mixed-use zoning to prevent urban sprawl.

DESIGNING WITH CLIMATE

Climatic site conditions include sun path, wind patterns, drainage, natural vegetation, and landscape features. The sun path should be considered throughout the process of the dwelling's configuration and orientation to maximize passive solar gain in the winter and minimize it in the summer. The dwelling can also be oriented to take maximum advantage of wind patterns for cooling purposes. Additionally, the natural drainage of the site can be enhanced to make use of rainwater and runoff for outdoor irrigation. Furthermore, natural landscape features can be preserved to contribute to the sense of place.

Climatic conditions, which vary from region to region, need to be considered in each site. The built environments of Palm Springs and San Francisco, California, are examples of the result of a disregard for climate during early design stages. Palm Springs has been landscaped with vegetation that does not belong in a desert, while San Francisco, a mountain range, has had a gridiron street pattern imposed on it as if it were a flat plane. In both cases climate and topography could have been integrated into the design to create a sustainable environment. In Palm Springs, planners could have embraced the natural flora of the desert and utilized adobe houses rather than constructing a superficial oasis. In San Francisco, designers could have utilized the hilly terrain to its advantage for views or as a buffer from wind and sun rather than forcing a grid. Alternatively, in Village Homes in Davis, California, the entire community was designed to suit local environmental conditions by including numerous water- and energy-saving strategies. In the Eco Village in Ithaca, New York, the designers concentrated the homes in two pockets rather than creating sprawl, leaving most of the greenfield property uninhabited.

Climate and topography need to be key considerations in the design of a community to maximize the sustainability of each home. Guidelines will be offered below for cold, temperate, hot, arid, or humid climates. Another condition of note is microclimate, which happens when the atmospheric conditions of a particular zone are different from those of the surrounding area. Design for sustainability can create suitable microclimates by tree planting, for example, to slow wind speed in the interest of energy efficiency.

Since larger surface areas lead to greater heat loss, it is generally more energy efficient for a dwelling to be designed in the form of a cube rather than as an elongated rectangle. The length-to-width ratio, however, may vary depending on climate. According to Numbers (1995) the most energy-conserving ratios of length to width are 1.1–1.3:1 for cold climates, 1.6–2.4:1 for temperate climates, 1.3–1.6:1 for hot and arid climates, and 1.7–3:1 for hot and humid climates, as illustrated in figure 2.2. Since in cold climates it is of primary importance to avoid heat loss, the resulting dwelling configuration should be close to a cube with a ratio between 1.1:1 and 1.3:1. Furthermore, north-facing windows should have minimal area with well-insulated walls. In temperate climates, there is less stress on the building skin, and the configuration becomes less significant, allowing for an elongated shape. The increase in environmental stress on dwellings in hot, arid climates is reflected by the ratio of its configuration, which is less elongated than homes in temperate climates. In warm or humid climates, however, cross ventilation becomes increasingly important and should be attained through a stretched configuration with openings at either end.

The siting of a dwelling with respect to a hill is also largely affected by weather. In cold or temperate climates, it is important to shelter the dwelling from cold wind. Since wind velocity increases at the ridge of a hill and cold air subsides at the bottom of a valley, it is best to locate a house halfway between the valley and the ridge to avoid both undesired extremes. On the other hand, for hot, arid climates, cold air, which settles

FIGURE 2.2 Examples of dwellings suitable for various climatic conditions. The ratio between interior space and envelope area will depend on the region and will affect energy consumption and determine heating and cooling costs.

Location	Northeast	East	South	Southwest	Northwest
Climate	Cold	Temperate	Hot and humid	Hot and arid	Temperate
Design					
Plan/ envelope ratio	1.3	1.6 to 2.4	1.7 to 3.0	1.3 to 1.6	1.6 to 2.4

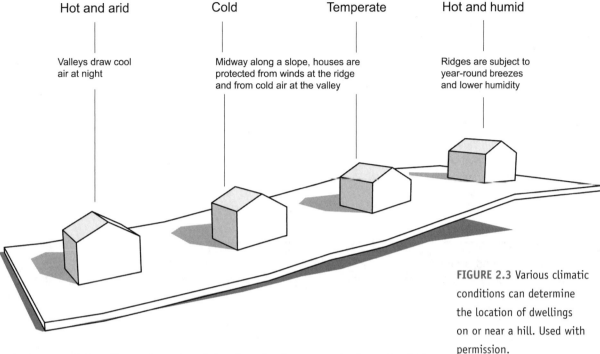

Hot and arid — Valleys draw cool air at night

Cold — Midway along a slope, houses are protected from winds at the ridge and from cold air at the valley

Temperate

Hot and humid — Ridges are subject to year-round breezes and lower humidity

FIGURE 2.3 Various climatic conditions can determine the location of dwellings on or near a hill. Used with permission.

at the bottom of the valley, is desired, and therefore dwellings in such places should be located lower. In addition, it is preferred that the home be sited in the valley on the south side of a landform to increase its exposure to low-angle winter sun rays. Finally, in warm or humid climates where cross ventilation is imperative, the dwelling should be sited on a hill's ridge to take advantage of strong winds, as shown in figure 2.3 (Numbers 1995).

Designing for Passive Solar Gain

Ancient Greeks and other indigenous societies oriented their towns and homes to maximize winter sun and summer shade. Yet, with the development of central cooling and heating systems, coupled with the availability of cheap energy, society has lost interest in siting dwellings for passive solar gain. With natural resources diminishing and the cost of energy rising, it is becoming increasingly vital to understand the benefits and methods of proper building orientation. It is necessary to note that the following section deals with dwellings in the Northern Hemisphere, which vary from those located in the Southern, yet the general concepts examined apply to both. For Southern Hemisphere dwellings it is also important to recognize that a north-facing building will maximize passive solar gain rather than one with a south-facing orientation.

A dwelling should be oriented to receive the most direct sunlight throughout the day, with its elongated side facing south. It is imperative that the dwelling be oriented toward true south and not magnetic south, which can differ by up to 20 degrees. To find true south, the location's declination must first be determined. The *declination* is the number of degrees east or west between compass (or magnetic) north and true north. It can be found by comparing a compass reading to plans prepared by a land surveyor. Once the declination is decided on, true south can be determined. With its elongated side on the

FIGURE 2.4 Homes should be oriented with their long elevation facing south or within 15 degrees of south to maximize passive solar gain. Used with permission.

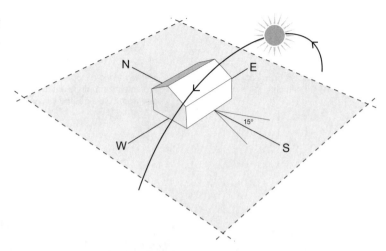

FIGURE 2.5 A dwelling must be clear of shadows from surrounding buildings. The minimum distance between homes on flat terrain depends on the height of the adjacent building and the sun's angle.

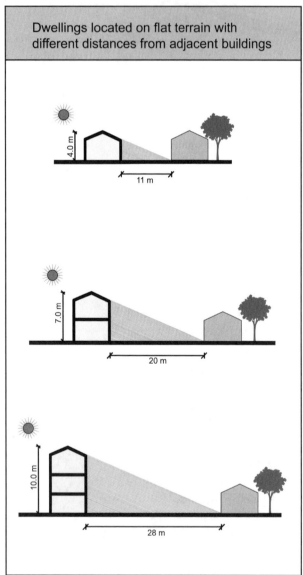

Dwellings located on flat terrain with different distances from adjacent buildings

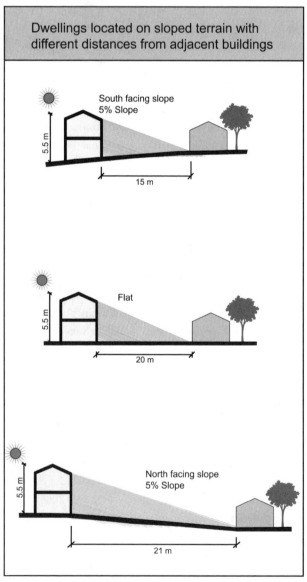

Dwellings located on sloped terrain with different distances from adjacent buildings

east–west axis, the dwelling will maximize its exposure to low-angle winter rays while minimizing exposure to high-angle summer rays with large roof overhangs. Exposure to the low-angle summer rays, which occur at sunrise and sunset, is also minimized since they land on the shorter east and west facades of the dwelling. Orienting the long elevation of the dwelling directly south is just a guideline, however, and an alignment within 15 degrees is sufficient, as illustrated in figure 2.4 (Numbers 1995). Furthermore, the dwelling should be sited where it lies in unobstructed sunlight. Placing a dwelling too close to adjacent objects or buildings should be avoided (fig. 2.5).

Since little to no sunlight will ever reach the north facade, openings on that side will not contribute to solar gain. Therefore, the number and size of windows on that side should be minimized to prevent heat loss. According to Numbers, only 5 to 10 percent of the composition of the north facade should be doors and windows in cold climates. South elevation, however, should be punctuated with large openings to allow sunlight to enter. South-facing windows are particularly beneficial to the dwelling, since the heat acquired through passive solar gain far exceeds any heat loss from the windows of that facade. To further reduce heat loss, the floor plan of the dwelling can be arranged to create an insulating buffer. Infrequently used areas, such as bedrooms, utility rooms, garages, or hallways, should be placed along the north side, while living areas, such as dining rooms, living rooms, and kitchens, should face south, as demonstrated in figure 2.6. This allows occupants to enjoy full exposure to sunlight in the living areas where they commonly spend most of their time.

FIGURE 2.6 An insulating buffer can be achieved through the careful placement along the northern facade of spaces used at night or infrequently.

Although having sunlight is essential during winter, exposure to sun rays should be limited in summer to prevent overheating and reduce dependency on central cooling systems. This can be easily achieved in two ways. The first deals with the width of the roof's overhang. Since the altitude of the sun varies between summer and winter, the overhang can be adjusted so that it shades the dwelling from summer rays while allowing winter sunlight to enter, as shown in figures 2.7 and 2.8. The second way is to plant or utilize existing trees along the south side. Since deciduous trees are in full foliage in summer and lose their leaves by winter, they will limit sunlight during summer but allow it to freely enter during winter. Different species of trees

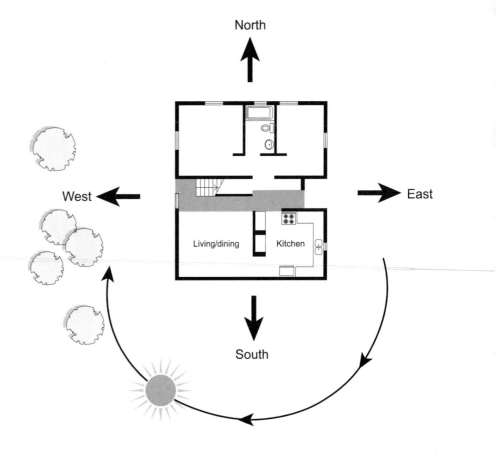

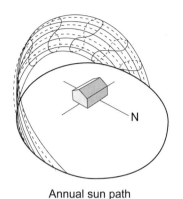

Annual sun path

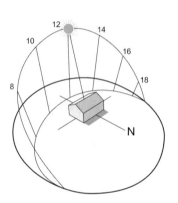

Sun location
at summer solstice

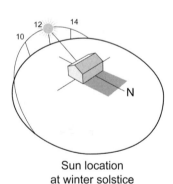

Sun location
at winter solstice

FIGURE 2.7 The seasonal varying sun paths.

also have various levels of transparency (fig. 2.9). Trees that allow more light to pass through when they are bare during winter are preferable. When faced with a choice between coniferous and deciduous trees, for example, the deciduous trees would make a more sustainable choice since coniferous trees allow only 8 percent transparency while deciduous trees allow 50 percent (Thomas 1996). Choosing deciduous trees allows more sun into the dwelling during winter months and provides shading from the sun during the summer. The chosen tree species should also respect the local vegetation and climatic conditions of the environment. Choosing to plant coniferous trees in the desert would not be a sustainable choice because of the scarcity of water, for example.

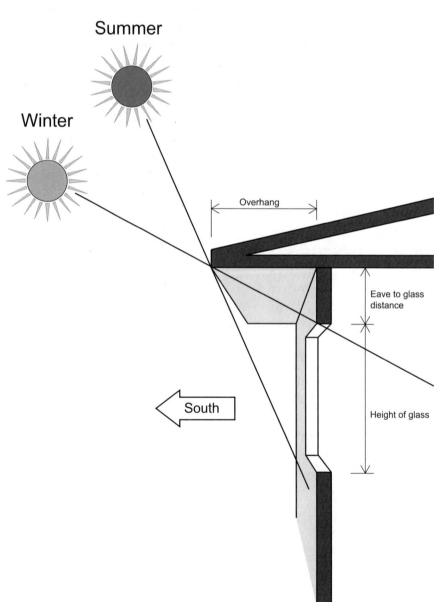

FIGURE 2.8 The width of the roof's overhang needs to be designed in relation to the orientation of the facade and the height of the window.

Coniferous tree
8%

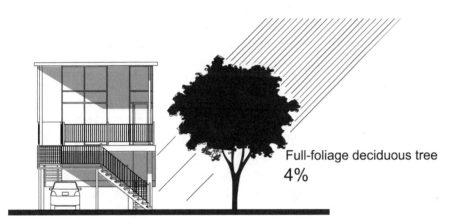

Full-foliage deciduous tree
4%

Bare deciduous tree
50%

Considering Wind Direction

Wind can be used along with the sun to generate power, which will be elaborated below. This section looks into passive ways to consider winds in site planning. Summer breezes can be used to cool a dwelling instead of an energy-consuming system. Winter winds should be avoided in cold climates since they cause significant heat loss.

To design a dwelling that effectively uses winds requires an understanding of the wind pattern of the site. The prevailing wind conditions will vary from location to location, and the direction of prevailing winds differs from summer to winter, but some general assumptions can be made about factors that affect wind speed. The *Venturi effect* relates to the increase in velocity of a moving medium that occurs when it passes through a constricted opening to maintain the same volumetric flow per unit of time. Any object, therefore, that constrains the wind path should positively channel and accentuate summer breezes. Having a dwelling in a direct wind path may prove problematic in winter if not dealt with properly. Objects such as water, landforms, vegetation, and adjacent buildings all contribute to the Venturi effect. Recorded data regarding wind conditions are commonly kept by local weather stations and can be consulted. Local weather media networks, which commonly have websites, are easy-to-access sources of information for those who wish to find out about wind direction. Once the information is found, it can be entered into computer programs, such as Rhino 4.0, which will suggest a siting for the dwelling.

Once local wind conditions have been determined for summer and winter, the design process may continue. The primary goal for the orientation and landscaping of a dwelling is to capture cool summer breezes while avoiding harsh winter ones. As a general rule, the elongated side of the dwelling should be oriented within 60 degrees of the prevailing summer wind. This will allow the breezes to pass through the dwelling and cool it. In addition, designers can use the Venturi effect to augment the speed of breezes. They can use existing landforms and trees or new strategically placed ones to channel summer breezes toward the house, as illustrated in figure 2.10.

For colder climates, landforms and trees can be used to buffer the dwelling from harsh winter winds and channel them away. Objects that buffer the dwelling are commonly referred to as *windbreaks*. It is important that windbreaks are not completely impermeable, since a solid windbreak will produce a low-pressure area on the building's leeward side. Semipermeable windbreaks such as trees, which are shown in figure 2.11, and fences are preferred. While studies differ on the best distance from windbreak to

FIGURE 2.10 Proper tree planting can help capture summer breezes while avoiding cold winter winds.

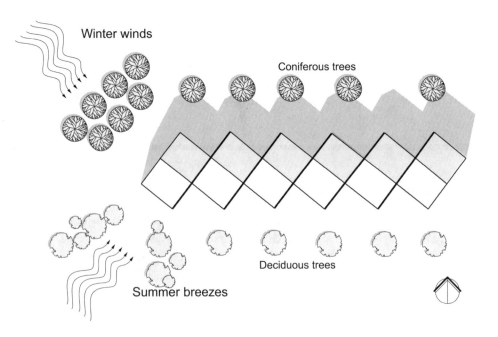

Winter winds

Coniferous trees

Deciduous trees

Summer breezes

FIGURE 2.11 Dense configuration of evergreens along the northern facade can be an effective wind barrier.

dwelling, they all agree that windbreaks should not be placed too close to the dwelling, to avoid excessive shade. At the same time, the windbreaks should not be so far away that they create a wind tunnel between the dwelling and the windbreak. According to Pantoja (1983), it is most effective to place windbreaks at a distance of 1.5 to 2.5 times the height of the building. In addition, woodland windbreaks should be located at a distance approximately ten times the tree-to-house height ratio, as shown in figure 2.12. However, if the dwelling is located in a hot climate zone that requires cooling even during winter months, winter winds should be treated as summer breezes are to maximize their contact with the dwelling.

FIGURE 2.12 The distance from the trees to the house should be about ten times the tree-to-house height ratio (*a*). The number of rows of trees needed to make a good windbreak varies from species to species (*b*).

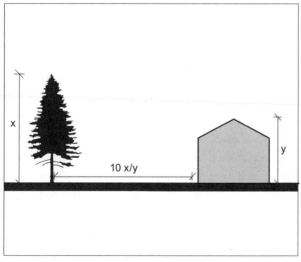

a

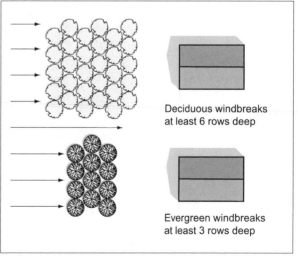

Deciduous windbreaks
at least 6 rows deep

Evergreen windbreaks
at least 3 rows deep

b

The design of a sustainable dwelling should address both wind direction and passive solar gain—not one or the other. Generally a solution can be found that satisfies both requirements, but occasionally the desired orientation based on wind patterns conflicts with the desired orientation for maximum passive solar gain. According to Numbers (1995), siting to maximize passive solar gain should take precedence, since the energy gain from an advantageous solar configuration exceeds the energy loss that might be incurred from an undesirable orientation based on wind patterns.

PRESERVING AND RESTORING FLORA AND FAUNA

In addition to passive solar gain and wind, the preservation of flora and fauna must also be considered while designing. It is highly critical in site planning where the relation between the dwelling and its natural surroundings is of outmost importance. A leading advocate for appropriate planning is the Sustainable Sites Initiative, which is an interdisciplinary effort by the American Society of Landscape Architects, the Lady Bird Johnson Wildflower Center at the University of Texas at Austin, and the United States Botanic Garden to create voluntary national guidelines and performance benchmarks for sustainable land design, construction, and maintenance practices.

In general, not only is vegetation crucial to maintaining the natural plant and animal biodiversity, it also helps with storm-water retention, prevents soil erosion, enhances air quality, helps sequester carbon, improves curb appeal, and buffers the dwelling from wind, noise, and sun. Instead of clearing land and landscaping artificially, designing a home should minimize harm to local flora and fauna, as shown in figure 2.13. Prior to design, the site should be surveyed to locate all its trees—mature and healthy ones as well as those that are decaying and in need of pruning, as illustrated in figure 2.14. It should then become clear which trees can be removed and which ones will be given priority in preservation. Norms suggest that a mature tree is any tree with a trunk circumference of 18 in. (45 cm) or more, measured from 40 in. (1 m) above ground level, as illustrated in figure 2.15 (Lamontagne and Brazeau 1996). The footprint of the dwelling needs to avoid areas where mature trees are densely located as shown in figure 2.16. Instead, it can be located either where no tree grows or where there are decaying ones that will be removed. If siting a dwelling over healthy trees cannot be avoided, those trees should be relocated when possible.

When trees are relocated, it is important that the adequate root-ball-size hole is dug and appropriate earth-moving equipment is used. Lamontagne and Brazeau (1996) suggest that for every 1 in. (2.54 cm) of tree trunk, a 10 in. (25.4 cm) to 12 in. (30.5 cm) diameter root-ball hole should be dug. Additionally, they advocate that the relocating hole should have adequate drainage, achieved through a downward-sloping trench dug at the base of the hole, and that enough room should be maintained for quality topsoil backfill around the root-ball. Furthermore, to ensure that trees are not damaged during construction, they should be adequately pruned, watered, fertilized, and protected prior to construction. Trees should also be fenced off to prevent damage or soil compaction around the roots, which deprives them of oxygen (Fisette and Ryan 2002).

In addition to trees, it is also important to preserve wetlands. The US Environmental

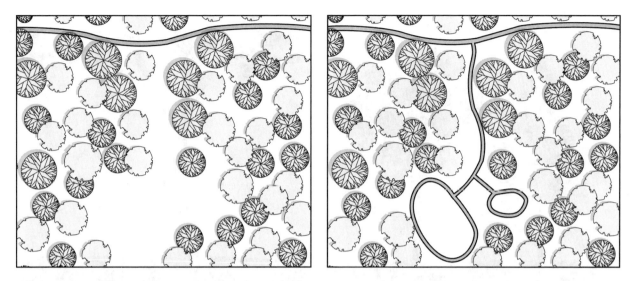

FIGURE 2.13 A home or cluster of homes needs to be constructed in a natural clearing in the forest to avoid natural assets.

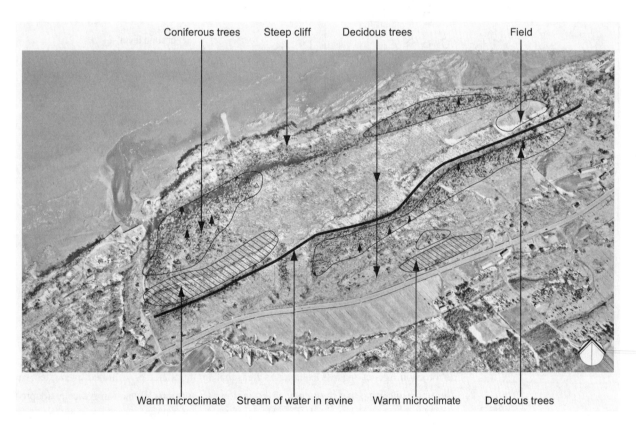

Coniferous trees   Steep cliff   Decidous trees   Field

Warm microclimate   Stream of water in ravine   Warm microclimate   Decidous trees

FIGURE 2.14 Prior to the start of design, a site needs to be surveyed and all its natural assets recorded, as was done in the residential development near Quebec City, Canada.

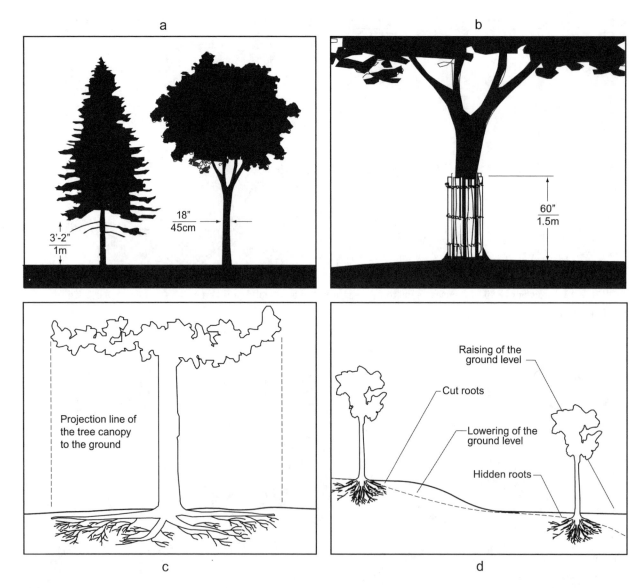

FIGURE 2.15 Mature trees, which need to be protected, are those with a circumference greater than 18 in. (45 cm) measured from 40 in. (1 m) above ground level (*a*). They can be guarded from mechanical damage with protection that is 60 in. (1.5 m) tall (*b*). Excavation should not occur around the spread of a tree's branches, to avoid root damage (*c*). Lowering soil levels may destroy the tree's root system, while raising the soil level may cause suffocation of the roots (*d*).

Protection Agency regards *wetlands* as areas that are inundated or saturated by surface water or groundwater at a frequency and duration that supports vegetation typically adapted for life in saturated-soil conditions. Wetlands are beneficial to the environment since they aid in flood control, collect storm water, purify runoff water, and create a natural habitat for flora and fauna. They are also heavily protected by federal laws and state ordinances. When roads or dwellings must be built near wetlands, they should be constructed at the height of the land. A pedestrian trail or bike path can be built around a wetland's edges to act as a buffer, and it can be enjoyed by the residents as a natural amenity area.

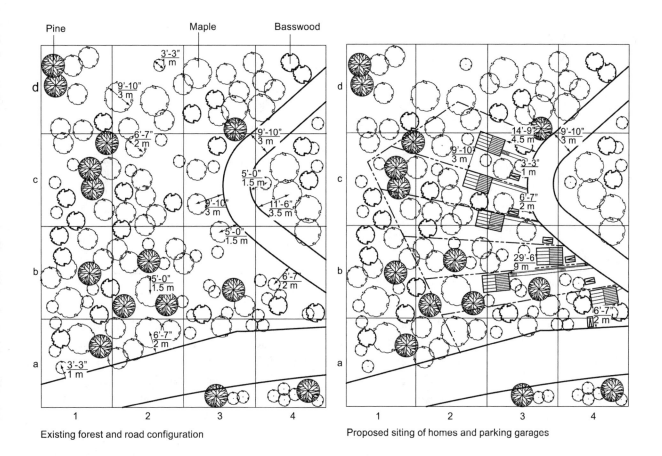

Pine · Maple · Basswood

Existing forest and road configuration

Proposed siting of homes and parking garages

PRESERVING TOPOGRAPHY AND NATURAL DRAINAGE

Dwellings should be designed with the natural topography of the site. Often a hilly terrain is regarded as too challenging to build on and is flattened or cleared instead. Not only is this costly, but it destroys the natural ecosystem and impairs natural drainage. This approach can lead to irreversible and unpredictable ecological challenges and should be avoided whenever possible. As a rule of thumb, any building type at any density can be constructed on a 0 to 5 percent slope. Small detached homes and duplexes are suitable for these slopes. Where the slope exceeds 10 percent, buildings can be custom designed. Slopes significantly exceeding a 10 percent gradient should be avoided since construction becomes too costly and soil erosion a significant concern. Additionally, on slopes greater than 5 percent, roads and walkways need to be located adjacent to the dwelling, to reduce cutting and filling costs. For safety, driveways in northern climates where roads can be icy should not exceed a 12 percent gradient.

To avoid sharp changes in elevation, dwellings and roads should be built parallel to contour lines, which are the lines on a topographical map that show the altitude of each location. Homes can also be designed perpendicular to them, since they provide opportunities to build stepped or split-level units. On the other hand, roadways should not be built perpendicular to contour lines, to minimize the amount of land that is disturbed, as illustrated in figure 2.17.

FIGURE 2.16 In a forested area, the siting of roads and homes should be adjusted according to the location of trees.

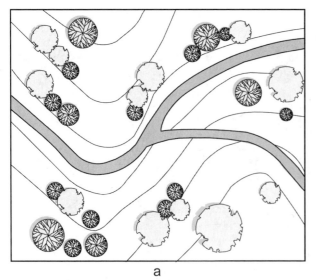

a

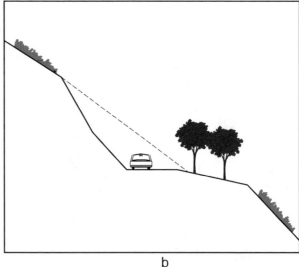

b

FIGURE 2.17 The path of a road should follow the site's contours (*a*). On sloped sites, roads can be constructed on existing flat areas rather than on new ones, which are both costly and environmentally damaging (*b*).

To stabilize a slope and prevent erosion, several steps can be taken during construction. The rate of erosion is likely to be affected by the porosity of soil, gradient of slope, and volume and velocity of water runoff. Excavation, therefore, should be kept to a minimum during construction to preserve local vegetation, which helps stabilize the soil. Drive *piles* or sink *step-down footings* for foundations when soil erosion is a concern. Such foundations avoid the massive excavation commonly done for a full basement by intervening in fewer spots, in the case of piles, or by creating shallow ones when footings are used. Since water-saturated soil erodes more easily, it is important that the soil be drained immediately. Therefore, a system should also be constructed to enhance the natural site drainage that will carry the runoff water to a retention pond or a nearby lake to allow water to slow and sleet to settle down.

In the design of the dwelling's drainage, it is important that the new system works with the site's natural drainage and does not fundamentally alter it or make it redundant. The natural drainage of the site provides water for flora and plays a large role in maintaining the existing ecosystem. When a drainage system for storm water is installed, surface runoff is eradicated and the local vegetation is forced to find water from other sources or face extinction. Instead, the dwelling should utilize the natural drainage of the site but ensure that excess water has a place to go to prevent flooding during periods of heavy rainfall.

Several interventions can enhance the natural drainage of a site. Instead of introducing curbs and sewers along roadways, keeping vegetated land along roadways should help them respond to flash flooding (fig. 2.18). Roadways should also be sloped so that water drains off them and onto the adjacent vegetation. This way the vegetation can absorb some of the water and filter it while naturally draining the site and restoring the water table level. Additionally, landscaped depressions along the road will reduce storm-water runoff as well as filter pollutants. Another method is to build the road out of porous materials and allow storm water to be absorbed by the roads and eventually contained by the site's natural drainage, as illustrated in figure 2.19.

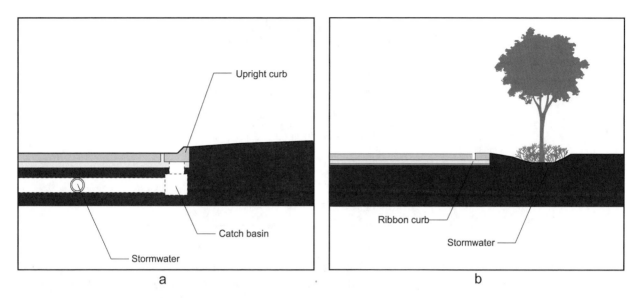

a

b

FIGURE 2.18 A comparison between conventional drainage (*a*) and an environmentally sensitive system that supplements the natural drainage of the site (*b*).

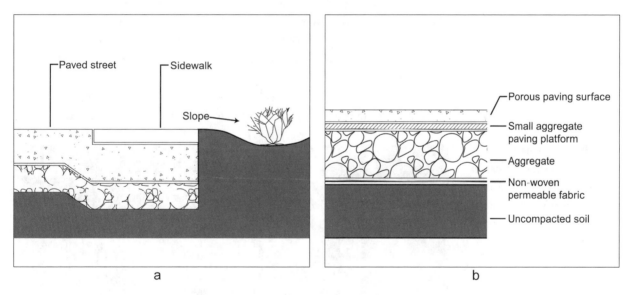

a

b

FIGURE 2.19 Impervious roadways and sidewalks are sloped to drain water toward the natural drainage system (*a*). A porous material can be used to allow water to go through the road and to its natural drainage system (*b*).

Gulf Island Residence

Location: Gulf Islands, British Columbia, Canada

Design: BattersbyHowat

Completion: 2004

Site area: 0.4 acres (0.162 hectares)

Total floor area: 2,368 sq ft (220 m²)

Number of floors: 2

Situated near the waterfront in the Strait of Georgia, Gulf Island Residence was constructed using a sensitive approach to the site's natural characteristics and existing amenities. To minimize the environmental impact on the site, the footprint of an old cottage was reused and removal of any trees was avoided (fig. 2.20). The site plan kept the existing pedestrian and vehicular paths and the septic field and well, which were retrofitted. Materials and construction methods were adopted to accommodate the climatic conditions and the building conventions of the region. To support the local economy and minimize site damage, prefabricated structural sections were incorporated.

Oriented to maximize solar gain and minimize heat loss, a long stretch of windows occupies the southern elevation while the north and east elevations are minimally fenestrated to protect the inhabitants' privacy and limit noise (figs. 2.21, 2.22). All windows

FIGURE 2.20 The new construction reuses the foundation of the old cottage and incorporates existing utilities and trees. Used with permission.

FIGURE 2.21 A 3 ft (90 cm) deep roof overhang and existing trees provide shading on the extensive southern glazing while allowing passive solar gains during the winter. Used with permission.

FIGURE 2.22 On the north elevation, concrete walls, wooden rainscreen, and zinc roofing create an opaque surface to minimize heat loss, offer privacy from neighboring lots, and limit noise. Used with permission.

have low-emissivity coating and are filled with argon gas to enhance energy efficiency. On the south side, a cantilevered roof overhang and existing trees shade the dwelling from the sun during the summer while letting in its warmth during the winter. The strategic placement of the windows and the open floor concept encourage natural breezes and light to penetrate the house (figs. 2.23, 2.24).

Prime attention in sustainable design is often paid to aspects associated with the building itself. Energy-efficient windows, local materials, and open plan design are some of the considered aspects. Yet, the performance of a dwelling will be greatly improved if considerations are given to site planning first. As demonstrated here, nature can become the architect's partner in achieving sustainability.

FIGURE 2.23 The glazed southern elevation permits significant passive solar gain. Used with permission.

FIGURE 2.24 The partition-free main floor allows for greater spatial flexibility and facilitates flow of natural light and breezes throughout the house. Used with permission.

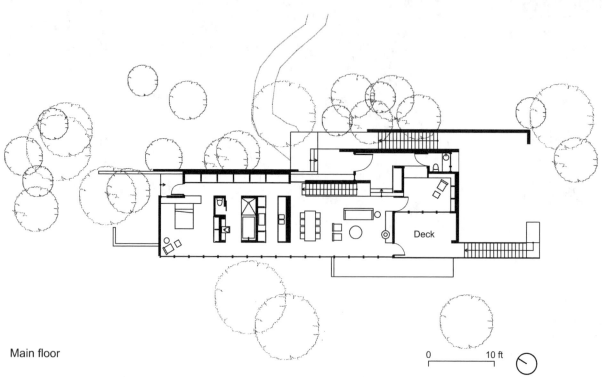

Main floor

0   10 ft

CHAPTER 3

Sustainable Residential Design Concepts

Some believe that sustainability is achieved when dwellings are designed for and equipped with "green" technologies. But green technologies alone cannot make a dwelling sustainable. How the home performs also largely depends on the manipulation of its form and function—design that is most efficient for its intended use. This chapter illustrates several residential concepts, such as aging in place and multigenerational dwellings, that contribute to sustainability from social, economic, and cultural perspectives with consequences for local and global environments. Technological issues are addressed in later chapters.

ARCHITECTURAL SOLUTIONS FOR SUSTAINABLE LIVING

Socioeconomic realities with direct effects on sustainable living need to be considered in the design of contemporary dwellings. Chief among these realities is the transformation of the family. Statistics show that single parents, singles, and seniors constitute larger percentages of the population than half a century ago. These households, at times, cannot find suitable accommodation within conventional market-sector dwellings. Rethinking space needs of all users and introducing design concepts in response to new lifestyle and demographic trends are, therefore, paramount if the building of sustainable communities is to be pursued.

Key features of such an approach are diversity and choice. At present, most residential developments are segregated by price and type of homes. As demand for sustainable living grows, affordable housing in walkable, transit-oriented communities near services is becoming harder to find. Mixing dwelling types and land uses enables people with a range of incomes and backgrounds to reside side by side, fostering greater social equity and integration. Building homes for seniors, for example, along with dwellings for young households will attract extended families and create a mutual support system. Some design approaches for adapting to changing demographics and lifestyles include live-work dwellings, aging in place, and multigenerational, small-size, and adaptable housing.

LIVE-WORK DWELLINGS

Once associated with a limited number of occupations, telecommuting and working out of the home have expanded to include a wider range of activities. The availability and affordability of personal computers, combined with advances in telecommunications, have made work at home a practical and economically viable alternative for many. Homeowners can also claim tax deductions for home-based businesses and avoid environmentally unfriendly daily commutes. By some accounts, daily commuters who drive to work an hour each way spend about 5 years of their lives at the wheel. The emissions from motor vehicles increase health risks and also pose an imminent threat to the environment at large. Between 70 and 90 percent of carbon monoxide emissions in cities are emitted by motor vehicles. Commuting's effect on mental health due to stress and time taken from family is also long lasting.

Used as a full-time or part-time work space, a home office is an important investment for a growing number of self-employed workers. When properly designed, the live-work arrangement provides efficient and personalized space in addition to a flexible schedule, which can help one to balance career and family life.

For working from home to be successful, thought must go into creating an environment that minimizes distractions and encourages productivity. It is insufficient to assume that one can work effectively from a makeshift setup (Dietsch 2008). The home office must be a well-integrated work space that prioritizes functionality, practicality, and comfort. The frequency of meetings with coworkers and clients, the storage requirements, and daily tasks are among a multitude of factors that influence office design. Although each home office is unique, certain basic design principles can be applied to ensure a successful union of personal and professional areas.

Interior dividers and level changes are common architectural devices that effectively differentiate home from work. The office should also be flexible and allow for future expansion and changes in function. Multipurpose shelving and movable partitions permit a variety of storage and spatial arrangements within the same room. In addition, large windows that provide ample natural light are necessary since home offices are commonly used during the day. According to Farley and Veitch (2001), working in rooms with exposure to natural light was found to enhance productivity and well-being, including improved overall satisfaction. Finally, comfortable, ergonomic furniture and a pleasant aesthetic will also improve productivity.

Home offices can be integrated into almost all housing types. Figure 3.1 illustrates areas in a home that can be used as office space. In the case of a multilevel dwelling, a spacious office can occupy the entire ground floor. The kitchen and living spaces would be moved to the upper levels, while partitions on the lower floor would be modified to accommodate larger meeting areas and storage rooms. When a smaller space is sufficient, the office can be located in a room at the periphery, ideally accessible through a secondary entrance. If the house has minimal floor space, movable partitions can allow the office area to be extended or reduced according to the homeowner's needs. Oftentimes, an addition that accommodates an office becomes an astute short- and long-term investment that not only improves the homeowner's work environment but increases the resale value (Dietsch 2008).

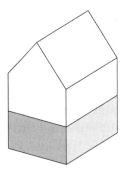

Occupying an entire floor

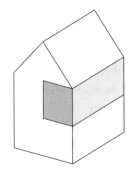

Occupying a portion of a floor

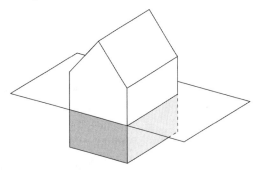

Occupying a basement

Occupying an attic

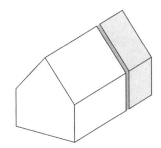

Addition to a house

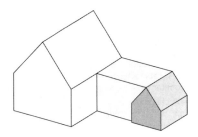

Ancillary structure

AGING IN PLACE

FIGURE 3.1 Possible home office locations in dwellings.

As a result of declining birthrate and increased life expectancy, the population of seniors has been steadily growing since the 1960s. Projections in the United States suggest that the number of people age 65 and over will nearly double between the years 2009 and 2034, which will have a significant effect on the economy and society (US Census Bureau 2009).

Contrary to popular belief, only 11 percent of all North American seniors live in assisted-living arrangements. The majority, according to Lawlor and Thomas (2008), plan to spend the rest of their lives in their own homes. Similar to the general population, most seniors live alone or with family, in an apartment or a house. *Aging in place* is an approach to creating communities and dwellings that support the needs of seniors or can be adapted to do so. It ensures secure, independent living that gives seniors greater autonomy and a better quality of life. From an economic perspective, aging in place delays the need for families or the state to provide new, costly living accommodations for seniors, thereby contributing to economic sustainability. Although the aging process brings about a decrease in physical stamina and mobility, with ongoing medical advancements seniors now live longer and lead dynamic and socially active lives. This means that aging in place is a viable solution for elderly people who can live autonomously.

Thoughtful barrier-free design can create spaces that simplify daily tasks for those with reduced mobility or dexterity. Minimizing physical obstacles and level changes can increase the ease with which a person circulates (Fischer and Meuser 2009; Chen 2004). If stairs are necessary, they should be accompanied by handrails, while interior changes in flooring materials should be seamless. An abundance of natural and artificial lighting improves depth perception and visual acuity. Smaller details can also simplify day-to-day tasks. Free-standing benches and wall-mounted shelves provide temporary spaces to sit and to place objects. As illustrated in figure 3.2, counters and sinks built with minimal bases can be comfortably used by either standing or seated people in bathrooms and kitchens. Special features can also be offered by developers, as shown in figure 3.3.

FIGURE 3.2 Barrier-free designs take into consideration the needs of occupants with reduced mobility and dexterity.

Although variable expenditures are associated with adapting an existing house, the costs are reduced when a barrier-free strategy is implemented in the initial design phase. Architects and builders will, therefore, have to consider strategies for functional and flex-

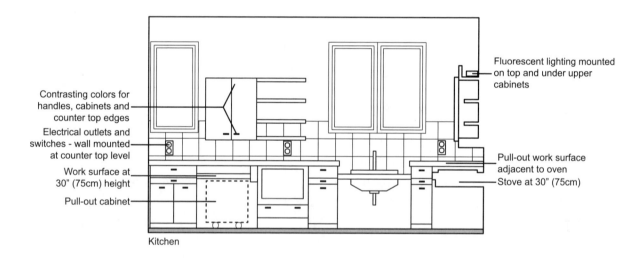

Contrasting colors for handles, cabinets and counter top edges

Electrical outlets and switches - wall mounted at counter top level

Work surface at 30" (75cm) height

Pull-out cabinet

Fluorescent lighting mounted on top and under upper cabinets

Pull-out work surface adjacent to oven

Stove at 30" (75cm)

Kitchen

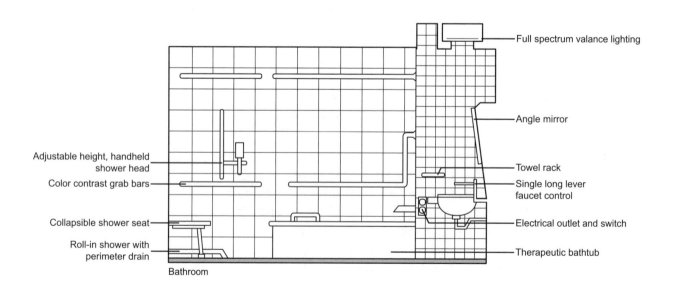

Adjustable height, handheld shower head

Color contrast grab bars

Collapsible shower seat

Roll-in shower with perimeter drain

Full spectrum valance lighting

Angle mirror

Towel rack

Single long lever faucet control

Electrical outlet and switch

Therapeutic bathtub

Bathroom

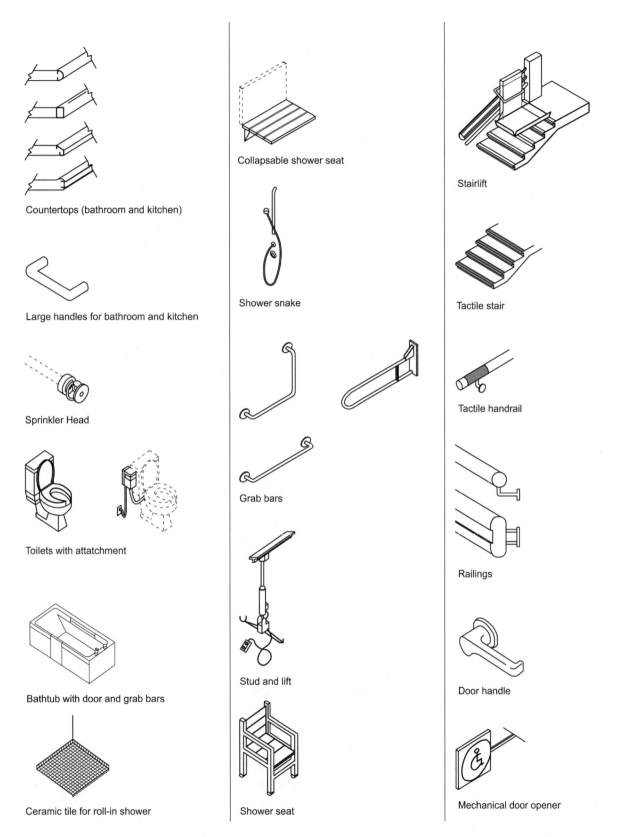

Countertops (bathroom and kitchen)

Large handles for bathroom and kitchen

Sprinkler Head

Toilets with attatchment

Bathtub with door and grab bars

Ceramic tile for roll-in shower

Collapsable shower seat

Shower snake

Grab bars

Stud and lift

Shower seat

Stairlift

Tactile stair

Tactile handrail

Railings

Door handle

Mechanical door opener

FIGURE 3.3 Special products can be offered in residential projects with large populations of seniors.

ible houses early on. In addition, city planners will also have to consider the needs of rapidly increasing numbers of seniors. Changes ranging from creating microclimates on streets with strong winds to installing grab bars or nonslip sidewalks in public places are some of the large-scale interventions considered.

MULTIGENERATIONAL LIVING

Before the rise of the nuclear family, it was much more common for extended families to reside under a single roof. Higher housing and childcare costs and an increased life expectancy have sparked a renewed interest in multigenerational living. The extended family usually lives in two or even more separate, self-contained households that are connected in some way. Although each family unit is responsible for its own independent dwelling, the units are interconnected through the use of shared spaces. Similar to aging in place, *multigenerational housing* promotes a sustainable lifestyle from both social and economic perspectives. Socially, it makes older members of the family feel involved and wanted, creates an intergenerational support system, and allows the transfer of cultural traditions from one generation to the next. Elderly people who live alongside their offspring have the opportunity to maintain an active autonomous or semiautonomous routine. The younger generation provides emotional security and physical assistance when needed. Families with children also benefit from the presence of grandparents, who offer support in child rearing, participate in the education of their grandchildren, and help preserve cultural traditions. Economically, it lessens the burden of caring for seniors on governments and individual households, thereby furthering sustainability. For example, pooling together financial resources and sharing expenses lessens the burden of home ownership for all (Zhao 2001).

The multigenerational dwelling can accommodate the unique and intricate relationships that inevitably exist between family members. For this reason, its design must meet several requirements relating to privacy, independence, and interaction. To maintain these attributes, each unit should contain all essential amenities, such as a kitchen, bathroom, and living area. Oftentimes, the homes need to have separate entrances so that one household is not required to pass through the space of the other. Integration of shared spaces is, however, of equal importance. Living rooms, dining rooms, terraces, and gardens reinforce family ties. Adaptability and barrier-free accessibility are additional requirements of such housing types. As the families evolve, so too should their dwellings. If one of the households needs to move to a new location, the vacant unit could easily be altered and rented to provide supplemental income.

Four main arrangements are commonly associated with multigenerational housing. Each is characterized by the specific spatial relationship that exists between the self-contained units. In the case of the *garden suite,* two independent units are located on the same lot where the backyard becomes a vital connection space, as shown in figure 3.4. The larger home is typically a permanent, single-family unit while the smaller one is generally movable and can be sited according to convenience. In contrast, *side-by-side units* follow the same form as semidetached houses and townhouses. Both units have ground-level access and are separated by a partition wall. The spatial relationship between the two main entrances and the removal of certain interior partitions can create communal spaces. *Superimposed units* are defined by level changes. While one unit has ground-level entry, the second can be accessed from an interior or exterior stairway. The traditional two-story duplex and three-story triplex are designed in this way, and, not surprisingly, these residences commonly house two or more generations. The elder generation often occupies the ground-level floor because of its increased accessibility. If the house is taller than two stories, the larger, presumably younger family inhabits the upper levels. The levels can be joined or disconnected through the addition or removal of stairs and mezzanines, according to the family's changing needs. Finally, *accessory apartments*, which are also referred to as granny flats, are built into existing single-family homes. Well-lit basements, garages, attics, and infrequently used rooms are the most readily convertible spaces. Secondary entrances can be added if they do not exist already. Because the accessory apartment is contained within the larger house, this combination fosters the strongest relationship between households (Zhao 2001).

FIGURE 3.4 A garden suite at the rear of an existing building. Used with permission.

SMALL-SIZE HOUSING

The average size of the North American home has increased considerably since World War II. A survey shows that the average North American home has grown from about 1,000 sq ft (93 m^2) in 1950 to 2,340 sq ft (217 m^2) in 2004, while the average household size has been reduced from about 3.4 to 2.6 persons in the same period. This means that the median area per person tripled, from 290 to 900 sq ft (27 to 84 m^2) (Wilson 2006). The reality is, however, that a growing number of households cannot afford to purchase or maintain such large dwellings.

LEED for Homes establishes criteria for dwelling sizes. Credit points are given to small units and deducted from oversized homes. For example, the size of a one-bedroom home should not exceed 800 sq ft (74 m^2), and three bedrooms should not be bigger than 1,900 sq ft (177 m^2).

In this chapter, small-size housing is that whose area ranges from 500 to 1,000 sq ft (46 to 93 m²) and that is an efficient and economically sustainable solution for individuals or small families who wish to benefit from home ownership. Environmentally, these units limit the resources needed for construction, including the land necessary, and once occupied, they consume less energy.

The challenge in designing a small home is to maximize its efficiency. Through rational planning, the designer must ensure that all basic living needs, such as resting, eating, working, and bathing, are met. A number of design strategies can improve the spatial quality of a small area. Large windows can expand the perceived space beyond the boundaries of the walls, as shown in figure 3.5. Natural light should reach far into rooms to create the brightest and most spacious atmosphere. In addition, higher ceilings increase interior volume and further diminish any unwanted feelings of enclosure (Chan 2007).

FIGURE 3.5 Large windows can expand the perceived space beyond the boundaries of a small dwelling. Used with permission.

Versatility and practicality are essential features of a small home. An open plan that contains few or no subdivisions increases adaptability and allows multiple functions to be assigned to the same space (Morcos 2009). Built-in and convertible furniture allows public spaces to have a wider range of potential uses. This economizes area by reducing the required number of enclosed rooms. The main spaces devoted to public and private

functions can, therefore, occupy the maximum available area. Different floor materials, small level changes, and furniture placement can also be used to define smaller spaces within a larger area.

Movable partitions can be incorporated if more privacy is required. Traditional Japanese wood homes, for example, utilize translucent paper screens to transform interior spaces and to mediate between public and private domains (Chan 2007). Figure 3.6 demonstrates how a movable partition can be arranged according to the needs of the occupant. During the day, the partition can be positioned to allow the public eating and living areas to occupy more than half the home's floor space. If homeowners wish to

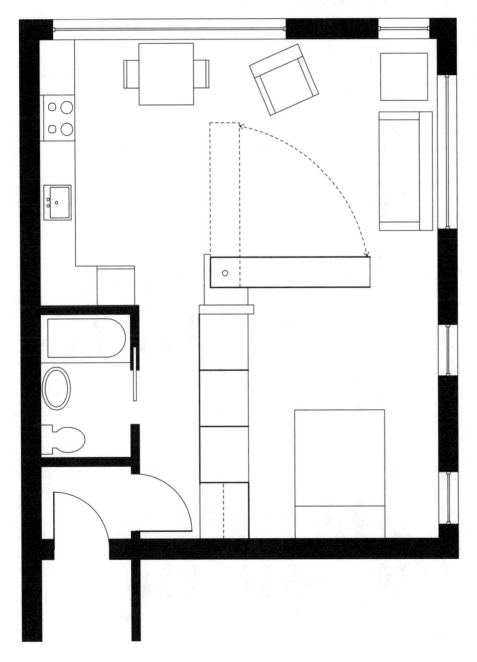

FIGURE 3.6 The inclusion of a movable partition in a small dwelling allows rooms to expand or contract.

expand their bedroom area, the same partition can be rotated. Integrating a bookshelf or storage space within the partition would further increase its practicality.

Small-size housing is valuable in higher-density communities—most often in urban settings. However, it can also be considered for suburban locations where densification is a priority. For this housing type to become accepted, however, cultural attitudes will have to shift toward a greater appreciation of efficient use of fewer resources and less personal space.

FLEXIBLE AND GROWING HOMES

The post–World War II definition of a household—breadwinner father, stay-at-home mother, and their children—has evolved to include a greater diversity of family compositions. Figure 3.7 illustrates how the makeup of a contemporary household may vary throughout its life cycle. Despite these socioeconomic realities, most dwellings offered by builders fail

FIGURE 3.7 A scenario of a contemporary family's life cycle.

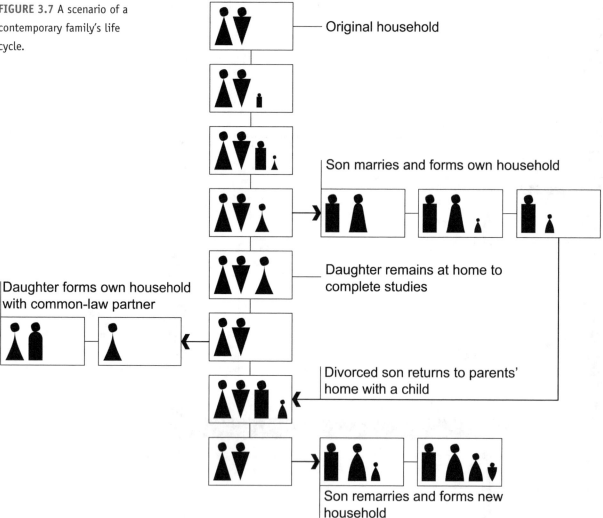

Original household

Son marries and forms own household

Daughter remains at home to complete studies

Daughter forms own household with common-law partner

Divorced son returns to parents' home with a child

Son remarries and forms new household

to suitably accommodate the changing needs of today's families. In regard to mobility, between 2002 and 2003, over 40 million households relocated to different dwellings (US Census Bureau 2010). Rather than retrofit or expand, growing families chose to move to larger homes. Similarly, to avoid costly maintenance, empty nesters tend to relocate from a single-family home to an apartment once their children move out. Flexible design prepares the entire structure for transformation. Interior layout can be altered by changing the locations of partitions as well as expanding or shrinking the size of the unit.

Integrating homeowner participation and flexibility in dwelling design promotes economic and social sustainability. Residents feel that they have a say in their living environment, and as a result participation in and contribution to community life increase. Economically, home ownership becomes more affordable when individuals can select features that address their current and future needs with their limited resources. Some can reside near transit lines, eliminating the need to rely on private cars. Some may also have lower utility bills as a result of their choices. The possibility of customizing before occupancy and making alterations over time is much greater when flexible design strategies are considered in the initial planning phase. The ability to frequently adapt a dwelling to the changing needs of a household allows families to reside and evolve within their community. Rather than attempt to predict the needs of their clients, builders can offer homes that can easily be retrofitted to suit an array of demographic backgrounds.

Manipulating entrances and vertical arrangements allows a multistory single-family dwelling to be converted into two or more independent units. In the case of a three-story building, a larger family may use two floors while a second, smaller household may reside on the third story. Alternative arrangements include using one of the levels as a home office or housing three related households in the same structure. To permit various options within and between dwellings, one can take advantage of a range of technological innovations such as flexible utility conduits, floor moldings, and demountable partitions, which are illustrated in figure 3.8.

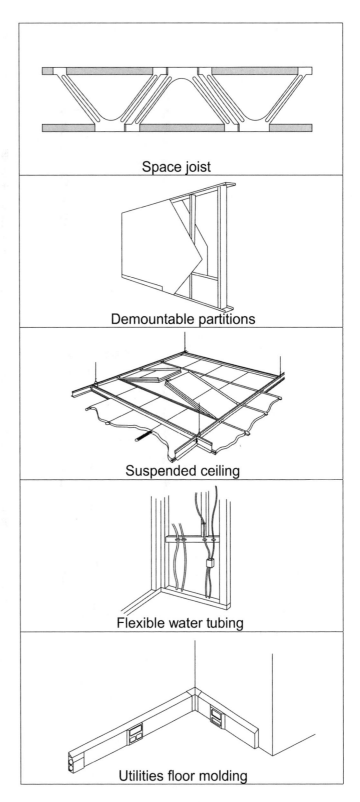

FIGURE 3.8 Some technologies permit adaptability, disassembly, and reuse of the home's spaces and components.

FIGURE 3.9 Identical open basement floor area in an affordable housing project was partitioned and finished by the occupants according to their unique means and space needs.

Expansion is another flexible design approach that works with the original volumes of a home. Two strategies can be used: add-in and add-on. In an *add-in*, the space is left unfinished, similar to that of a loft. Growth within the home occurs through adaptation and use of this area. Partitions and extra finishings are gradually added in response to ongoing space needs. Second stories, attics, and basements can all be designed to accommodate interior expansion. For example, basements that were built with larger windows and standard ceiling heights can be converted from storage spaces to living areas, as illustrated in figure 3.9.

Narrow homes are suited to this flexible housing strategy because all bearing walls are positioned at the perimeter. Avoidance of any inside, load-bearing elements will free up the interior space. Semipermanent or movable partition walls offer the possibility to create

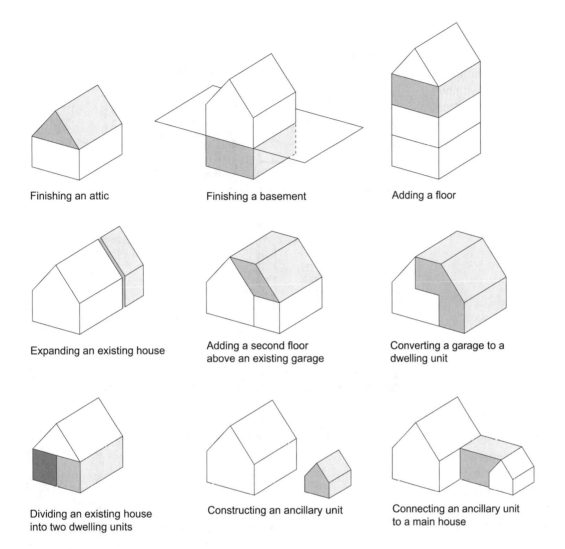

Finishing an attic

Finishing a basement

Adding a floor

Expanding an existing house

Adding a second floor above an existing garage

Converting a garage to a dwelling unit

Dividing an existing house into two dwelling units

Constructing an ancillary unit

Connecting an ancillary unit to a main house

a large number of floor-plan variations. The add-in strategy also coincides with a growing do-it-yourself, or DIY, trend. After land, one of the most expensive aspects of construction is finishes (Broadbent 2006). Partially finished spaces offer homeowners the opportunity for savings by allowing occupants to complete their home as they are able.

The potential to expand a house beyond its original perimeter is another characteristic of flexible housing. Planning for the *add-on* method foresees construction of a new addition to a home (fig. 3.10). The dimensions of the lot, along with municipal setback distances and maximum roof heights, determine the direction of the expansion. Adding on or designing for such expansion will require that the site's natural features are accounted for. Trees and vegetation will have to be initially planted where they will not need to be uprooted at a later stage. For add-on growth to be possible, structural framing must be designed to support future additional loads. The choice of materials and the dimensioning of a house also affect the feasibility of the expansion. Concrete block and masonry walls are difficult to dismantle and may impede future construction. In contrast, modular structural and partition systems, which are designed to be disassembled easily, facilitate changes to the house.

FIGURE 3.10 Methods of adding space to and transforming a dwelling unit.

The owner of the unit on the third floor and the mezzanine is a single mother, age 41, with two adolescent school children.

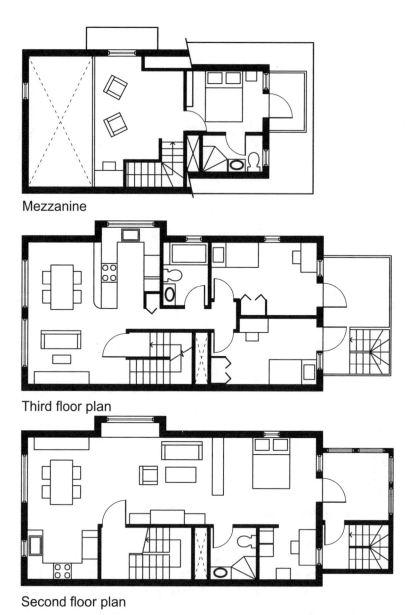

Mezzanine

Third floor plan

The owners of the second floor unit are a young couple without children who have been married for three years and who, until the purchase of their home, rented a one-bedroom apartment in a suburb not far from the city center.

Second floor plan

The owner of the ground floor unit is a widower, age 57, who has worked as a civil servant for many years and has been offered an early retirement package due to budget cuts.

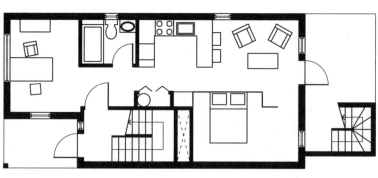

Ground floor plan

FIGURE 3.11 Plans showing a variety of layouts made by households occupying floors of a three-story Next Home structure.

The Next Home

Location: Montreal, Quebec, Canada

Design: Avi Friedman, Architect

Completion: demonstration in 1996, with various site adaptations in 1998 and 1999 since the concept seemed to respond to a market need for small, adaptable dwellings

Total floor area: 2,800 sq ft (260 m²)

Number of floors: 3 and a mezzanine

The Next Home was constructed on the campus of McGill University in Montreal, Canada, as a demonstration unit after research on societal changes, technological innovations, and environmental concerns (Friedman 2002). Through the implementation of flexible design strategies, the Next Home adheres to a holistic view of sustainability that combines economic, social, and environmental considerations. The adaptable nature of the design provides an effective initial fit to the lives of its occupants and facilitates response to future changes. Built from prefabricated panels, the dwelling utilized a menu of features to create units that respond to diverse household requirements.

The floors of the Next Home were dimensioned to provide the maximum number of potential spatial relationships. At 20 ft (6.1 m) wide and 40 ft (12.2 m) long, the home allows builders to take advantage of standardized, modular dimensions to reduce material waste and construction costs. Three-story structures can be detached, semidetached, or constructed in rows to both increase urban density and reduce infrastructure costs. Figure 3.11 demonstrates

FIGURE 3.12 A partition between the second-floor living room and bedroom is also used as a closet.

FIGURE 3.13 A variety of kitchen types were offered as a preoccupancy choice to buyers.

FIGURE 3.14 Front elevation of one of the Next Home structures, near Quebec City, Canada.

a scenario of choices made by the occupants of the demonstration unit who occupy different levels of one three-story structure. A vertical service core contains water supply, drainage, ventilation, and electrical systems. Its accessible, central location facilitates servicing and adaptability to future changes.

The creation of a catalog of components encouraged homeowners to customize their interior and exterior, using digital visualization media (Feng 2000; see fig. 3.12). Roofs, dormers, and balconies could be selected to create a distinct facade that simultaneously matches the overall aesthetic of the neighborhood. The absence of interior load-bearing partitions allowed floor-plan variation and was conducive to future add-in expansion.

While a couple with children may select a larger kitchen, a single person who occupies another floor might choose to purchase a smaller kitchen with compact appliances. Figure 3.13 shows some kitchen options. Similarly, the bathroom in one of the units might be conventional, whereas an elderly occupant using a wheelchair will need a spacious bathroom that does not hinder mobility.

The Next Home's emphasis on flexibility and homeowner participation led to the design of dwellings that reflected contemporary diverse demographics. The unit was constructed in several locations and was suitably adjusted to the needs of the occupants (fig. 3.14).

CHAPTER 4

Unit-Planning Principles

D esigners often underestimate the effect of the dwelling's layout on sustainable living. According to a study by the Building Research Establishment (BRE 2005), achieving sustainability can be realized cheaply or even at no additional cost to the occupant. Before elaborating on specific technical aspects, it would be of value to review general unit-planning strategies. The issues that are referred to in this chapter include shape, overall size, height, relation to other units, and interior organization.

COST-EFFECTIVE COMFORT

The notion of sustainable housing is often associated with such technical considerations as environmentally safe materials and energy-efficient envelope design. There are, however, several basic planning decisions made at the preliminary design stage in addition to site selection and orientation that can significantly affect the economic, environmental, and social aspects of a housing development. Manipulating variables such as the unit's dimensions, configurations, size, and grouping can reduce heat loss and the amount of construction materials required, leading to cost savings for both builder and occupant without compromising living comfort.

In the United States, for example, the approximately 1.4 million new homes that are constructed each year consume 40 percent of all lumber and plywood sold (Sabnis et al. 2005). The amount of wasted construction materials is also large. A 2007 study by the Nebraska Energy Office demonstrated that, on average, 8,000 lb (3.6 tonnes) of waste is produced when a 2,000 sq ft (190 m^2) home is constructed. Most of it—35 percent is lumber and manufactured wood products, 15 percent dry wall, and 12 percent masonry materials—will eventually end up in landfills (Paschich and Zimmerman 2001). Planning dwelling units efficiently will reduce their environmental footprint, save time, lower costs, and reduce waste and pollution.

If planned efficiently, the dwelling can be comfortable with no increase in construction costs. In fact, the owner will likely be rewarded with life-cycle cost savings (Fuad-Luke 2004). Early investments in good design can lower operating and maintenance costs and increase the home's value. A nominal increase in the original capital investment, as little as an additional 0.3 percent, can greatly improve the eco-performance of an average-size home. With careful planning it is possible to improve the operational and environmental aspects of a home without compromising living comfort and to create a product that is more affordable and more marketable to both builders and buyers (BRE 2005).

DESIGN PRINCIPLES

Designers and builders can consider six basic preliminary design strategies to achieve sustainable homes: minimizing size, simplifying configuration, stacking floors, joining units, dimensioning for modular design, and optimizing interior space. Each of these strategies is explained in the following sections.

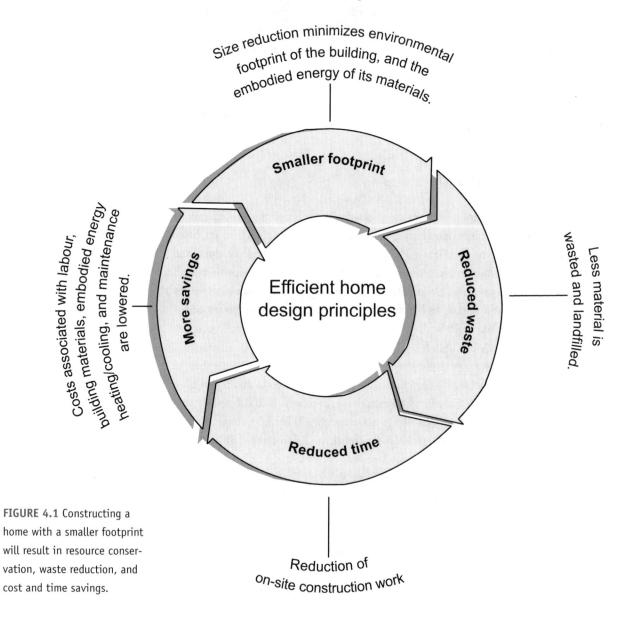

FIGURE 4.1 Constructing a home with a smaller footprint will result in resource conservation, waste reduction, and cost and time savings.

Minimizing Size

In general, the bigger the house, the greater its carbon footprint will be because of the manufacturing and shipping of building products and, once occupied, its operation (Low et al. 2005). Energy consumption is, to a significant extent, also proportional to house size. In the United States, for example, 100 million homes out of a total of 130 million account for 20 percent of the climate-changing greenhouse gas emissions from housing (Sabnis et al. 2005; US Census Bureau 2009). Therefore, downsizing a house will limit the amount of resource consumption and save time and money, as shown in figure 4.1.

By downsizing from 3,000 to 2,000 sq ft (279 to 186 m²), for example, a homeowner could save one-third of the cost per area and could put the savings into better materials and superior craftsmanship (Wilson 2006). It can also be argued that, when affordability is an issue, approximately 800 sq ft (74.3 m²) is needed to house two occupants, and another 200 sq ft (18.6 m²) can accommodate every additional person (Friedman 2002).

Simplifying Configuration

Complex designs might be visually interesting, yet they are not the "greenest," because most heat losses occur through floors, ceilings, and walls. The dwelling shape can, therefore, influence its energy efficiency by affecting the amount of exposed surface area through which heat can flow (Ireland 2007).

Complex envelopes have many corners and a longer perimeter, which require more materials and labor to construct and, as a result, cost more. Examples of complex and simple envelopes are shown in figure 4.2. Furthermore, a complex shape results in more wall and roof surfaces exposed to the elements, higher heat absorption during the day, and greater heat losses at night. On the other hand, buildings with fewer corners might require fewer windows, thereby avoiding costly labor and materials.

The ratio of floor area to perimeter should be maximized. With the same floor area and height, simplifying the building configuration minimizes the number of corners, overall building perimeter, and total wall surface area, leading to a smaller exposed envelope and an efficient use of interior space. For various building configurations with the same floor area, an increase in the floor-area-to-perimeter ratio augments the reduction in wall surface when a more complex building configuration is changed to a simpler one. When the building configuration is changed from a square to a circle, for example, 11 percent less wall is required to enclose the same floor area. Therefore, not only is the space more efficiently used, the

FIGURE 4.2 A building with a complex envelope (*a*) will consume more materials and lose more energy than one with a simple shape (*b*).

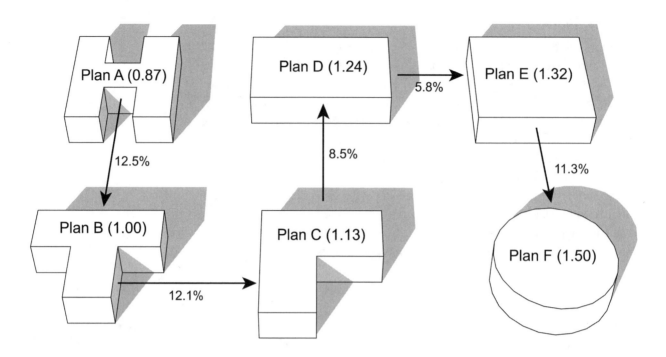

Plan configuration	Wall area sq.ft. (m²)	Energy required (KWh)
Plan A (H)	1,720 (160)	2,856
Plan B (T)	1,505 (140)	2,501
Plan C (L)	1,320 (123)	2,198
Plan D (rectangle)	1,205 (112)	2,001
Plan E (square)	1,140 (106)	1,894
Plan F (circle)	1,010 (94)	1,679

FIGURE 4.3 Buildings with simpler configurations and fewer corners have higher floor-area-to-perimeter ratios (numbers in parentheses on plans). The energy used and heating costs in such structures are also lowered.

consumption of energy is more manageable. Simplifying the shape of a typical home reduces exposed wall surface, which minimizes the associated annual energy consumption and, as a result, its heating cost, as shown in figure 4.3.

A dome-shaped structure is the most energy-efficient design because it encloses the greatest volume but has the least surface area. Although a circular building achieves the minimum wall area and energy consumption, it is not practical, because curved walls are more difficult and costly to build. Furthermore, its circular layout challenges effective planning for functional interior layout. For those reasons, a square is preferable to a circle and still maintains a minimal floor-area-to-perimeter ratio (Chueca 2009).

Dwellings are rarely designed as a perfect square either. As with the circular shape, it is difficult to plan efficiently the interior of a square. Rectangles therefore are the most practical choice for a simplified shape. Rectangular designs require less land, can fit on narrower infill lots, are easier to group, and therefore have reduced energy and material costs. What should the proportions of the sides of the rectangle be? The answer depends on many variables, such as chosen module, available lots, orientation, interior division, proportion of rooms that must be fully lit, and municipal bylaws. As elaborated in chapter 2, a rectangular home can also benefit from passive solar gain. An elongated building with an east–west axis will expose the longer south side to maximum heat gain in the winter (Halliday 2008).

Stacking Floors

Approximately half the energy losses from a home are through the walls, floor, and roof, with the rest attributed to openings or to air leaks due to poor joints and seals (Sabnis et al. 2005). When two or more floors are stacked, materials and energy consumption are lowered substantially because of the reduction in exposed area.

For the question of whether the basic configuration of the house should be tall and stacked or low and spread out, the answer is not necessarily a matter of style or local climate. At times, low-rise houses may look more appealing, allowing more possibilities for privacy and outdoor features such as decks and porches. Single-story ranch houses or bungalows, for example, may also benefit from passive solar gain when their longitudinal facades face south. With regard to energy consumption, however, the tall and stacked home has less roof surface for a given volume and does not lose heat through the roof as quickly when warm air rises. Second, a smaller roof means less area available to absorb sunlight, which in turn minimizes overheating and subsequent cooling demand. Third, a smaller roof means fewer construction materials, less waste, and lower costs. Most savings, however, will result from the reduction of the dwelling's footprint and expenses associated with the excavation and construction of a foundation. Accordingly, the cost of a two-story house will be reduced compared with a one-story building with an equivalent area (Gonzalo and Habermann 2006). Figure 4.4 compares heat loss in stacked and unstacked dwellings.

FIGURE 4.4 A tall and stacked house has less envelope surface relative to floor area compared with a spread-out low-rise house, which lowers warm air leakage.

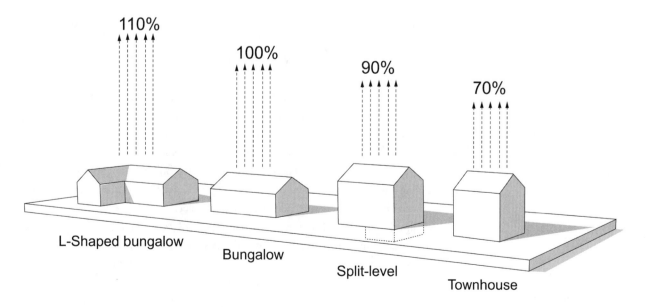

110%

100%

90%

70%

L-Shaped bungalow

Bungalow

Split-level

Townhouse

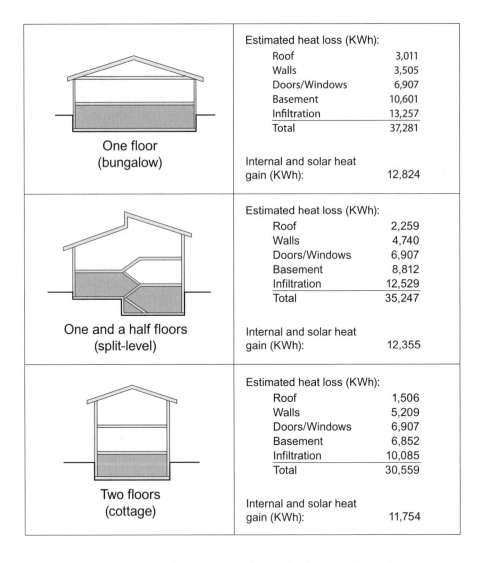

FIGURE 4.5 Various floor stackings result in different surface-to-volume ratios and energy consumption, with the highest value for one-story bungalows and the lowest for two-story cottages

One floor (bungalow)

Estimated heat loss (KWh):	
Roof	3,011
Walls	3,505
Doors/Windows	6,907
Basement	10,601
Infiltration	13,257
Total	37,281

Internal and solar heat gain (KWh): 12,824

One and a half floors (split-level)

Estimated heat loss (KWh):	
Roof	2,259
Walls	4,740
Doors/Windows	6,907
Basement	8,812
Infiltration	12,529
Total	35,247

Internal and solar heat gain (KWh): 12,355

Two floors (cottage)

Estimated heat loss (KWh):	
Roof	1,506
Walls	5,209
Doors/Windows	6,907
Basement	6,852
Infiltration	10,085
Total	30,559

Internal and solar heat gain (KWh): 11,754

Variation in floor stacking for a single-family dwelling leads to different housing forms, such as one-story bungalows, one-and-a-half-story split-level homes, or two-story detached cottages. From a material and energy usage point of view, bungalows have a higher average surface-to-volume ratio (0.38) compared with split-level homes (0.25) and therefore require more construction materials and are less energy efficient, as shown in figure 4.5. In all climates, attached units like row houses are most efficient because there are only two exterior walls and the opportunity for cross ventilation. For a given floor area, apartments use less energy than row houses, row houses less than semidetached, and semidetached less than detached houses. It is important also to vary the building heights and breaks in the building line of row houses and apartment complexes to prevent continuous shadowing and allow for increased sunlight to all the units on the block (Thomas 2005).

Finally, despite the environmentally friendly aspects of stacking houses, issues related to style and the occupants' preferences are things that designers must consider. Problems associated with limited outdoor space for people living in the upper units, or efficient circulation for housing complexes five to six stories tall, will need to be addressed by the designer.

Joining Units

When dwelling units are joined together, they are more energy efficient (fig. 4.6). Land use efficiency is also improved; since more land can be kept open for common use, natural vegetation and wildlife are preserved (Gonzalo and Habermann 2006). Clustering buildings also reduces the infrastructure needed for driveways, roads, underground sewers, water provision, and electrical systems. Fewer disturbances, as a result, will affect the site and the surroundings area (fig. 4.7). Finally, by clustering units, a considerable amount of time and material spent on the envelope will be saved.

When a garage is needed, there are several considerations. From an indoor air quality perspective, if the site is large enough, a fully separate garage is preferable over an attached one. In the case of an attached garage, a very tight air seal in the common wall between the garage and the home is needed to prevent or minimize the amount of au-

FIGURE 4.6 In joined units, the amount of exposed wall area is reduced substantially as one or more exterior walls are eliminated, enabling construction efficiency and energy savings.

Single-family detached		Total: 400
100	100	100	100

Estimated heat loss (KWh):

Roof	1,506
Walls	5,209
Doors/Windows	6,907
Basement	6,852
Infiltration	10,085
Total	30,559

Internal and solar heat gain (KWh): 11,754

34% reduction

Semi-detached		Total: 256
64	64	64	64

Estimated heat loss (KWh):

Roof	1,506
Walls	3,261
Doors/Windows	6,907
Basement	5,002
Infiltration	10,085
Total	26,761

Internal and solar heat gain (KWh): 11,291

26% reduction

Rowhouse		Total: 184
64	28	28	64

Estimated heat loss (KWh):

Roof	1,506
Walls	1,313
Doors/Windows	6,907
Basement	3,156
Infiltration	10,085
Total	22,967

Internal and solar heat gain (KWh): 10,761

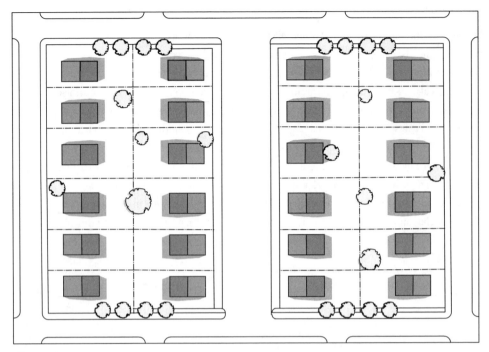

Common

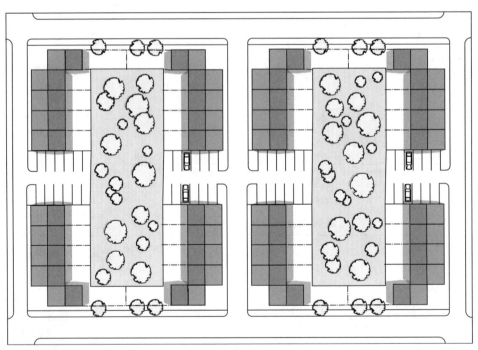

Mid-density

FIGURE 4.7 Joined units can share land and utility runways, reducing construction cost and leaving more space for natural landscape and the preservation of wildlife.

tomobile exhaust that can leak into the house and reduce the air quality. In general, a housing configuration with an indoor garage is discouraged because it fosters poor air quality when the car's engine runs (Sassi 2006). From an energy-efficiency standpoint, however, including a garage within the structure is preferred since fewer construction materials and less space heating are required. Various alternatives to location of a garage are shown in figure 4.8. There is, as with other considerations, often a trade-off among several strategies to achieve sustainability, and a chosen design needs to prioritize the most important environmental and health needs.

In single-family housing subdivisions that have poor public transit service, municipalities commonly mandate several on-lot parking spots per unit. Reducing the number of required parking spaces from two to one space per dwelling, for example, can triple the site's dwellings capacity from 10 to 32 units per acre (Thomas 2005). This further proves the importance of having a community where shops, transit stops, and other public amenities can be reached by a short walk.

Dimensioning for Modular Design

Experience shows that, compared with construction of modular dwellings, the construction of randomly dimensioned homes requires more cutting and fitting, resulting in increased waste, more time spent, and higher labor costs. *Modular dimensioning* involves standardizing room size for structural framing members and sheathing, including dry-

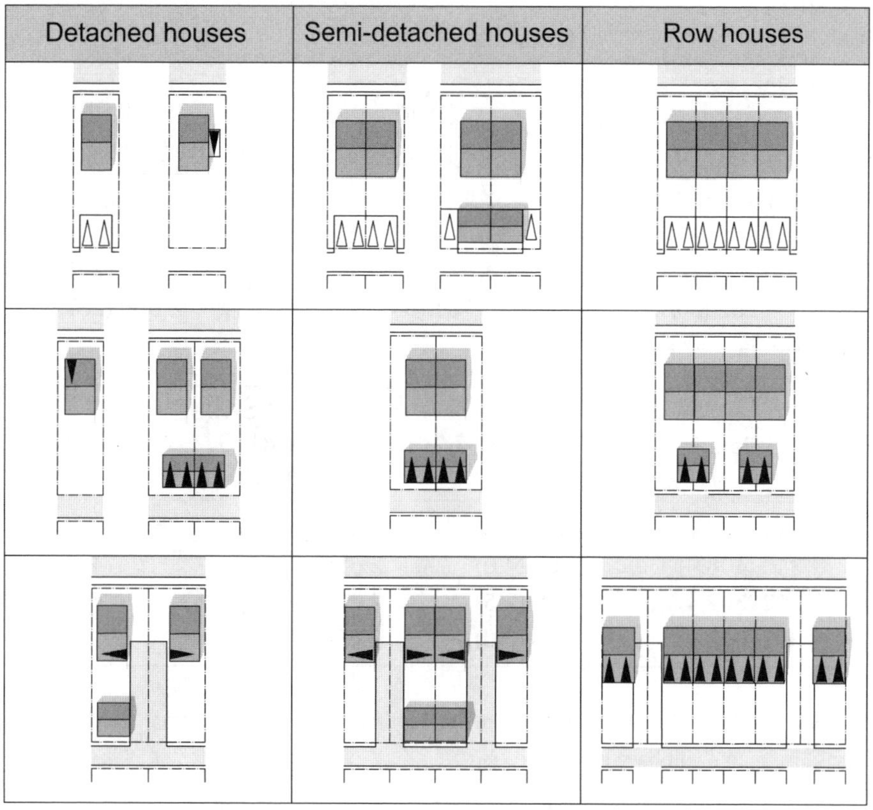

FIGURE 4.8 Various relationships between the location of a garage and the main house in higher-density residential situations.

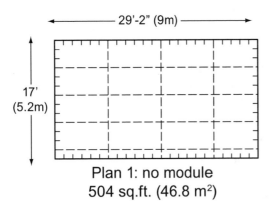

Plan 1: no module
504 sq.ft. (46.8 m²)

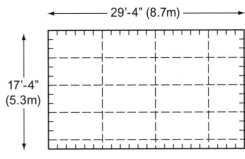

Plan 2: 16" (400mm) module
508 sq.ft. (47.2 m²)

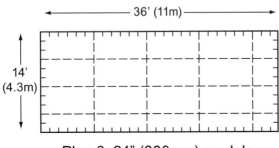

Plan 3: 24" (600mm) module
504 sq.ft. (46.8 m²)

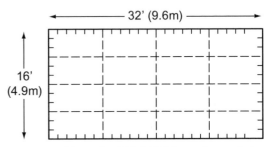

Plan 4: 48" (1220mm) module
512 sq.ft. (47.6 m²)

Plan module	Joists ft (m)	Studs ft (m)	Sheathing sq.ft. (m²)
Plan 1: no module	1,240 (378.2)	1,840 (561.1)	2,502 (232.5)
Plan 2: 16" (400mm)	1,261 (384.4)	1,706 (520.1)	2,511 (233.3)
Plan 3: 24" (600mm)	984 (299.9)	1,834 (559.2)	2,609 (242.4)
Plan 4: 48" (1220mm)	992 (302.4)	1,751 (534.0)	2,560 (237.9)

Plan module	Joists		Sheathing	
	Ordered ft (m)	Wasted ft (m)	Ordered sq.ft. (m²)	Wasted sq.ft. (m²)
Plan 1: no module	1,324 (403.6)	83 (25.4)	2,688 (249.7)	185 (17.2)
Plan 2: 16" (400mm)	1,340 (408.4)	79 (24.0)	2,688 (249.7)	174 (16.2)
Plan 3: 24" (600mm)	992 (302.4)	8 (2.5)	2,688 (249.7)	78 (7.3)
Plan 4: 48" (1220mm)	992 (302.4)	0 (0.0)	2,560 (237.9)	0 (0.0)

FIGURE 4.9 Four building configurations with similar shape, floor area, and perimeter. Due to its modular design, which also respects standard industry product dimensions, plan 4 will have no waste.

walls, studs, and joists, leading to savings and decreasing the amount of discarded materials (Carpenter 2009). Modular designs also allow advanced calculation and off-site fabrication of large structural panels, further lowering costs and saving time.

In wood-frame constructions with standardized dimensions of building modules, one configuration could be slightly more beneficial than another, despite their equal areas, as illustrated in figure 4.9. In plan 2, the building configuration is closer to a square and therefore requires a smaller number of studs than plan 3, for example. On the other hand, a slightly higher number of floor joists are provided for the first two plans, which are wider and require tighter joist spacing of 12 in. (405 mm). In general, designing for 4 ft (1,220 mm) modules in plan 4 and 24 in. (600 mm) stud spacing in plan 3 alone can reduce lumber use by 8 percent. The significant advantage of modular design is the reduction of construction waste that is not reusable and must be landfilled. Despite the similarity in material requirements for different modules, the amount of wasted material varies significantly. The amount of wasted joists and sheathing is higher in plans 1 and 2 (between 6 and 7 percent) where the modules have a smaller spacing, since those wasted cutoffs are too small to be reused. This accounts for only one dwelling unit. One could imagine how much this amount would be for an entire neighborhood. For example, when the 83 ft (25.4 m) of wasted joists in plan 1 is multiplied by the number of dwellings to be constructed, the total waste is significant. In plan 3, with a larger modular configuration, less material is wasted in cutoffs. The result of efficient modular design is not only reduction of needed material; it also includes reducing jobsite waste generated from disposed packaging, such as cardboard and plastic.

Optimizing Interior Space

A small-size house, as already noted, will have a smaller environmental footprint. Yet, its interior space must also be designed efficiently. In roof design, for instance, the use of conventional prefabricated trusses results in the creation of unused yet heated volume above the top floor's ceiling. Choosing other types of roof trusses can allow additional used space, as shown in figure 4.10, where an attic is possible.

A large part of the heat loss occurs through basements. Compared with slabs-on-grade and crawl spaces, a full basement requires more material, labor, and construction time, especially when it is made of concrete. Full basements can be eliminated where they are not required for climatic reasons (i.e., protection against frost damage) or seismic reasons (i.e., providing greater stability to the structure). Some recommend preserved-wood foundations, particularly in the form of prefabricated panels for dry and energy-efficient basements. According to Kennedy et al. (2002), it is estimated that the use of wood in-

FIGURE 4.10 Choice of a specially designed roof truss allows turning the roof into a habitable space.

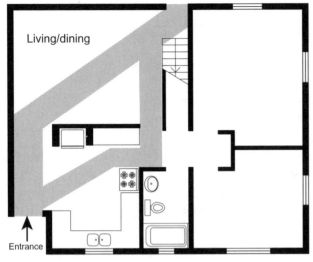

Living/dining

Entrance

Inefficient circulation

Living/dining

Entrance

Efficient circulation

FIGURE 4.11 Efficient use of small spaces can be attained by minimizing circulation paths and hallways.

stead of concrete will reduce the amount of embodied energy by about 30 percent. It must be noted, however, that, when considering the use of wood versus concrete for foundations, one should recognize the advantages and the disadvantages of both. Wood foundations will consume more natural solid sawn lumber, whereas the production of concrete will require more energy. Those aspects will be elaborated in chapter 6.

Another strategy for efficient design is to minimize length of circulation paths and hallways (fig 4.11). Where larger spaces are desired that don't increase the overall size of the home, a designer can emphasize horizontal lines, use fewer partitions, gently slope the ceilings upward toward the openings, or suggest lighter colors. An open plan will also contribute to better interior heat management, as there will be fewer walls to block passage of warm air from room to room, as shown in figure 4.12. Pipe, duct, and conduit runs could also be reduced by grouping of spaces with similar functions, such as with back-to-back bathroom, kitchen, and laundry areas (Thomas 2005).

FIGURE 4.12 Heat will travel more easily between spaces of a dwelling with fewer walls.

Remington Court

Location: Seattle, Washington, USA

Design: HyBrid Architecture

Completion: 2009

Site area: 0.09 acres (0.04 hectares)

Floor area: 1,530 sq ft (142 m²)

Number of floors: 3

Third floor

Remington Court is a four-unit project featuring three townhouses and a detached single-family house. Built as an urban infill project among small-scale dwellings, the project elegantly demonstrates principles of sustainable design that allow flexible planning, energy efficiency, and a reduced footprint.

Within a simple rectangular plan, the three-story townhouses offer a broad range of spatial flexibility (fig. 4.13). Designed to allow a complete separation from the upper floor, the first level is equipped with its own entrance, roughed-in plumbing for a future kitchen, and removable partition walls. The first floor can be converted into a separate unit and be used as a living or work area without undergoing heavy alteration (fig. 4.14). The second level contains the main living space and a kitchen in an open configuration (fig. 4.15). On the third level, the master bedroom incorporates modular wardrobes, which offer yet another strategy for flexible spatial configuration. The wardrobes, fitted with fixable casters, also serve as floor-to-ceiling partitions to create separate spaces.

Strategically oriented, this energy-efficient building encourages natural light and breezes to penetrate its interior (fig. 4.16). Daylight and ventilation are maximized

FIGURE 4.13 The floor plans offer spatial flexibility to accommodate a variety of personal needs and lifestyles. Used with permission.

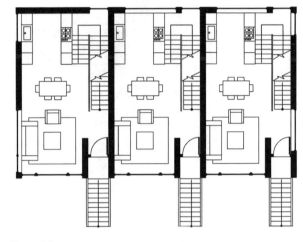

Second floor

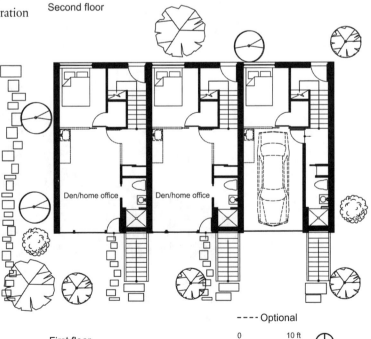

Den/home office   Den/home office

First floor

---- Optional

0   10 ft

FIGURE 4.14 The front stoops engage the street and invite the residents to interact with their neighbors. The elevated main entry allows for the conversion of the first floor into a separate unit. Used with permission.

FIGURE 4.15 The open configuration of the main living area encourages natural daylight and ventilation while providing maximum spatial flexibility. Used with permission.

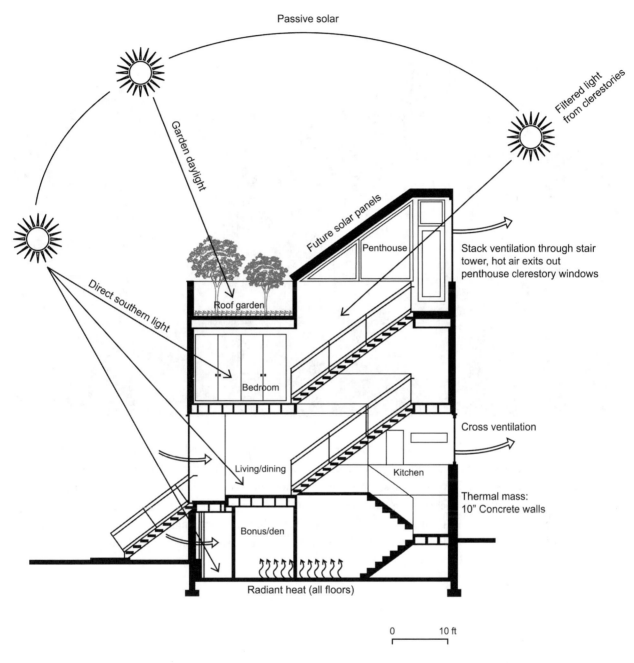

Passive solar

Filtered light from clerestories

Garden daylight

Future solar panels

Penthouse

Stack ventilation through stair tower, hot air exits out penthouse clerestory windows

Direct southern light

Roof garden

Bedroom

Cross ventilation

Living/dining

Kitchen

Thermal mass: 10" Concrete walls

Bonus/den

Radiant heat (all floors)

0   10 ft

through the floor-to-ceiling windows on the southern facade, the penthouse clerestory windows, and the open stair that connects all four floors (fig. 4.17). In closed areas such as the bathrooms, transoms are installed on the north and south partition walls to reduce the need for artificial lighting during the day.

In addition to using passive technologies, the building optimizes its energy efficiency through its super-insulated walls and roofs, thermal mass with 10 in. (25 cm) concrete walls, radiant heat from polished concrete floors, and green roof. By the joining of the three units, each dwelling benefits from further reduction in heating cost. The thermal mass of the building envelope helps mitigate temperature fluctuations and cre-

FIGURE 4.16 The project's orientation facilitates passive solar gains and natural ventilation.

FIGURE 4.17 The penthouse stair towers with operable clerestory windows enable stack ventilation and ample daylight. The rooftop decks incorporate vegetable gardens designed to absorb rainwater. Used with permission.

ates an acoustic barrier. The rooftop garden designed for each unit features a deck and a vegetable garden primed with 9 in. (23 cm) of planting medium. By providing a surface for heat and storm-water absorption, the green roof helps slow down interior heating and reduces the building's environmental footprint. It also helps to minimize the *urban heat island effect*, which happens when urban areas have higher temperatures than rural areas because of the use of materials in the built environment that retain heat.

CHAPTER 5

Constructing a Home

According to a projection by the Intergovernmental Panel on Climate Change on the environmental effects of construction, unless practices are fundamentally altered, the worldwide building industry could double its greenhouse gas emissions between 2004 and 2030, that is, GHG emissions could go from 9.5 billion to 17.2 billion tons (8.6 billion to 15.6 billion tonnes) (UNEP/GRID-Arendal 2008). This requires the adoption of not only appropriate design strategies but sound construction principals. Whereas the previous chapter dealt primarily with design principals, this chapter delves into the technical aspects of sustainable construction. It provides a guide for the design of an improved envelope, efficient framing, and construction details as well as prefabrication.

THE BUILDING ENVELOPE

A building envelope is the physical separator between the indoor and outdoor environments. According to Winchip (2007), a principle goal of building envelope design for a sustainable dwelling is to minimize emissions and optimize energy consumption, preferably using renewable energy. Another objective is to maintain the occupants' thermal comfort and uniform temperatures by controlling heat transfer from the surfaces of the envelope and by ensuring that it is airtight (Carpenter 2009). The third goal is to eliminate moisture problems related to thermal bridges and damp basements, especially by reducing condensation during humid summers. Finally, a properly designed envelope can reduce noise and risk of injury due to such things as shattered windows from fire, high winds, and falling ice caused by ice dams on sloped roofs (Harvey 2006). The construction of a high-performance building envelope may cost more, but over the building's lifetime, savings to the occupant and the environment will result from lower energy consumption and downsized heating and cooling systems (Keeler and Burke 2009) (fig. 5.1).

Apart from openings, the envelope's opaque areas (e.g., walls and roofs) can be considered static. Its functions include heating and cooling, through shelter and insulation, and reduction of temperature swings through *thermal mass*—the ability of materials to store thermal energy (Gonzalo and Habermann 2006). The glazed elements of the building, such as windows and skylights, may be more dynamic in response to short- and

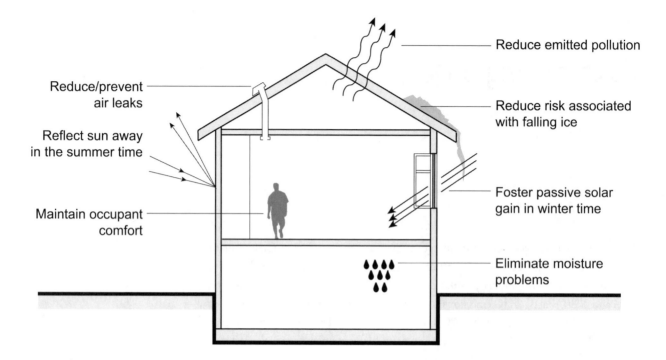

Reduce emitted pollution

Reduce/prevent
air leaks

Reduce risk associated
with falling ice

Reflect sun away
in the summer time

Foster passive solar
gain in winter time

Maintain occupant
comfort

Eliminate moisture
problems

FIGURE 5.1 Functions of a building envelope designed for sustainability.

long-term changes in interior and exterior conditions. In addition, they have other functions, such as letting in daylight, providing a view, and passive solar gain.

As a starting point, designers need to modify the envelope in response to challenges and opportunities presented by the orientation of the different facades, as outlined in chapter 2. Second, the enclosure can be kept warm by placing insulation as close as practically possible to the exterior. This allows the envelope to contribute to the thermal mass, helps to even out temperature fluctuations, and raises the radiant temperature of the interior, which will be discussed next. Third, the design should aim for durability through the choice of quality materials. Finally, proper construction practices will ensure minimum air leakage into and out of the house (Gonzalo and Habermann 2006) (fig. 5.2).

THERMAL MASS AND ITS DISTRIBUTION

It is commonly recognized by scientists and green builders that high thermal mass depends on the way the building is constructed and is needed to stabilize daytime temperature and nighttime cooling. Thermal mass is particularly effective in hot, dry climates, such as in deserts, when the temperature difference between night and day is large, about 18°F to 35°F (10°C to 20°C) (Halliday 2008). In hot, humid climates, the temperature drop between day and night is only 9°F to 19°F (5°C to 10°C). The home's thermal mass will absorb and store the sun's free energy, releasing it at night if the indoor temperature drops below the wall temperature, which will lessen the need to heat the dwelling in the winter. In summer, the same principles are in effect, but because of a *thermal lag* of passive heating, thermal mass successfully diminishes the amount of cooling required by decreasing the peak temperature that is reached during daytime (Schaeffer 2005).

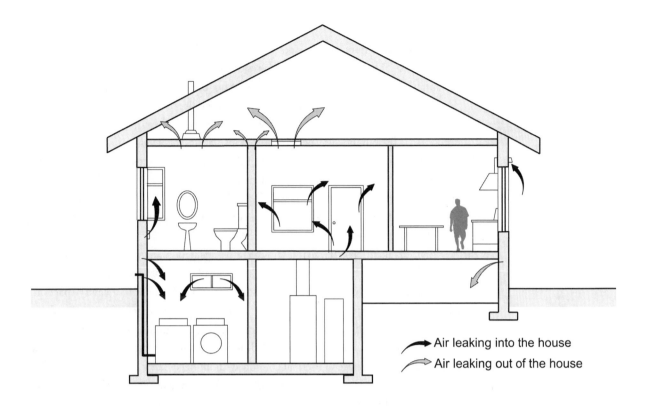

Air leaking into the house

Air leaking out of the house

FIGURE 5.2 Common points
of air leakage into and out of
a home.

Thermal mass needs to be designed properly to achieve a proper balance and avoid over-heating the building.

For best results, the elements of thermal mass should be exposed to direct sunlight and be in direct contact with conditioned and circulating air. A designer needs to avoid covering these components with elements such as false ceilings, drywall, and carpeting. Secure and controllable night cooling should also be provided where exposed thermal mass is intended to moderate daytime temperatures (Halliday 2008).

In general, all materials can be categorized according to their degree of thermal mass. Buildings constructed of hardwoods, softwoods, and masonry such as clay bricks, concrete blocks, and rammed earth have good thermal qualities, which slow down their response to changes in external conditions and limit internal temperature swings (Baker-Laporte et al. 2001). A concrete slab can also act as a thermal store, provided that it is not covered with a lightweight finish. Thermal mass increases with the thickness of the walls, floors, and roof. The thicker the materials, the greater the delay in the transfer of heat from the outside ambient climate to the inside surface. For a typical exterior wall 12 in. (30 cm) thick, the thermal lag is 8 hours for concrete and 10 hours for brick (Harvey 2006). A building with low thermal mass behaves in the opposite manner and is typically made of metal, such as a steel-framed structure and lightweight cladding panels. This gives a fast thermal response to changes in external conditions and results in large temperature swings. In dwellings, constructing walls with high thermal mass in the living areas and low thermal mass in the sleeping spaces will be a suitable strategy, since the occupants spend more of their daytime in the living areas (Kwok and Grondzik 2007). The various components of the envelope and their construction practices are outlined next.

The Value of Insulation

At the outset it is important to note that one should not confuse insulative value with thermal mass. They are two different physical aspects of a building. Insulative value is the ability of a product to block the transfer of hot or cold air from one place to another. The thermal mass quality of a material refers to its ability to store heat.

During winter, there is an inevitable constant flow of heat from the indoors to the outdoors via the building envelope. Without insulation, the inside surface of roofs, walls, and floors could be 14°F to 25°F (8°C to 14°C) colder than in insulated buildings (Ireland 2007). The large temperature gradients, causing warm air to rise and cool air to fall, create drafts inside the home and also need to be considered. In the insulation category, LEED offers credit points according to the type of insulation, its properties, and whether it can be recycled once its useful life has ended.

Batt, blanket, loose fill, foam, and reflective insulation are the most common types used in buildings. The small air pockets in the insulating material reduce heat transfer. When insulation is poorly installed by stuffing too much of it into a cavity space, the air pockets are compressed and the insulation loses its performance value. Insulation may also inadvertently act as an air and moisture barrier, requiring ventilation to prevent indoor air pollution. Good insulation will result in a higher surface temperature and, therefore, a greater sense of thermal comfort without necessarily raising interior air temperature. An air temperature difference of 1.8°F (1°C) may result in a savings in heating of 6 percent (Hegger et al. 2006).

A material's insulation ability is measured as a resistance value, or R-value, which is the resistance of 1 in. (25.4 mm) of that material to heat transfer, in units of °F ft² h/Btu.

FIGURE 5.3 Places that require particular attention when insulating a dwelling.

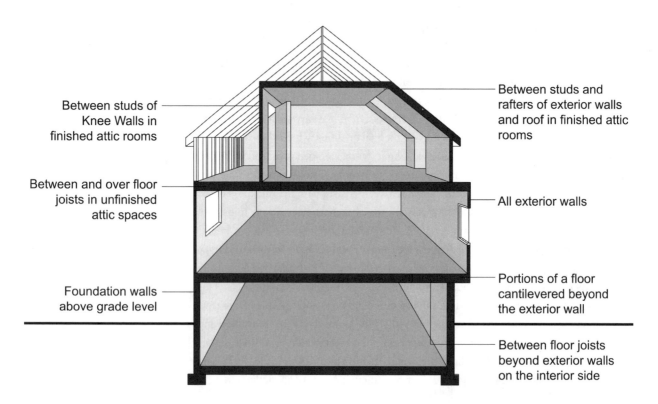

Between studs of Knee Walls in finished attic rooms

Between and over floor joists in unfinished attic spaces

Foundation walls above grade level

Between studs and rafters of exterior walls and roof in finished attic rooms

All exterior walls

Portions of a floor cantilevered beyond the exterior wall

Between floor joists beyond exterior walls on the interior side

The metric notation of R-value is RSI. The inverse of the R-value is the *U-value*, short for Btu value, which measures actual heat flow, gained or lost, through an area of material over time for every degree of temperature difference between the inside and the outside (Ireland 2007). Generally, insulators are materials with an R-value of 2 or more. To reduce heat loss, one needs to use a material with a high R-value or increase the material's thickness. However, it is important to note that the relationship between R-value and thickness is not directly proportional, since R-value decreases slightly with each increase in width. For example, fiberglass insulation has an R-value of 3.7 per 1 in. (25.4 mm), but a 3.5 in. (89 mm) thickness of fiberglass has a value of only R-11, which is less than 3.5 times 3.7 (Ireland 2007). The payback period on investments in insulation is approximately 2 to 5 years (BRE 2005).Yet, a sharp rise in the cost of heating has made investment in better insulation worthwhile. In addition, the immediate environmental returns are also noticeable.

Insulation is needed on all components of the building envelope, and typically more is needed in the ceilings. The US Department of Energy recommends R-values for various components of the home, depending on regional climate. These values need to be taken as the minimum level of necessary insulation, and builders should generally use R-values that are between 1.2 and 1.3 times higher (Johnston and Gibson 2008). Locations in a dwelling that merit special attention when insulating are shown in figure 5.3.

Walls

Adding wall insulation to optimize thermal comfort and reduce energy consumption usually involves a choice of interior and exterior insulating methods.

Interior insulation is good for reducing both the response time and the energy required to bring a room up to comfort levels, and it is usually less costly than exterior insulation. The disadvantages of interior insulation are that it reduces room size and that in existing buildings it involves replacing skirtings, architraves, pipe work, wiring, and any other fixed items. In addition, this method precludes the use of the building's thermal mass for heat storage because of the layering of walls. Also, thermal stresses in the outer skin increase the risk of condensation, and it becomes impossible to avoid *cold bridges*, also called thermal bridges, which are the spots in which cold and warm air travel easily between interior and exterior. Interior insulation is also prone to thermal bridges at the joints of walls and ceilings. Controlling interior condensation, humidity, and moisture can be problematic (Gonzalo and Habermann 2006). There are, however, insulation methods, such as those using foam, that can be injected into a poorly insulated wall from the exterior. These methods make the insulation of old structures possible and efficient and cost effective.

External wall insulation (EWI) systems are a composite system of thermal insulation affixed to the wall and a weather-proofing finish to protect against the elements. According to Energy Saving Trust (2006), there are three types of EWI: wet-render systems, dry-cladding systems, and bespoke systems. *Wet-render* EWI utilizes finishes that are cementitious renders, polymer and fiber-reinforced cementitious renders, polymeric coatings, and insulating renders. *Dry cladding* uses finishes made of rigid boards, panels, and

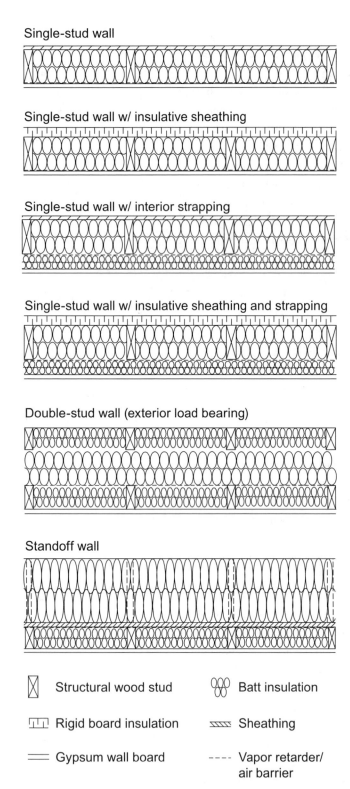

Single-stud wall

Single-stud wall w/ insulative sheathing

Single-stud wall w/ interior strapping

Single-stud wall w/ insulative sheathing and strapping

Double-stud wall (exterior load bearing)

Standoff wall

Structural wood stud   Batt insulation

Rigid board insulation   Sheathing

Gypsum wall board   Vapor retarder/
                     air barrier

FIGURE 5.4 Energy-efficient wall alternatives that maximize insulation and minimize thermal bridging. The lower part of each section represents the wall's indoor face.

tiles. Wet render and dry cladding are typically proprietary systems that are accredited by a third party. *Bespoke systems* are custom-made combinations of the first two types (Energy Saving Trust 2006). Energy-efficient wall alternatives that maximize insulation and minimize thermal bridging are shown in figure 5.4.

Roofs

Heat losses from roofs are high because of the relatively large surface area and upward radiation. Adding insulation is often quite easy, and payback periods are short. Water vapor and condensation must be controlled by appropriate use of vapor barriers and ventilation. Pitched-roof insulation is an easy, low-cost option where insulation material, usually batt, mineral wool, or rigid foam panels, is placed horizontally. Where the attic space is insulated, the insulation can be inserted between the rafters. To leave room for ventilation of any kind of roof, one needs to include baffle components, as shown in figure 5.5 (Johnston and Gibson 2008).

Attic and roof-space insulation is essential for an airtight assembly. Roof trusses should, therefore, accommodate consistent insulation beyond the top plates of exterior walls. Several types of roof trusses, such as raised-heel trusses, shown in figure 5.6, allow greater amounts of insulation, especially over the exterior wall's top plates, where heat loss is typically the highest.

On flat roofs *inverted decks*, where the insulation is placed on top of the membrane and the structure, allow the roof slab to act as thermal storage and reduce the risk of condensation (Stirling 2009). An inverted deck, also called a warm deck, has the advantage of protecting a weatherproof layer against thermal stress, but if the existing roof finish has reached the end of its useful life, a warm-deck solution may have a more attractive payback period since it is easier to replace.

Floors

Insulating floors, especially basement floors and crawl spaces, is important because heat moves from high- to low-temperature areas. Although generally heat rises, heat will also move down and out through the base-

FIGURE 5.5 Vent baffles are placed on every second roof truss to increase ventilation of roof space.

FIGURE 5.6 Raised-heel trusses facilitate the introduction of more insulation and help reduce thermal bridging.

ment or a bottom floor's concrete slab to the ground, because the ground is generally cooler, everywhere, year round (HGTVpro 2010). The cost of placing insulation under existing concrete floors is not likely to be economically justifiable unless the floor needs to be replaced for another reason, such as moisture, deterioration, or inadequate load-bearing capacity. Heat loss can, at times, be reduced by ensuring there is effective drainage around the building perimeter and by adding external insulation below ground level. Another alternative is to place insulation over an existing floor and cover it either with a *screed coat*, a layer of material, commonly cement, used to create a smooth surface level between the structure and the finish floor, or with a proprietary flooring system, which is usually easier to insulate (US DOE 2009).

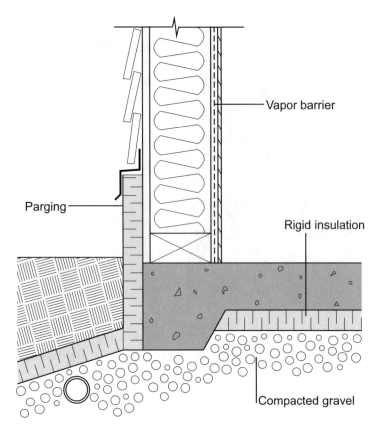

Vapor barrier

Parging

Rigid insulation

Compacted gravel

FIGURE 5.7 Method of insulating slab-on-grade foundation.

Heat loss from a *slab-on-grade* foundation, that is, concrete poured over soil, is greatest at the edges—it is not constant over the entire floor (OR DOE 2008). Insulating the edges of the slab will have as good an effect as putting insulation under the slab, as shown in figure 5.7. The U-value calculation for the floor must take into account both the size and the edge conditions of the slab. Additional insulation of a suspended timber floor is usually provided either by a continuous layer of semirigid or flexible material laid above the joists and below the floor finish or by a semirigid material between the joists. The U-value is calculated as a combination of the floor finish, air spaces, and overall insulation above the structural floor.

EFFICIENT FRAMING AND CONSTRUCTION DETAILS

When wood-frame buildings are constructed, minimizing the amount of lumber and making sure that it was harvested from sustainable forests are the first basic steps. Having too many studs does improve the structural integrity but can reduce the space for insulation, which can hinder the building envelope's performance. "Optimal value engineering" research shows that up to 20 percent of the wood used for framing could be removed without compromising the building's integrity (Johnston and Gibson 2008). Sustainable framing methods conserve building materials, such as lumber and steel, and save energy while creating a durable home. Advanced framing techniques reduce construction waste, minimize embodied energy of materials, increase cost savings, and economize energy consumption.

Efficient framing can be achieved through any number of techniques. One is using larger module configurations or wider spacing between components. For example, using larger studs that are 2 in. by 6 in. (50 mm by 150 mm) instead of conventional studs, which are 2 in. by 4 in. (50 mm by 100 mm), and spacing them at 24 in. (610 mm) on center rather than 16 in. (405 mm) will save studs that cost approximately $1,000 (US) for a 2,400 sq ft (220 m²) home, and it will save nearly 5 percent on labor costs (US DOE 2009). The extra space in the wall cavity used for insulation improves the wall's R-value and saves about 5 percent on heating and cooling bills per year (Johnston and Gibson 2008; US DOE 2009).

Another lumber-saving technique is to frame the floor with open-web joists, instead of solid sawn lumber, and align floor joists with wall studs to remove the double top plate. Open-web joists, which are shown in figure 5.8, are twice as strong, span longer, and often include metal components. Finger-jointed studs are another efficient framing

FIGURE 5.8 Engineered open-web floor joists have replaced those made of solid sawn lumber.

Partition joints

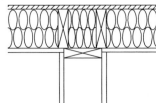

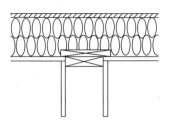

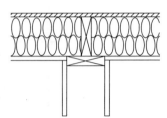

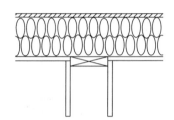

Corner joints

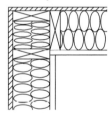

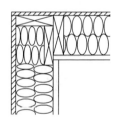

Structural wood stud	Batt insulation
Rigid board insulation	Sheathing
Gypsum wall board	Vapor retarder/ air barrier

FIGURE 5.9 A smaller number of studs can be used in partition joints and corners to save lumber and reduce heat loss through thermal bridging.

product because they are made of smaller sections. They are reliably straight and do not twist, split, or warp, as conventional studs do.

Advanced framing at the corners of exterior walls and interior partitions involves using two studs instead of three or four, which can eliminate the use of lumber simply for nailing purposes and provide more room for insulation to prevent cold spots, which cause condensation (Johnston and Gibson 2008). Proper corner design strategies that save framing lumber are illustrated in figure 5.9.

Controlling airflow across the building envelope is a fairly simple process, since many common building materials, such as plywood, wafer board, drywall, and polyethylene, are effective barriers (Keeler and Burke 2009). The problem lies in the manner in which these materials are assembled, particularly at the joints between sheets of the same material and at the intersections of different building components. Most air leakage occurs in areas where the envelope is pierced, such as window and door openings, service and utility penetrations, and intersections with floors, roofs, and basement walls (Jones 2008).

Function		Mechanism	Solution	Materials/process
Control heat flow	Heat loss	Conduction	Insulation; avoid thermal bridges, particularly at foundation wall, floor/wall junctions, roof/wall junctions and window frames.	Batt, rigid board, blown or sprayed insulation; careful detailing to avoid thermal bridges
		Radiation	Reflective coatings (where air spaces are present); low-emissivity coatings in glazing units.	Aluminum-coated papers; proprietary coatings
		Convection	Keep air spaces narrow and/or interrupt convective currents with grid patterns; fill in wide air spaces with insulation.	Use appropriate designs/processes, e.g., apply adhesives for rigid boards on foundation walls to form squares/rectangles
		Air leakage	See "Control Air Flow"	
	Heat gain	Solar	Control heat gain for summer and winter conditions through appropriate design and window size, location and orientation.	Overhangs; solar shading devices; low-emissivity windows
Control air flow	Infiltration/ exfiltration	Diffusion	Provide continuous layer of sheet materials that are impervious to air.	Air barriers; rigid sheet materials (drywall, plywood, etc.) or membranes (polyethylene, aluminum, etc.) or a combination of both
		Leakage	Seal all gaps to form a continuous air-tight building envelope, particularly at windows, electrical boxes and service penetrations.	Sealants, caulking beads, tapes and gaskets; polyurethane foams; air-tight boxes and wraps for electrical fixtures
Control moisture flow	Water	Gravity	Slope exterior finishes and flashings away from wall at joints; slope grade away from foundation wall; use overhangs with drips (where applicable).	Weather barriers: olefin sheets, building paper, tar coatings, polyethylene, exterior finishes, waterproof paints, etc.
		Capillary action	Keep exterior finishes away from soil; interrupt flow of water form soil with a weather/moisture barrier.	Flashing materials: metal, plastic, etc.; gaps sealed with sealants, caulks and gaskets
		Momentum	Keep exterior finishes away from soil; use appropriate flashing materials and details; provide roof overhangs.	
		Pressure difference	Use rainscreen principle i.e. provide a sealed, drained air space between exterior finishes and wall to equalize pressure difference.	
	Vapor	Diffusion	Provide a continuous layer of sheet materials that are impervious to vapor; located on the warm side of the insulation to control outgoing vapor.	Vapor diffusion retarders (VDRs) or "vapor barriers": aluminum-coated kraft paper, polyethylene, vapor-resistant paints, extruded polystyrene; multiple layers of building paper and other materials may also act as VDRs.

FIGURE 5.10 Summary of solutions and materials necessary to control heat, air, and moisture flow.

Thermal bridges between studs and plates, where floors intersect the walls, and at foundation walls could be eliminated by applying the following three strategies. First, a builder needs to place the insulation on either side of a conductive material to interrupt heat flow or change and reorient the conductive material to eliminate the cold bridge altogether. Ideally, the thermal resistance will remain throughout the entire wall. Second, a continuous vapor barrier on the wall's warm side will prevent condensation from forming inside the wall. Third, the air barrier should be as continuous, rigid, and durable as possible to withstand rupture and dislocation. Some of these strategies are summarized in figure 5.10, and proper practices are shown in figure 5.11.

FIGURE 5.11 To avoid air leakage, a receptacle needs to be properly sealed (*a*) and a vapor barrier should be installed around doors (*b*).

FIGURE 5.12 Computer-aided prefabricated panelized production reduces waste and improves quality.

PREFABRICATION AND RESOURCE EFFICIENCY

Prefabrication methods can offer many advantages over conventional construction. The assembly of units, panels, or components under factory-controlled conditions yields a higher-quality product that generally results in more energy-efficient homes. The sheltered plant offers greater possibilities for quality control compared with on-site construction where the workers are subjected to varying external climatic conditions. Because of the quick and efficient factory assembly, some of which is fully automated, as shown in figure 5.12, the effect of poor weather conditions on construction is reduced, as is the potential for damage due to inadequate material storage and vandalism. Cleanup time and material costs are also reduced with less waste (Thomas 2005).

The quality of prefabricated wall systems can be evaluated in terms of three interrelated characteristics: craftsmanship, technical performance, and durability. The system's craftsmanship governs its potential to achieve consistent levels of performance from one application to another. The wall's technical performance, particularly with respect to its airtightness, will affect the rate of deterioration due to condensation. Fire and sound resistance, critical for dividing walls, will contribute to the quality of the unit's interior environment. The panel's durability depends on the various materials' resistance to elements and on the probability of exposure to the elements, given the panel's design (Arieff and Burkhart 2002).

Prefabricated panel systems (PPSs) are generally capable of technically outperforming walls built using conventional construction methods. PPSs, particularly those with urethane or isocyanurate foam, provide excellent insulation value for their thickness. This is due partly to their continuous thermal break across the joints, particularly with the double-spline variation. These panels also result in the tightest assemblies because of

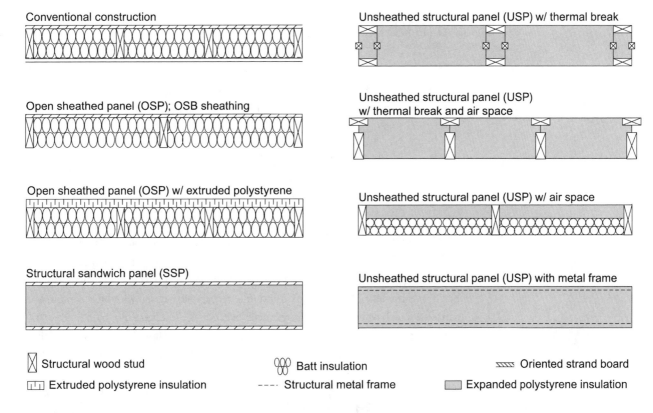

Conventional construction

Open sheathed panel (OSP); OSB sheathing

Open sheathed panel (OSP) w/ extruded polystyrene

Structural sandwich panel (SSP)

Unsheathed structural panel (USP) w/ thermal break

Unsheathed structural panel (USP)
w/ thermal break and air space

Unsheathed structural panel (USP) w/ air space

Unsheathed structural panel (USP) with metal frame

Structural wood stud

Batt insulation

Oriented strand board

Extruded polystyrene insulation

Structural metal frame

Expanded polystyrene insulation

their exceptionally well-fitted joint systems and the possibility of extending the exterior skin below the floor level, allowing for a continuous barrier across the end of the floor section. The inherent simplicity of the design makes these panels high performing. The critical nature of the lamination process, however, requires a relatively high level of quality control. Among the questionable characteristics of these systems is a tendency to ridge at the joints because of inadequate allowance for thermal expansion and a possibility of panels delaminating (Arieff and Burkhart 2002).

Many types of prefabricated systems, subsystems, and components can be combined at various stages of assembly to provide a complete package. Eight types of panel are applicable to wood-frame residential construction and can be divided into three categories, as illustrated in figure 5.13 and explained on the following pages.

FIGURE 5.13 Sections of energy-efficient prefabricated wall systems.

Annie Residence

Location: Austin, Texas, USA

Designer: Thomas Bercy/Bercy Chen Studio

Completion: 2002

Site area: 0.25 acres (0.101 hectares)

Total floor area: 1,292 sq ft (120 m²)

Number of floors: 2

The house, designed for two families, is constructed of a modular steel frame and prefabricated ThermaSteel panels (fig. 5.14). The panelized composite structure consists of modified expanded polystyrene (EPS) as an insulating material and a light-gauge galvanized steel frame. EPS is a nontoxic and fully recyclable material with high compressive capacity, which makes the panels free of air leakage. The built-in vapor barrier allows the panels to breathe while also preventing mold growth. The lightweight, durable, and thermally efficient panels can be quickly assembled, and when fitted, they provide excellent

FIGURE 5.14 The modular construction uses exposed steel frame and prefabricated infill panels to reduce construction waste and increase thermal efficiency. [with permission]

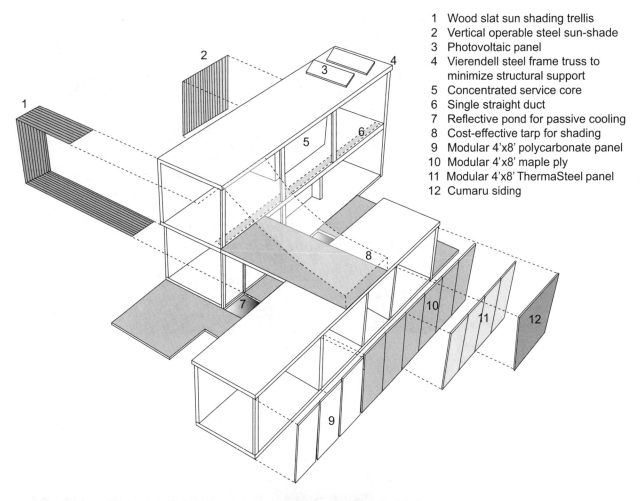

1 Wood slat sun shading trellis
2 Vertical operable steel sun-shade
3 Photovoltaic panel
4 Vierendell steel frame truss to minimize structural support
5 Concentrated service core
6 Single straight duct
7 Reflective pond for passive cooling
8 Cost-effective tarp for shading
9 Modular 4'x8' polycarbonate panel
10 Modular 4'x8' maple ply
11 Modular 4'x8' ThermaSteel panel
12 Cumaru siding

FIGURE 5.15 Expanded axonometric of the dwelling's building components.

FIGURE 5.16 Interior walls and ceilings are constructed with modular maple plywood panels, and sealed concrete serves as a finished floor.[with permission]

FIGURE 5.17 Spatial continuity between the exterior
and the interior is seam-
lessly achieved through the
flush-glazed hallway and the
reflecting water pool connecting the two pavilions. [with
permission]

FIGURE 5.18 The retractable nautical tarp over the rooftop deck and the wood-slat trellis on the west elevation provide cost-effective means for shading. [with permission]

insulating qualities and resistance against rot and termites. Constructing with an exposed frame and preinsulated panels significantly reduces the amount of building materials and finishes required, as well as construction waste. Designed according to a 4 ft by 8 ft (1.2 m by 2.4 m) module system, the house further incorporates modularly dimensioned maple plywood for interior walls and ceilings (figs. 5.15 to 5.17).

Built on a slab-on-grade foundation, the house requires only minimal finishes on its polished concrete floor. The sealed concrete conserves resources by eliminating the need for extra layers of flooring and finishes. Vierendeel steel-frame trusses (i.e., trusses with holes in their web to reduce weight) incorporated in the second level lessen the number of vertical structural supports on the lower level by acting as bridges, thereby creating an uninterrupted spatial continuity.

For increased efficiency, all the service areas of each pavilion, such as kitchens, bathrooms, and utility rooms, are contained in a central core. By gathering the plumbing and heating and cooling systems in the center, the service core maximizes its size and energy and material efficiency.

The building incorporates cost-effective means of shading, such as the retractable nautical tarp over the roof deck and the wooden trellis on the west elevation (fig. 5.18). Both create pleasant shades while allowing adequate lighting and ventilation. Through a combination of rigid and batt insulations, the roof attains an R-value of 54.

CHAPTER 6

Building Materials

Building materials need to be carefully considered, from harvesting through the reuse or dismantling of the building. The best materials are *green building materials* (Yudelson 2007). Commonly, products that use natural local resources or recycled ingredients in place of virgin ones, recycle any waste generated by their processes, have low embodied energy, are biodegradable, have minimal derivation from petrochemicals, and are designed for reuse and recyclability are considered the most sustainable (Woolley and Kimmins 2000). Green building materials are also nontoxic, nonhazardous, energy and water efficient, durable, and environmentally responsible in manufacturing, occupancy, and demolition. Architects and builders have an opportunity to influence the sustainability of a manufacturing process by specifying which building materials will be used. Importance should be given to products that have ISO 14000/14001 environmental labels, which encourage demand for and supply of products that stress the environment the least (GBES 2009).

This chapter examines various building materials, illustrates how to evaluate their sustainability through a step-by-step process, and discusses conventional materials as well as a few of the most environmentally responsible available.

LIFE-CYCLE ASSESSMENT PRINCIPLES

Building materials can be classified in a number of ways. The most common categories are naturally occurring and manufactured. *Naturally occurring* materials include organic materials such as wood, bamboo, and straw as well as minerals and rocks, such as metal ores, stone, and earth. *Manufactured* products are derived from natural resources through physical, mechanical, or chemical processing and include cement and synthetics such as plastics and paints (Sassi 2006). Another aspect that will influence choice of materials is their source. Ideally all materials will be used near their place of harvesting and manufacturing to avoid pollution due to transport and to provide local employment.

Throughout the design phase when materials are considered, there are many opportunities to reduce the environmental impact of a dwelling. The selection process begins with a life-cycle assessment of materials, from manufacture to disposal (Keeler and Burke 2009). The main aspects to be considered are how the extraction or manufacturing, transport, and disposal of the materials affect climate change, fossil fuel and water resources, and general environmental and human health (Anderson and Howard 2000). A decision about applying a technique or selecting a material is most often based on life-cycle cost analysis, which was defined by Haworth (1975) as a financial technique through which the time-phased costs of a project over a specific planning period can be comparatively evaluated. This analysis is also referred to as a *cradle-to-grave assessment*. Currently, more environmentalists are advocating a *cradle-to-cradle* study that promotes the reuse and recycle of products instead of their disposal (Yudelson 2007). A leading advocate of the cradle-to-cradle approach is William McDonough, who articulated the subject in a book by the same name (McDonough and Braungart 2002). In addition, a number of organizations, such the US Green Building Council through LEED, have provided guidance, sources, and rating systems of sustainable materials (Meisel 2010).

FIGURE 6.1 The life cycle of building materials and the environmental aspects associated with their production.

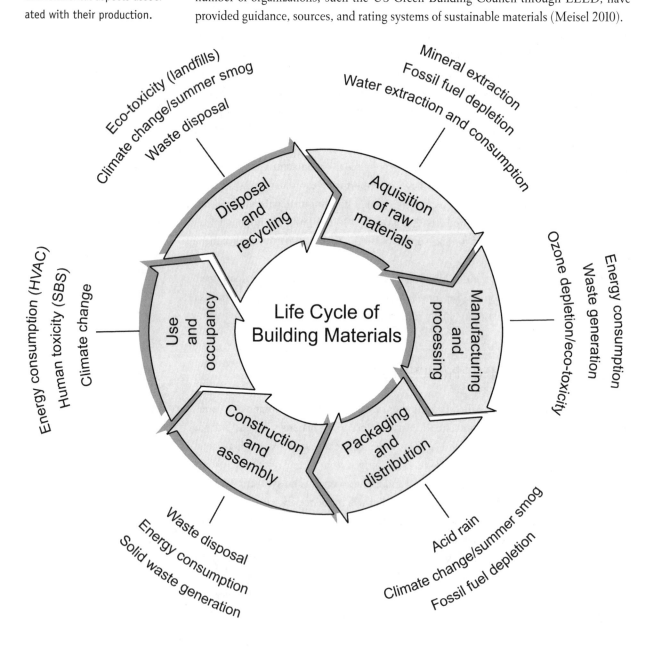

The cradle-to-cradle approach brings the process full circle in a closed loop that conserves energy and resources and minimizes waste. The process involves six major phases, as shown in figure 6.1: acquisition of raw materials, manufacturing and processing, packaging and distribution, construction and assembly, use and occupancy, and finally disposal and recycling. One of the measurements of a material's environmental impact is *embodied energy*, which is the energy used in its production (Thomas 2005) (fig. 6.2). This value, however, takes into account only energy consumption and does not evaluate other critical issues such as hazardous waste generation and health concerns. Each of these phases will be discussed below.

Acquisition of Raw Materials

As noted in chapter 1, resources are considered *renewable* when they can be naturally replenished and their acquisition remains sustainable, and they are considered *nonrenewable* when they are available on Earth in limited and finite amounts (fig. 6.3) (Calkins 2009). During acquisition, raw materials are mined, quarried, harvested, or extracted

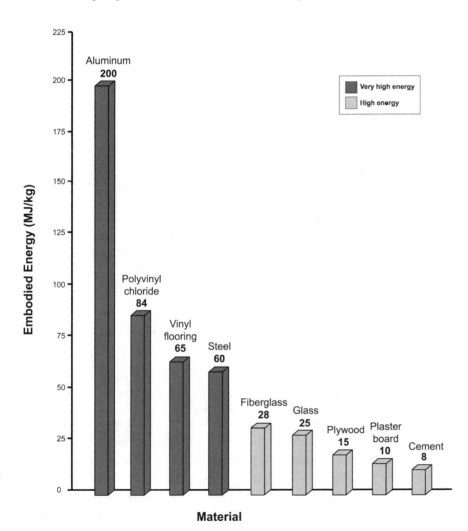

FIGURE 6.2 Embodied energy used in the production of various products.

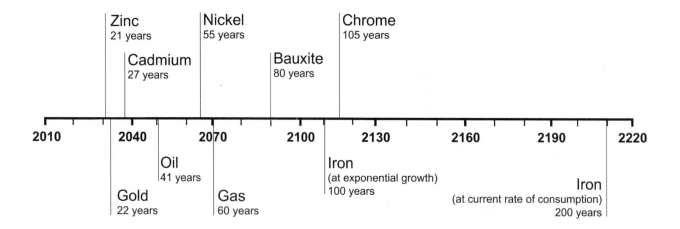

FIGURE 6.3 Projected availability duration of natural resources used in common building materials.[with permission]

from natural resources. The process is capable not only of depleting those resources but of damaging the surrounding area.

Careful consideration should be given to the acquisition process so it does not damage land, water, air, or wildlife habitat (by law, it must not threaten endangered species). The acquisition should also avoid producing undesirable by-products such as contaminated solid and toxic or hazardous liquid and gaseous waste. The first step in building with sustainable materials is, therefore, to avoid depletion of natural resources by using well-managed renewable resources such as wood or ones that are considered unlimited, like earth (Hegger et al. 2006).

Processing and Manufacturing

The processing and manufacturing of materials involve some degree of both energy consumption and waste generation. By-products, postconsumer materials, and industrial scrap can be reused and recycled by incorporating them into the same manufacturing process or into new applications to save virgin raw materials (GBES 2009). Contaminated wastes need either to be treated prior to disposal or destroyed through incineration. A similar procedure takes place for hazardous wastes that cannot be recycled, to reduce their adverse effects on the environment.

This step in building with sustainable materials is to select those that consume less energy and to minimize waste disposal by recycling or reusing waste generated at the source or by other manufacturers.

Packaging and Distribution

After the materials are manufactured, their packaging and distribution commence. Packaging requires additional resources, while distribution consumes fuel for transportation. Inefficient or unsustainable packaging and distribution of a material can compromise its overall sustainability. It is necessary to use recycled, biodegradable, or postconsumer materials, since packaging commonly accounts for a large portion of construction waste that later clutters landfills. When these packaging products are recyclable, their negative attributes are reduced. Likewise, a green building material that is properly packaged becomes unsustainable if it needs to travel a long distance. Desired products will be those that are manufactured, distributed, and used locally (Halliday 2008).

Construction and Assembly

During construction and assembly, one or more products may be combined physically or chemically to create the final building material. It is important, however, to avoid permanently binding recyclable materials to nonrecyclable ones, so that they can be recovered with ease at the end of their useful life. Sustainable construction and assembly are mindful of the future, when these materials will need to be dismantled for reuse or recycling (Baker-Laporte et al. 2001).

Use and Occupancy

Use and occupancy also affect the environment since most materials will require at least some maintenance at this life stage. When an untreated component made of natural renewable resources requires the use of hazardous and harmful maintenance products to stay useful and acceptable in appearance, its sustainability is greatly reduced. If the material is not durable, it will require not only ample attention but also frequent replacement, which may produce more waste. To accurately compare materials to determine the most durable alternative, one must consider embodied energy, waste generation, resource depletion, and effects on the ecosystem. Therefore, this step in building with sustainable materials involves choosing products with longevity and durability that require little maintenance or replacement over their lifetime (Keeler and Burke 2009).

Recycling or Disposal

The life cycle of a material does not end after its initial use. During the final stage, recycling or disposal, a material can either be reintroduced into the life-cycle loop or be responsibly disposed of through composting or incineration. These allow the retrieval of some of the material's original embodied energy. After a dwelling has served its useful life, it may be partially or fully demolished. Some products can be salvaged, refurbished, and reused for similar applications or recycled as raw materials to be turned into other components. Ideally, materials and assembled products, such as windows and doors, can be dismantled so that they may be reused with minimal processing. If reuse is not possible, then recycling back into an equivalent material or product is the next option, but it requires significantly more reprocessing. *Downcycling* is reprocessing a material into a lower-grade form, which still is useful because it economizes virgin materials. These processes can be repeated several times before a material is finally retired to a landfill or incinerated (Sassi 2006). Materials that have no postconsumer value should be avoided. Through the careful selection of materials, sustainable alternatives can be substituted for materials that cannot be recycled or reused.

For recyclable and reusable building materials to be environmentally advantageous, there needs to be a collection program and, more importantly, a market demand. Otherwise, even when a collection program is in place, materials can still find their way to landfills if no one is using them. It is not enough to build materials that have the potential to be recycled if they are virgin. It is more sustainable to begin with recycled and reused materials.

CRADLE-TO-CRADLE ASSESSMENT OF COMMON BUILDING MATERIALS

The cradle-to-cradle process is further explained below through the evaluation of several materials used in residential construction, including concrete, metal, wood, sealants, flooring, paints, and thermal insulation. The environmental considerations for each, which include resource depletion, waste generation, energy consumption, ecosystem effects, and emissions, will be examined at the life-cycle stages.

Concrete

Concrete is formed from a mixture of water, sand, and gravel solidified together by a binding agent called cement (CAC 2010). Using fly ash, the production of which is illustrated in figure 6.4, in the manufacture of concrete can reduce its environmental impact (KGS 2006). A by-product of power generation in coal-fired plants, fly ash can be used as a supplementary cement material to replace a portion of virgin cement in the concrete mixture, reducing its associated mining impacts. Using fly ash also improves the structural properties of concrete, making it stronger, less permeable, more durable, and more resistant to chemical attack (Headwaters Resources 2008).

The acquisition of raw materials for the production of concrete is very energy and resource intensive. It requires extensive mining and quarrying for crushed rock, sand, limestone, clay, and coal, as illustrated in figure 6.5.

The acquisition of these materials can lead to a number of adverse effects. Mining can cause deforestation, topsoil loss, and erosion. Also, water runoff from mining operations can spill into freshwater and harm local flora and fauna (Mehta 2001). The processing and manufacturing stage may contribute to improper disposal of rinse water used for the fabrication of concrete components. Furthermore, dust emissions, carbon dioxide, sulfur dioxide, and partially combusted organic materials can reduce air quality when they are emitted during the combustion of coal or natural gas, which occurs in high-temperature kilns used for making cement (Allen 2004). The batching, mixing, transport, placement, consolidation, and finishing of concrete also require considerable energy. Although the packaging for concrete is minimal, its distribution requires large trucks to either mix and transport liquid concrete or deliver large prefabricated components. Both methods create additional dust and carbon dioxide emissions. After concrete is assembled and constructed, it is a durable, fire-resistant, and stable material throughout its occupancy and use, causing minimal adverse im-

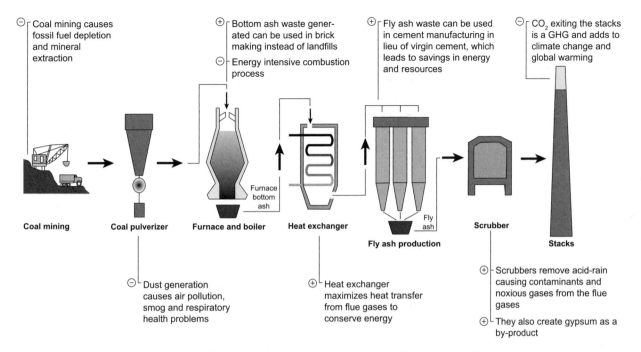

FIGURE 6.4 Fly ash, a by-product of coal-fueled electric power generation, used in concrete production.

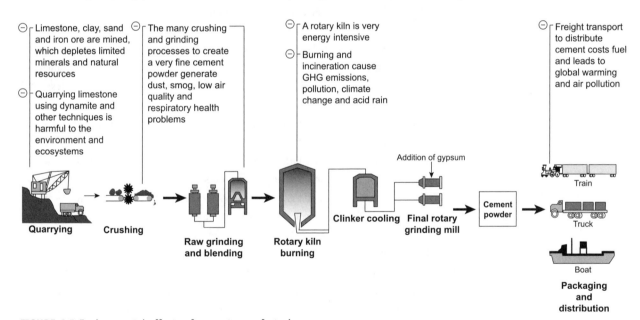

FIGURE 6.5 Environmental effects of cement manufacturing.

pact. As noted above, compared with wood, for example, the insulating potential of concrete is relatively low, yet it can be an excellent thermal-mass material for heat absorption. During its final life stage, the waste generated from its demolition may be minimized if the concrete can be crushed and downcycled as aggregate into new batches of concrete. It can be 100 percent recycled and reused as aggregate in road-beds or as a granular material (CAC 2010).

To further reduce the negative environmental effect of concrete, careful dimensioning should be practiced to avoid the need for on-site adjustment. The formwork for casting concrete should be waxed or treated with synthetic nonstick materials to allow easy removal of the forms. Soil contamination should be minimized by limiting the amount of water used to wash equipment and wet concrete for curing, thereby reducing wastewater and preventing runoff.

Metals

Two of the primary metals used in construction are aluminum and steel. Since they have different environmental impacts throughout their life cycles, they will be examined separately.

Aluminum is a highly workable, lightweight, durable, and strong metal that, depending on its finish, can require little maintenance. Its acquisition involves mining for bauxite ore, a finite resource that comprises roughly 8 percent of Earth's crust (Calkins 2009). High-grade bauxite deposits can be found only in tropical and subtropical countries such as Australia, Jamaica, and Brazil. Extracting the raw material necessitates a process called *strip mining*, where large tracts of land are cleared of trees and soil so that the bauxite layer can be harvested (IAI 2008). The bauxite is used to produce alumina, a fine white powder that is then processed to manufacture aluminum.

To minimize the negative environmental effects of the mining process, the soil that was removed should be replaced and vegetation replanted. Whether this happens depends to some degree on the country's reclamation laws, which aim to reduce long-term ecosystem damage. Even when aluminum is carefully mined, some tropical forests and species are likely to be lost.

Large quantities of waste are often generated during the processing and manufacturing of aluminum. Its production causes emissions of sulfur dioxides and nitrogen oxides, which contribute to global warming, acid rain, and smog; toxic emissions of fluoride and carbon monoxide; discharges of heavy metals into sewers; the contamination of land with fluoride and carbon sludge; and the contamination of water with fluorine and hydrocarbons (Fernandez 2006) (fig. 6.6). Even when airborne emissions from the manufacturing of aluminum are treated or destroyed, a small amount of carcinogenic hydrocarbons will inevitably be emitted. Fortunately, the disposal of these wastes is strictly regulated and most of them can be recovered or treated, which reduces their adverse effects on the environment.

Large quantities of water are also required to process aluminum, but most of it can be treated and recycled afterward. The heavy metal slag and large amounts of wastewater produced from the fabrication and finishing process are treated and disposed of at controlled disposal sites.

Another drawback of aluminum is the amount of energy that is required for manufacturing, accounting for 1.4 percent of the global energy consumption annually (Bauer and Siddhaye 2006) (fig. 6.7). To lower energy consumption during manufacturing, recycled aluminum can be used rather than bauxite ore. The distribution process of aluminum also consumes a large amount of fuel, since all of the high-grade bauxite ore deposits are great distances from the places of aluminum manufacture and use.

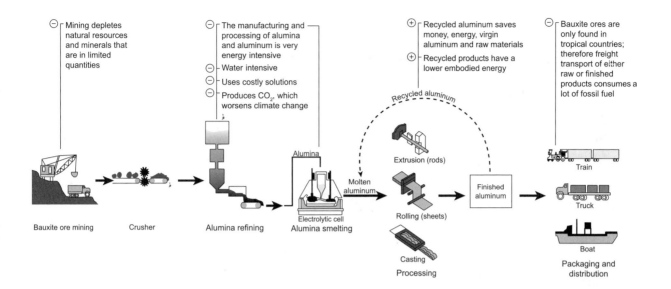

Mining depletes natural resources and minerals that are in limited quantities

The manufacturing and processing of alumina and aluminum is very energy intensive
Water intensive
Uses costly solutions
Produces CO_2, which worsens climate change

Recycled aluminum saves money, energy, virgin aluminum and raw materials
Recycled products have a lower embodied energy

Bauxite ores are only found in tropical countries; therefore freight transport of either raw or finished products consumes a lot of fossil fuel

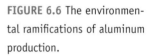

Recycled aluminum

Bauxite ore mining   Crusher   Alumina refining

Alumina

Electrolytic cell
Alumina smelting

Molten aluminum

Extrusion (rods)

Rolling (sheets)

Casting
Processing

Finished aluminum

Train

Truck

Boat

Packaging and distribution

FIGURE 6.6 The environmental ramifications of aluminum production.

Construction with aluminum is very advantageous because of its light weight and strength. Furthermore, it requires little maintenance because of its durability. Nevertheless, while it is very sustainable during use and occupancy, during its demolition is not. Architectural details should avoid mixed-material assemblies, to facilitate recycling and reduce the negative environmental effects of aluminum. Recovery systems in the building industry should also be established. The least harmful of the finishing processes, and therefore the most environmentally preferable, are anodizing and powdered-paint coating.

Steel is an alloy made of iron and carbon. Like aluminum, it is strong, durable, and workable. Steel, however, corrodes and requires more maintenance and more frequent

FIGURE 6.7 The energy-intensive manufacturing and processing of aluminum.

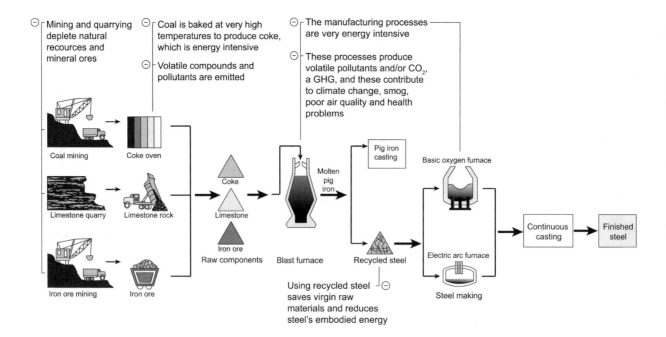

FIGURE 6.8 Environmental ramifications of steel processing and manufacturing.

FIGURE 6.9 The energy-intensive manufacturing of steel.

replacement than aluminum. During the acquisition of raw materials for steel, mining of iron ore is needed, which, when not regulated, may result in mineral depletion and damage to land and wildlife habitat. Concerns for water quality also arise from the disposal methods of the milling operations shown in figure 6.8.

Steel is manufactured by integrated smelting processes (fig. 6.9). These processes generate air-polluting combustion emissions. While these pollutants have been reduced significantly over the last decade by more efficient production processes, the emissions are still enough to harm the environment. The manufacture of steel is slightly less environmentally damaging when compared with aluminum, since iron can be found around the world, unlike bauxite ore.

Construction and assembly are highly efficient, taking advantage of prefabricated methods. Steel is one of the most recyclable construction materials available, since it can be easily separated from the waste stream magnetically and then processed into a high-quality alloy (Fernandez 2006).

To increase its sustainability, recycled steel should be used in place of raw materials. According to the Canadian Sheet Steel Building Institute (CSSBI 2008), every ton of steel recycled saves 2,500 lb (1,150 kg) of virgin iron ore, 1,400 lb (635 kg) of coal, and 120 lb (55 kg) of limestone. Methods to manage emissions from the manufacturing processes need to be further developed to minimize air pollution.

Wood

The advantage of trees is their potential to be harvested sustainably and the fact that wood is biodegradable. The main environmental concern regarding forests is overharvesting. Several North American management practices, however, have been put in place to ensure that forests are replanted after they are harvested. The Forest Stewardship Council (FSC) is an international nonprofit organization that ensures that wood products come from sustainably managed forests. Unfortunately, sustainable practices are not in place everywhere, and the harvesting of exotic imported woods, such as mahogany, ebony, zebrawood, and rosewood, has great potential to endanger their forests and species living in them (Baker-Laporte et al. 2001). When sustainably managed, the manufacturing and processing of wood require minimal energy input and do not generate excessive waste, since the log only needs to be cut into dimensional lumber. In addition, the waste can be recycled into wood chips for composite products, incinerated for energy generation, or ground up and used as compost, as illustrated in figure 6.10.

When sustainable management is not practiced, however, waste generation becomes a major concern. It is important, therefore, for the protection of the environment to select lumber from certified and well-managed sources and to ensure that endangered species are not harvested. The effects of packaging and distribution of wood also vary from source to source. If wood is purchased from local sources, transportation and packaging can be kept to a minimum.

The use of wood during construction requires fairly minimal energy input since it is relatively light and very easy to handle, as shown in figure 6.11. The standardization and modularity of dimensional lumber greatly aid this process. When wood is treated properly, it can last far beyond the useful life of a dwelling and requires little maintenance. The demolition and renovation of structures made of wood, however, is sometimes a concern. While much of the wood debris can be recycled and reused, more often than not it finds its way into landfills. One of the reasons is that municipal recycling operations rarely collect wood products, and they are commonly disposed of by contractors into landfills. Also, the wood often contains nails or other scrap metal, which is hard to separate. Fortunately, wood is highly biodegradable (Hegger et al. 2006).

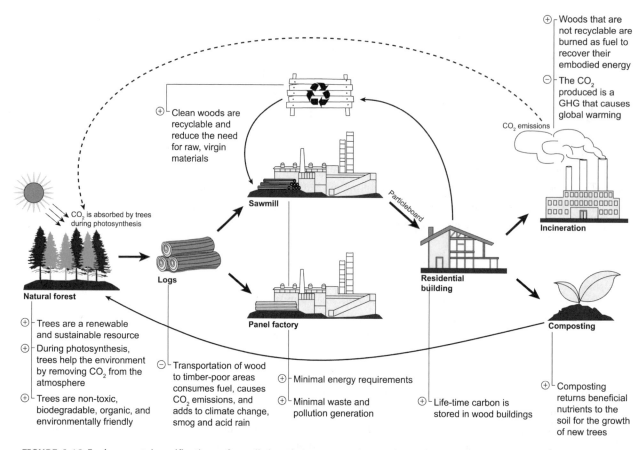

Woods that are
not recyclable are
burned as fuel to
recover their
embodied energy

⊖ The CO_2
produced is a
GHG that causes
global warming

CO_2 emissions

⊕ Clean woods are
recyclable and
reduce the need
for raw, virgin
materials

Sawmill

Particleboard

Incineration

CO_2 is absorbed by trees
during photosynthesis

Logs

Residential
building

Natural forest

Panel factory

Composting

⊕ Trees are a renewable
and sustainable resource

⊕ During photosynthesis,
trees help the environment
by removing CO_2 from the
atmosphere

⊕ Trees are non-toxic,
biodegradable, organic, and
environmentally friendly

⊖ Transportation of wood
to timber-poor areas
consumes fuel, causes
CO_2 emissions, and
adds to climate change,
smog and acid rain

⊕ Minimal energy requirements

⊕ Minimal waste and
pollution generation

⊕ Life-time carbon is
stored in wood buildings

⊕ Composting
returns beneficial
nutrients to the
soil for the growth
of new trees

FIGURE 6.10 Environmental ramifications of wood's harvesting, processing, and use.

FIGURE 6.11 Construction
using wood requires minimal
energy input.

FIGURE 6.12 Floor I-joists made of engineered wood.

A sustainable alternative to the traditional wood siding or joists, which was touched upon earlier, is *engineered wood*, which is made of wood fibers combined with bonding agents that create a composite lightweight product with superior strength, shown in figure 6.12 (Khatib 2009; Hegger et al. 2006). Use of engineered boards instead of common plywood for flooring and roof sheathing can lead to savings in embodied energy.

Thermal Insulation

Whereas in chapter 5 insulation was discussed from a functional perspective and with regard to technical aspects related to its method of application, this section articulates the subject from a material point of view. Environmentally conscious manufacturers of insulation use recycled materials such as glass, plastic, cotton, or newspaper in many of their products (fig. 6.13). Each product offers different advantages, and effectiveness depends on the type of application, building, and method of installation.

The environmental impacts of thermal-insulation materials vary significantly according to type. Thermal insulation can be broadly divided into four groups: fiberglass,

FIGURE 6.13 Composition of insulation products made of recycled materials

Type of insulation	Cellulose	Fiberglass	Mineral wool	Cotton	Spray polyurethane foam (SPF)
Raw materials	• Recycled newsprint • Boric acid • Natural additives	• Fibrous glass wool • Cured binder	• Basalt rock • Slag	• Natural denim • Cotton fibers	• Recycled plastic • Soya
Recycled content	• Post-consumer recyled newspaper	• Post-consumer recycled glass	• Recycled Slag (by-product of steel production)	• Post-industrial recycled denim • Cotton	• Post-consumer recycled plastic

mineral wool, cellulose, and foam. Of the four, cellulose insulation is made of the most environmentally sound material—recycled paper.

Cellulose insulation can be made from up to 85 percent recycled material, according to the Cellulose Insulation Manufacturers Association (CIMA 2010). During the manufacture and processing of the insulation, the recycled newsprint is reduced to fiber form in mechanical mills and then treated for fire resistance. This does not generate any significant waste and does not consume much energy. The distribution of cellulose insulation is most efficient when local sources are selected, reducing travel distances, fuel consumption, and greenhouse gas emissions. Since cellulose insulation is a loose fill, its application requires more energy than fiberglass and mineral wool. The demolition and renovation of cellulose insulation generates waste, since it is difficult to recycle because of the natural degradation and contamination that occurs during its use.

Fiberglass and mineral wool both require mining for raw materials, which may affect land, water, and air quality. Fiberglass, for example, requires the acquisition of sand, limestone for calcium and magnesium, and borax for boron, while mineral wool requires either diabase and basalt rock or slag from an iron ore blast furnace. Manufacturing and processing of fiberglass and mineral wool also emit small amounts of toxic gases, particulates, and volatile organic compounds (VOCs) (Hegger et al. 2006). These emissions are usually treated prior to their release but are still a concern. Most of the solid waste produced can be recycled back into the process.

FIGURE 6.14 Application of batt insulation is a manual process that requires minimal mechanized energy input.

Packaging and distribution of fiberglass and mineral wool are similar to those for all other types of insulation, with a need to minimize the distance between the source and the building site. Fiberglass and mineral wool come in a variety of forms, including batt, board, blanket, and loose fill (Jones 2008). Applications of fiberglass and mineral wool do not require a great energy input, as shown in figure 6.14. The finished products, however, contain fibers that may be carcinogenic and can compromise air quality if not adequately contained. During demolition and renovation, both fiberglass and mineral wool can be recycled or reused.

Foam insulation can be polyurethane, polyisocyanurate, extruded or expanded polystyrene, or phenolic. The first two are available as boards, and the latter two are either boards or foamed in place. Phenolic foam is produced from benzene, which is derived from crude oil and olefins that are extracted from natural gas. Polyurethane, polyisocyanurate, and extruded or expanded polystyrene are produced from pure, by-product, or waste-stream petrochemicals and their derivatives (Kwok and Grondzik 2007).

During the manufacturing and processing stage, all foam insulation types, other than expanded polystyrene (EPS), use ozone-depleting chlorofluorocarbons (CFCs) as blowing agents. EPS is blown with pentane gas, which is not ozone depleting but still contributes to ground-level smog. Unfortunately, the manufacturing process for foam insulation is extremely damaging to the environment. The CFCs are slowly being replaced with alternative blowing agents. The alternatives are, however, not all commercially available, particularly for polyisocyanurate and phenolic foams.

The use of foam insulation, shown on the house in figure 6.15, consumes minimal energy and produces little waste. Made up of large sheets, it is applied as plywood is, which makes it simple to affix. The demolition of a structure with foam insulation, on the other hand, produces a great deal of waste. Although polystyrene, a thermoplastic, can be heated and remolded into a new product, and polyurethane and phenol can be recycled as filler, foam insulation is challenging to recycle because of natural degradation and contamination (Fernandez 2006). For this reason, a great portion of discarded foam insulation is landfilled. Certain materials, however, can be recycled for use in other industries. For example, excess EPS from construction sites is melted down to make plastic as a raw material for the manufacturing of other products, such as laptops and cell phones (Garcia 2009).

Sealants

There are numerous sealant types with varying compositions, which makes it difficult to acquire detailed data on energy consumption, waste generation, and resource depletion. It is known that plastic resins deplete natural resources and consume energy during raw material acquisition since they are by-products of the petrochemical industry. The processing and manufacturing of sealants also consume energy and generate wastes.

FIGURE 6.15 Dwelling under construction cladded with rigid foam insulation.

On the positive side, the waste generated is often reworked into batches of defective product, rather than disposed of (Adhesives and Sealants Council 2010). The sealants are generally not recyclable or reusable after they have served their useful life, and they must be disposed of. Since most sealants are chemically based, strict regulations apply to the disposal of sealants and sealant waste. Furthermore, sealants can potentially off-gas contaminants indoors, and therefore it is important to use low-VOC and low-toxicity water-based formulations (US EPA 1997). Third-party standards, such as those of South Coast Air Quality Management District (SCAQMD) and Green Seal, promote the use of products that reduce the quantity of indoor air contaminants that are harmful not only to occupants but also to installers.

Flooring

Linoleum is a popular floor covering made from natural, biodegradable materials, which are primarily derived from linseed oil, resin, and cork powder, all of which are renewable resources (Hegger et al. 2006). During manufacturing and processing, any scrap linoleum produced can be recovered and reused. Its construction and assembly do not require a large amount of energy since linoleum is produced in sheets or tiles for easy assembly, as shown in figure 6.16. Linoleum is also very durable, greaseproof, waterproof, and fire resistant, making it a great product in terms of use and occupancy (Hardwood Floors 2006).

FIGURE 6.16 Installation of a floor covering made of linoleum.

Its packaging and distribution are its largest drawback, since it is often imported and travels long distances, usually from countries in the Far East. And following demolition or renovation, linoleum cannot be recycled easily since it is often affixed to another base material, such as plywood or concrete. If separated, however, it is known to be recyclable and biodegradable (Strongman 2008).

The main ingredient of *vinyl flooring* is polyvinyl chloride, or PVC. Vinyl flooring is a popular alternative to linoleum since it is cost effective, durable, and produced in most regions. Vinyl, however, adversely affects the environment at every stage of its life cycle, making any waste generated during the manufacturing process highly toxic (Calkins 2009) and the product itself a threat to the environment and human health if incinerated. Solid, liquid, and gaseous wastes generated during the fabrication of vinyl products are all managed by strict disposal regulations. Fortunately, most of the waste generated during manufacturing and processing can be recycled or incinerated. The packaging and distribution of vinyl flooring depend largely on the dis-

FIGURE 6.17 Some carpets are manufactured from recycled plastic containers, which lowers their environmental impact.

tance between the source and the final destination, while the construction and assembly consume minimal energy. At demolition and renovation there are very few collection or recovery systems in operation for vinyl flooring. Therefore, the recyclable material is, unfortunately, often disposed of.

Hard surfaces made of materials such as linoleum, laminate, wood, ceramic, and rubber can be certified with the FloorScore standard. Products with FloorScore certification contribute to good indoor air quality to protect occupants' health (Resilient Floor Covering Institute 2009).

The most commonly used carpets are made from petrochemical products (e.g., nylon, olefin, and polyester), while natural ones are made of wool (Hegger et al. 2006). Two primary environmental concerns about carpets arise during the manufacturing and processing stage. Styrene-butadiene (SB) latex is often used in carpets, cushions, and adhesives. During the production of SB latex, toxic waste materials are generated; as air pollutants, they can become a public health hazard for surrounding communities (ACME DIY.com 2010). Also, the fiber-dyeing process for carpets consumes large amounts of water. In addition, the carpet dyes contaminate the wastewater and can threaten water quality when disposed. Some carpets are made out of recycled plastic containers, shown in figure 6.17, which lessens the environmental impact from the acquisition of raw materials.

During the carpet's use, the main environmental concern is not the carpet itself but the cushion foams that may be used under it. Its durability during use and occupancy varies depending on the type of fiber used. Therefore, carpets must be carefully selected based on low emissions and qualities that reduce long-term maintenance and waste (ACME DIY.com 2010). Green Label and Green Label Plus are programs that set VOC limits for carpet and carpet cushions, respectively. Both programs ensure that products meet the most stringent criteria for low chemical emissions (CRI 2009).

In recent years significant progress was made in the area of recycling carpets. Leading the way was Ray Anderson's InterfaceFLOR revolution. His goal was to eliminate virgin materials and other natural resources from the production of carpets. In addition, technologies have been developed for the recycling of carpet backing and fibers into either new carpets or other products.

Paint

Most synthetic paints are made from petrochemicals, whereas natural paints are produced from renewable resources such as plant resin, ethereal oils, mineral fillers, and pigments. Paint is made of three major components: a carrier or matrix solvent that evaporates as the paint dries, a binder that contains resins and oils to keep the paint together and make it adhere to a surface, and pigments that give it color and durability (Hegger et al. 2006). The acquisition of raw materials for natural paints is noticeably more sustainable than for synthetic paints. The manufacturing and use of paints, however, produce several types of waste, many of which are hazardous, such as discharge from equipment cleaning, obsolete stock, and returns by clients. Most of the waste can be recovered and reworked into marketable products during manufacturing and processing.

The use of paint is fairly easy and requires little energy. The safe disposal of leftover paint can be achieved through municipal collection and recycling programs. Paint is also fairly durable and does not require a great deal of maintenance.

At the demolition and renovation stage, there is no way to recover the postconsumer paint, and it will likely find its way into a landfill; therefore, it is best to use biodegradable, natural paints (Yudelson 2007).

Insulated Concrete Forms (ICFs)

Insulated concrete forms (ICFs) are forms that are left in place after the concrete is poured for a foundation or wall (PCA 2009). The forms are generally made of foam insulation such as EPS and are filled with reinforced concrete to create a solid structure, as shown in figure 6.18. The sustainable benefits from ICF systems can be summarized in five points: optimized energy performance, durability, recycled material content, local materials, and improved indoor air quality (ICFA 2008). The energy efficiency is due to both the thermal mass of concrete that helps absorb and release heat slowly and the airtightness and continuous insulation of the system. Other benefits provided by the solid structure include sound insulation and resistance to fire, pests, storms, and high winds.

Structural Insulated Panels (SIPs)

Structural insulated panels (SIPs) are panels with a core of rigid foam insulation between an exterior and interior skin. SIP panels are custom designed, prefabricated, and assembled on site, which reduces waste, construction time, and labor costs (SIPA 2009). Their solid structure allows airtightness with high thermal insulation and minimum levels of air infiltration. In addition, this integrated system uses less wood than a conventional wood-frame house.

Roofing

Roofing materials have to withstand the most direct exposure to wind, sun, and snow. Therefore, weight, heat capacity, fire rating, durability, maintainability, and ease of installation need to be considered (Hegger et al. 2006). For instance, longer-lasting heavier materials may require stronger support for the extra weight. Lighter colors are advantageous in hot climates since they reflect heat and reduce the urban heat island effect. Various new types of shingles can also have reduced embodied energy.

Palms

Location: Los Angeles, California, USA

Design: Marmol Radziner Prefab

Completion: 2008

Site area: 0.124 acres (0.05 hectares)

Total floor area: 2,800 sq ft (260 m²)

Number of floors: 2

FIGURE 6.19 The floor plans of the Palms residence illustrate the modularity of the design. Used with permission.

Low Volatile Organic Compound (VOC) interior paint

Forest Stewardship Council (FSC) certified Eco-Timber flooring

Outdoor living

High-efficiency glass

Office

Recycled steel frame

Second floor

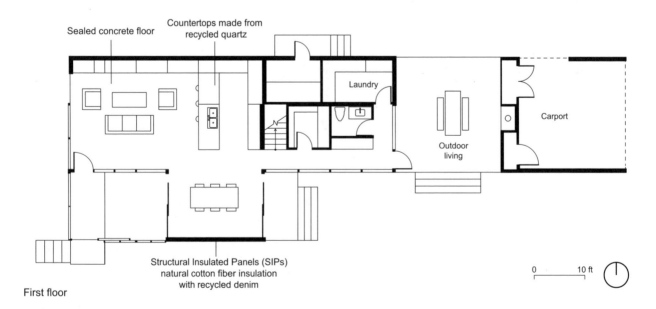

Sealed concrete floor

Countertops made from recycled quartz

Laundry

Carport

Outdoor living

Structural Insulated Panels (SIPs) natural cotton fiber insulation with recycled denim

0   10 ft

First floor

This custom-designed home was constructed using the maximum benefits of factory production and incorporating green building materials. Consisting of fourteen modules that measure 12 ft by 8 ft (3.7 m by 2.4 m), the dwelling was built from a recycled steel frame and SIPs (fig. 6.19). As an economic alternative to timber frame, the steel provides a superior material and dimensional consistency. It does not decay or deform and contributes to an improved indoor air quality, for it is not subjected to termite or mold growth and does not require any chemical bonding agents. Steel also significantly reduces construction waste and is fully recyclable. The panels incorporate natural cotton fiber insulation that contains 85 percent postindustrial recycled content and no toxic chemicals. Because of the superior thermal efficiency of the panels, a home constructed with SIPs saves energy, which can lead to a downsized HVAC system.

The exterior cedar siding built and added in the factory provides natural rot and

FIGURE 6.20 The cedar used for exterior siding is a highly durable material that maintains excellent weather and insect resistance. The heavy lattice wall on the west elevation provides shading and privacy while allowing natural lighting and ventilation. [used with permission

FIGURE 6.22 Ninety percent of the dwelling's components, including built-ins, flooring, and kitchen cabinets, were factory manufactured. Used with permission.

FIGURE 6.21 The dual-pane glazing with low-emissivity and ultraviolet-protecting glass allows the southern elevation to take maximum advantage of passive solar gains and external views. Used with permission.

insect resistance and an insulation value, which allows the wood to remain cool in summertime and warm in the winter (fig. 6.20). In addition, the dwelling takes advantage of southern orientation to maximize passive solar gain (fig. 6.21).

Factory assembly reduced waste and labor and maximized resource conservation by facilitating reuse and recycling. All the cabinetwork, including the built-ins, was made from walnut certified by the Forest Stewardship Council (FSC) and from medium-density fiberboard free of formaldehyde (fig. 6.22). The composite countertops were manufactured from recycled quartz. All interior paint was low in volatile organic compounds (VOCs). The second level incorporates FSC-certified flooring; sealed, polished concrete serves as a finished floor at the lower level.

CHAPTER 7

Energy-Efficient Windows

Windows play a significant role in achieving comfort by letting in natural light, solar warmth, and fresh air and permitting outdoor views. On the other hand, poor-quality windows can be the source of overheating or unwanted infiltration or exfiltration of air. Quality windows, therefore, influence the dwelling's energy consumption and consequently its sustainability. This chapter examines a window unit's energy performance and provides guidelines for its selection and installation.

WINDOW DEVELOPMENT

A window is a filter of conditions between the indoors and the outdoors, as illustrated in figure 7.1. Proper window design not only is energy efficient but also prevents interior glare and related fading and improves comfort. Since a window is, in fact, an opening in the building envelope, it must be made of high-quality materials and be properly installed to protect against the elements and unwanted moisture and heat migration (Jones 2008).

Historically, windows were the "weak links" in dwelling design because of their heat loss, unwanted heat gain, air leakage, and infiltration. Since glass is a good conductor, windows can account for up to 30 percent of a home's heat loss (Wenz 2008). With improved technologies, however, it is possible to have views without sacrificing comfort or energy efficiency. The selection of windows should be based on four aspects: appearance, function, energy performance, and cost. Function and energy performance are of particular interest in sustainable residential design. Function includes daylighting, glare control, thermal comfort, durability, ventilation, sound control, maintenance, and resistance to condensation. With respect to energy performance, the National Fenestration Rating Council provides standard rating and labeling systems for total window systems including glazing and frame (NFRC 2005). The labels include U-values, solar heat gain coefficients, air leakage rates, and visible transmittance (Jones 2008). Furthermore, with newly improved window technologies, which are summarized in figure 7.2, several attributes can be emphasized in sustainable residential projects: innovative glazing-unit structure, low-emittance coatings, low-conductance gas fills, warm edge spacers, thermally improved sash and frame, solar-control glazings and coatings, and improved weather stripping. Those principles and concepts will be explained and illustrated below.

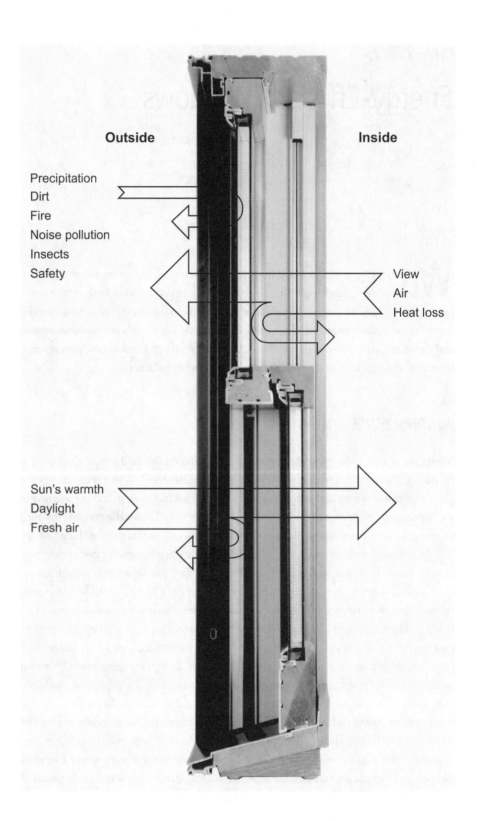

FIGURE 7.1 A window acts as a filter and a barrier for various conditions between the inside and the outside.

Outside

Inside

Precipitation
Dirt
Fire
Noise pollution
Insects
Safety

View
Air
Heat loss

Sun's warmth
Daylight
Fresh air

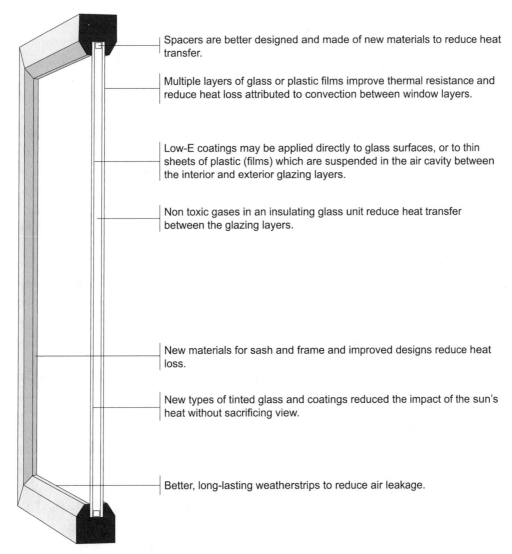

Spacers are better designed and made of new materials to reduce heat transfer.

Multiple layers of glass or plastic films improve thermal resistance and reduce heat loss attributed to convection between window layers.

Low-E coatings may be applied directly to glass surfaces, or to thin sheets of plastic (films) which are suspended in the air cavity between the interior and exterior glazing layers.

Non toxic gases in an insulating glass unit reduce heat transfer between the glazing layers.

New materials for sash and frame and improved designs reduce heat loss.

New types of tinted glass and coatings reduced the impact of the sun's heat without sacrificing view.

Better, long-lasting weatherstrips to reduce air leakage.

FIGURE 7.2 Technological innovations in contemporary fenestration products have improved their performance.

DAYLIGHTING

Spaces with well-thought-out natural light are considered desirable to work and live in. In addition, according to Adams (2004), a deficiency of daylight in northern latitudes can lead to health problems, such as seasonal affective disorder (SAD) and vitamin D deficiency. Using daylight instead of artificial light will also lead to substantial energy savings. Several studies also linked higher levels of productivity and improved well-being to a naturally lit room (Farley and Veitch 2001). To achieve LEED certification, 75 percent of all spaces in a building should be lit naturally.

Proper daylighting design addresses both the amount and the quality of light entering a room. Daylighting requirements will depend on the function of the building, hours of use, type of users, requirements for views, need for privacy, ventilation, and energy

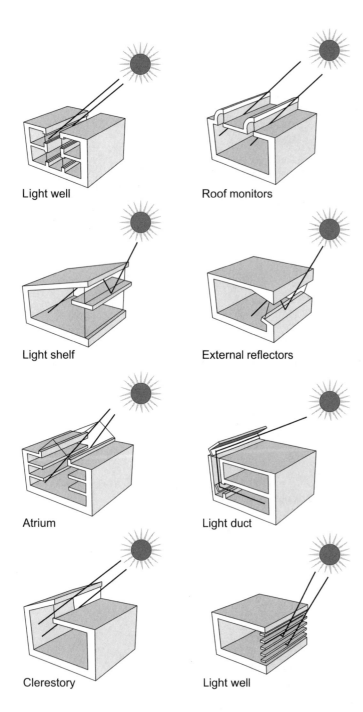

Light well

Roof monitors

Light shelf

External reflectors

Atrium

Light duct

Clerestory

Light well

FIGURE 7.3 Daylighting systems and devices.

use. Design for good daylighting depends on the position, form, and dimensions of the openings (fig. 7.3); the glazing materials used; and the location, form, and dimensions of the shading.

Operable windows are commonly known to be an important contributor to occupants' satisfaction since they offer the users a tool to control their own immediate environment In the design of the glazed areas, therefore, attention should be directed to window size, orientation, glazing type, frame type, construction details to prevent infiltration, means of solar control, and insulation. In addition, devices can be used to distribute the light more evenly. One example is the *light shelf*, shown in figure 7.3. Light shelves are designed to reflect light onto the ceiling and to the back of the room while reducing excessive light levels near the windows, thereby saving energy (Jones 2008).

As a rule of thumb, window area should equal approximately 20 percent of a room's floor area, to provide enough light, even during overcast days. Good planning for natural light depends on the size and shape of both the windows and the room. Light from a window can travel a distance of one and a half to two times the height of the window header. For a typical header located 84 in. (2.1 m) from the floor, light will reach a maximum of 12 ft 4 in. (3.8 m) into the room, not including sunrise or sunset times (Ireland 2007). Shallow-plan buildings, therefore, provide more opportunities for daylighting (as well as natural ventilation and cooling) than deep-plan buildings do. A guide for zoning daylight is the "2.5 H rule," where the depth of the room does not exceed 2.5 times the height (H) from the window's header to the floor (Kwok and Grondzik 2007). For corner rooms or those on top floors, skylights or windows in more than one facade will also improve daylight distribution. Locating windows on more than one wall will lead to better light distribution and uniformity (Gonzalo and Habermann 2006).

Often the window may be placed and sized to respond to different demands. For instance, high windows will ensure good daylight penetration into the rear part of the room, whereas wide ones will offer better views (Ireland 2007). Also, the level of daylighting at a point in a room depends to a large extent on the amount of sky visible through the window from that point. As a result, the provision of a significant amount of glazing near the ceiling is beneficial from a daylighting point of view. Tall narrow windows, for example, will provide a better daylight distribution in a room than low wide ones. Small windows create a spotlight effect on a specific area and a sharp contrast. To have light penetrate deeper into a room, a designer needs to use high windows, as illustrated in figure 7.4. Wider ones will cause a broader area of light to enter.

SHADING

While direct sunlight can be an attractive feature, particularly in winter, if it falls directly on occupants or worktops, it may be undesirable. Avoiding overheating is a challenge in window design, since heat gain can be significant. Summertime cooling costs, according to Jones (2008), can double in homes with unshaded windows. The right shading choice depends on the solar path across the site, the surrounding landscape or buildings that obstruct the sun, the season and time of day, the building orientation, and the latitude. Where the solar gain is excessive in summertime, the most effective way to reduce it is to use shading devices, which are illustrated in figure 7.5. A wide and ever-growing competitive range of devices is available, including internal and external products such as blinds, shutters, louvers, and structural add-on devices that can be fixed or adjustable to the sun's movement (Kwok and Grondzik 2007; Mintz 2009). A common device is the overhang, which was used in a Vancouver Olympic Village's building, designed by GBL Architects and shown in figure 7.6. When windows have fixed overhangs to minimize summer solar gains, they will also reduce daylight entry throughout the year. Movable shading or blinds, on the other hand, will reduce daylight only when they are in place. Venetian blinds may be used to reflect direct sunlight toward the ceiling, thereby avoiding discomfort and achieving greater penetration at the same time. Occupants, however, need to use such blinds properly to achieve the best effect (Prowler 2008).

Depending on orientation and location, a window's need for shading may be reduced if sensible glazing ratios are adopted. When the sun strikes, that radiation is partly reflected by the glass, partly absorbed by it, and partly transmitted through it to the indoors (Kwok and Grondzik 2007). A single-glazed window has an R-1 (RSI 0.18) resistance value to heat flow. The objective is to increase that number as much as possible by adding insulation, sealants, curtains, and shading devices. Just by closing the shutters or drawing the drapes, for example, an occupant will increase the value slightly to R-2 (RSI 0.35). Double-glazing will elevate the value a bit more to R-3 (RSI 0.53). These R-values, however, are unfortunately still not high

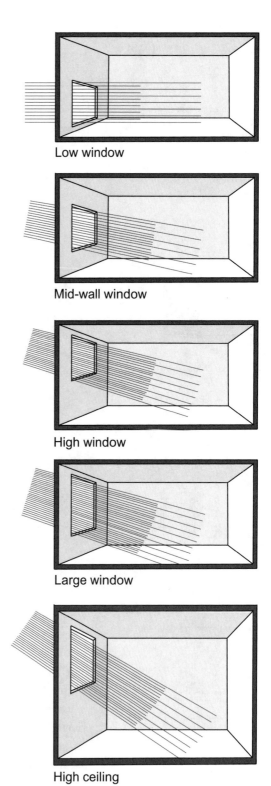

Low window

Mid-wall window

High window

Large window

High ceiling

FIGURE 7.4 The amount of daylight that enters a room will depend on a window's size and height above the floor.

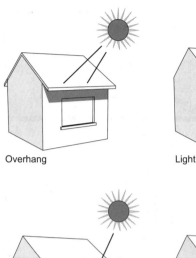

Overhang

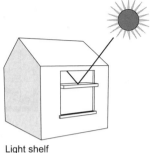

Light shelf

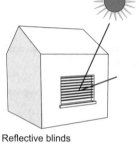

Reflective blinds

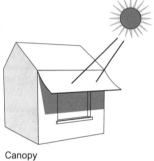

Canopy

Shadow overhang

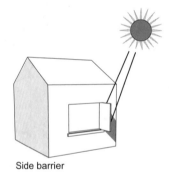

Side barrier

FIGURE 7.5 Various types of external shading devices.

enough to make any significant difference in balancing heat loss (Smith 2005).

A good window system may have insulated shutters, which can achieve R-values of R-9 to R-11 (RSI 1.6 to RSI 1.9). According to Wenz (2008), shutters with these R-values are almost as effective as a wall with a value of R-13 (RSI 2.3). Insulating shutters, such as rigid foam panels with a heat-reflective foil facing, should be made from recycled plastics, recycled aluminum, and foam blown in with zero-ozone-depleting agents (Wenz 2008). When closed after dark, insulating shutters can be useful in reducing heat loss. Creating a well-sealed air gap between the shutters and the glazing increases the shutters' effectiveness but can be difficult to achieve. External shutters are, therefore, preferable to internal ones. Managing the operation of external shutters is, however, not easy. In cold weather the occupants are unlikely to open windows to close shutters, defeating the very purpose of using them (Harvey 2006).

CONTROLLING AIR MOVEMENT

Fresh air may be supplied by natural or mechanical means or a hybrid system containing elements of both. Operable windows can aid in removing excess heat, humidity, and odors from the home via natural ventilation. This is particularly important for removing cooking odors and moisture created in kitchens and bathrooms, which can also reduce mechanical ventilation costs. Overheating may be reduced by ventilation mechanisms in carefully designed windows.

Well-designed naturally ventilated buildings generally have shallow plans. To maximize air movement through a space, at least one window should be on the facade that has prevailing winds and breezes, and windows need to be placed on the opposite side of the room as well, to direct the air's exit, as illustrated in figure 7.7. In the Northern Hemisphere, the prevailing summer winds are typically from west to east. As a result, western-facing windows are good for cooling during this season. Another inlet-outlet combination includes cool air entering from a low-lying window and pushing up and out the warmer and lighter air through a higher opening in the wall or ceiling on the opposite side, such as in cooling or wind towers (Ireland 2007; Harvey 2006). A wind catcher works in reverse, catching the cool breezes from the top and transporting them down the tower to the rest of the home.

FIGURE 7.6 An overhang shading device has been used on the south-facing facade of a building in Vancouver's Olympic Village. Used with permission.

As for window size, the best airflow for natural ventilation is achieved when air inlet windows are small and the exits are large, to increase the velocity of the air entering the room. For cellular rooms with windows on only one side, natural ventilation will be effective only to a depth of about twice the room height, which may need to be higher than in a mechanically ventilated building. The space saved by avoiding ducting in the ceiling or floor will offset any required increase in story height.

FIGURE 7.7 Natural ventilation is best allowed by opposite windows and a chimney effect.

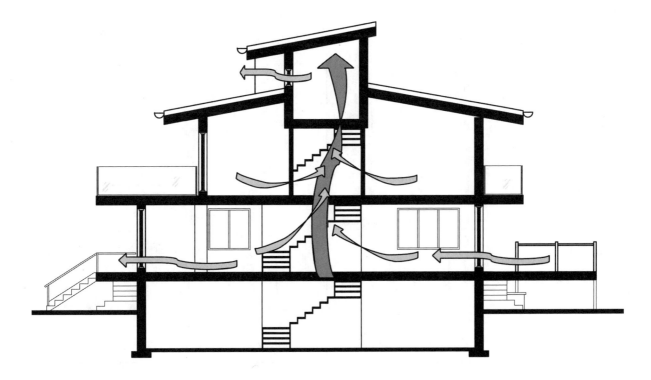

CONTROLLING HEAT LOSS

A window consists of frame and glazing. Within the frame, there are two components: the first is the outer frame, or *casing*, which is anchored to the wall, and the second is the interior frame, also known as the *sash*, which encloses the glazing and can be opened in a variety of ways. The *glazing unit* consists of two or more glass or synthetic plastic panes, separated by spacers and coated in various ways to control heat gains and losses (fig. 7.8) (Jones 2008).

Heat transfer in windows may involve one or more of the following processes: transmission of solar radiation, emission of infrared radiation, conduction of heat through all components (i.e., the glass, the frame, and the spacers between the panes), convection in the air between the panes of glass, and infiltration of outside air (Keeler and Burke 2009). These methods of heat transfer are illustrated in figure 7.9.

Conduction is the process by which heat is lost through the materials themselves, especially in metal-frame windows. It occurs through both the frames and the glass and depends on the properties of the materials themselves. *Convection* is heat transfer that occurs through windows by the movement of the air itself. Air is a relatively good insulator in terms of conduction, and motionless air provides no opportunity for convection to occur. Air trapped between two glass panes in a double-glazed or storm window, therefore, immediately improves the window's heat resistance ability. The optimum thickness of the gap between two panes of glass depends on the temperature difference between the inside and outside. The greater the temperature difference, the narrower the optimum gap spacing needs to be because convection will be triggered by large air spaces and large temperature

FIGURE 7.8 Basic window types and components that influence a window's thermal performance.

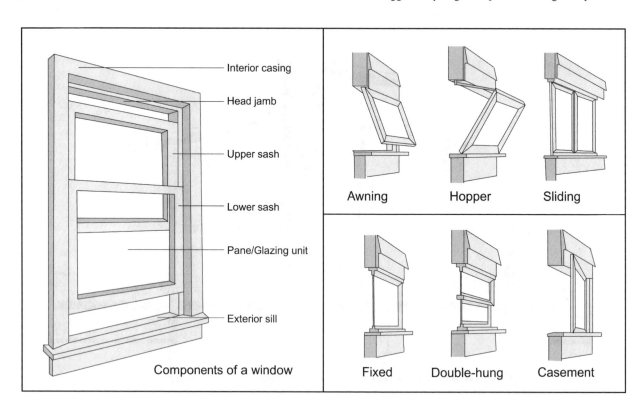

Interior casing

Head jamb

Upper sash

Lower sash

Pane/Glazing unit

Exterior sill

Components of a window

Awning   Hopper   Sliding

Fixed   Double-hung   Casement

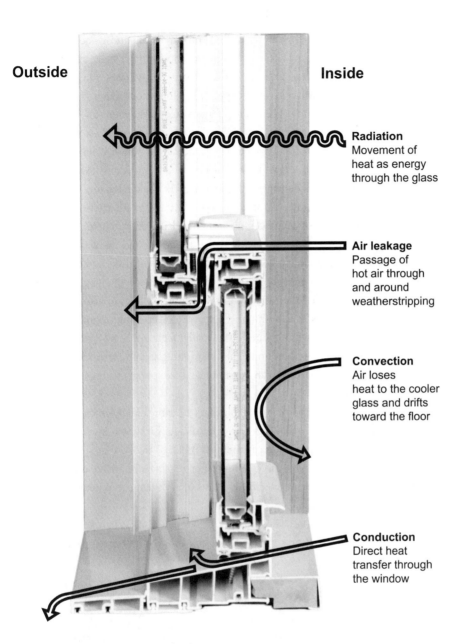

Outside

Inside

Radiation
Movement of
heat as energy
through the glass

Air leakage
Passage of
hot air through
and around
weatherstripping

Convection
Air loses
heat to the cooler
glass and drifts
toward the floor

Conduction
Direct heat
transfer through
the window

FIGURE 7.9 Methods of heat transfer through a window.

gradients (Harvey 2006). Glazing units are usually built with a 0.5 in. (12.7 mm) air space between two 0.25 in. (6.4 mm) sheets of glass, to give a total width of 1 in. (2.5 cm). As for the glass, the thickness is determined according to structural considerations.

Harvey (2006) suggests that coupled with edge losses from the glazing unit, conductive heat losses through the frame can account for 10 to 30 percent of the total heat losses from a window. The selection of an appropriate frame material is, therefore, not simply a question of appearance. Wood, for instance, is a good insulator but is easily damaged and has a high maintenance requirement. Metal requires much less maintenance but is a very good conductor. The selection of an aluminum frame, for example, which also requires a small amount of maintenance, must ensure that it is designed with a thermal break. A thermal break is a separation that uses materials with a lower thermal conductivity, such as cellular foam, rigid PVC, polyurethane, and wood, to keep frost from entering. Metal frames are also susceptible to temperature changes and will expand and contract significantly on a seasonal, daily, or even hourly basis. The joint between the glazing unit and the sash must, therefore, be flexible enough to accommodate any movement without breaking the glass. Vinyl frames are low maintenance but, like metal frames, are susceptible to temperature changes. Finally, some frames use a combination of materials, usually a wood core covered with either aluminum or vinyl. These are intended to take advantage of thermal qualities of wood while protecting it with either vinyl or aluminum and reducing the maintenance requirement (Baker-Laporte et al. 2001).

Infiltration of cold air and *exfiltration* of warm air across a barrier occur when air flows through an opening or cavity (Kwok and Grondzik 2007). There are three joints where this can take place in a window: between the frame and the wall, between the frame and the sash, and between the sash and the glazing unit. Infiltration is minimized by providing as airtight a joint as possible. In the joint between the frame and the wall, this is controlled entirely by the installation procedure. Infiltration losses between the frame and the sash depend on the number and type of operable components and on the types of gaskets, as shown in figure 7.10. Finally, radiative heat losses, which occur across an air space, are dependent on the ability of the glazing to transmit, absorb, and reflect *radiation*. These heat losses can be minimized by special coatings, which are applied to the glass surface.

Generally, windows with fewer operable parts are more energy efficient. The longer the joints, the more heat loss will occur through leakage. Fixed windows are best in this regard, but they have no ventilation capabilities. As far as the type of operation is concerned, pivoting components are more energy efficient, since they make use of compression seals. Sliding parts are least effective in terms of air leakage, but joint seals can also be provided (Winchip 2007).

Controlling the direction of heat flow is a complex task. When heat flows into a home from the outside on a warm, sunny day, it increases the indoor temperature and, as

FIGURE 7.10 Air infiltration losses between the frame and the sash depend on the type of operable components and the types of gaskets.

Outside

Inside

Heel bead sealant

Cap bead gasket

Cap bead gasket

a result, air-conditioning costs. On a chilly winter day, heat can escape from the home if there is poor thermal resistance in the window components. The thermal resistance of the glazing comes from the air space between the panes of glass and from the thin films of air at the inside and outside surfaces of the assembly that slow down heat transfer. The glass itself, however, has negligible resistance to heat flow (Smith 2005).

AIR LEAKAGE CONTROL

Because of inside and outside temperature and pressure differentials, a window may leak air from around the frame and the connection joints of an operable unit. Well-designed windows act as dynamic heat exchangers: warm air leaking to the outside transfers heat to the frame, and infiltrating cold air is warmed up by heat conduction through the very same frame (Harvey 2006). A good window, therefore, can prevent air or heat leakage, which affects energy control, comfort, and condensation potential.

Sealants and gaskets are used for the fixed component of the window, while weather stripping is used for the operable parts, as shown in figure 7.11. At the glazing-sash junction, wet or dry seals are used; in wood windows, wet seals are commonly installed (see "rain screen principle" below). Sealants are generally applied as cap beads at the outside of the joint. The application of similar seals on the inside, as cap and heel beads, is also equally important. In vinyl and aluminum sashes, dry and wet seals are used: a rubberlike grip can be installed on one or both sides of the glazing unit, and a heel seal will provide airtightness between the glazing and the sash (Baker-Laporte et al. 2001).

FIGURE 7.11 Air leakage between the sash and the frame could be controlled by weather stripping on the sash.

CONDENSATION AND RAIN PENETRATION CONTROL

Bulk moisture is a large quantity of water entering the building as rain/snow or groundwater. *Capillary action*, or wicking, is another way water can be transported across the building envelope through porous materials such as wood (Jones 2008). Water vapor in the air is also a cause for concern. The control of water vapor flow through a window is linked to the control of airflow, since vapor diffusion in window frame materials such as aluminum, steel, glass, PVC, and protected wood is very small. In unsealed double glazing, for example, exfiltrated

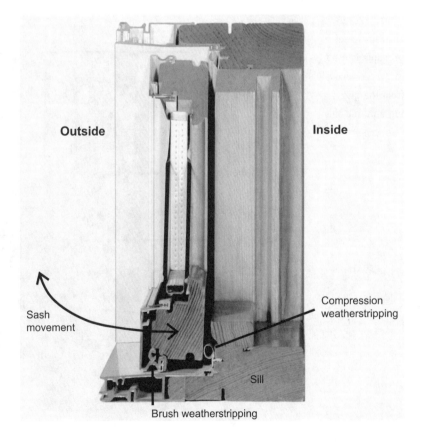

Outside

Inside

Sash movement

Compression weatherstripping

Sill

Brush weatherstripping

humid air can condense between the panes of glass and obstruct the view. Not only can condensation impair visibility, but the liquid matter can lead to the deterioration of the sash, frame, and sill as well as the interior finish and the supporting wall.

The relative humidity of the inside air and the temperature of the glazing, sash, and frame are the two conditions to act upon to solve this problem. To reduce the moisture level in indoor air, one must increase ventilation and decrease the use of humidifiers, wood for indoor heating, and the intensity of human activities. Wood heating may also cause static issues in the indoors. To increase the temperature of the window's indoor surface, several strategies can be used. The R-value (RSI) of the window component can be increased by additional air space, which is formed by a glass or plastic layer, inside, tightly covering either the whole window or the glazing only. In addition, the indoor warm air can be better circulated next to the windows, with the help of registers/radiators and fans or by removing barriers such as heavy curtains, air deflectors, and large furniture.

Finally, rain penetration can be avoided by applying the *rain screen principle*, which is based upon control of pressure forces that can move water through small openings, rather than the elimination of the openings themselves, at the interface of glazing-sash and sash-frame components (fig. 7.12) (Foster and Whitten 2008).

By the same token, the function of a *spacer bar* is to seal the unit so that no air or moisture enters the air space. It consists of a hollow metal section sealed with an organic compound. To ensure that there is no moisture, a chemical drying agent is put in the

FIGURE 7.12
The rain screen principle is used for water removal from the glazing unit and the frame.

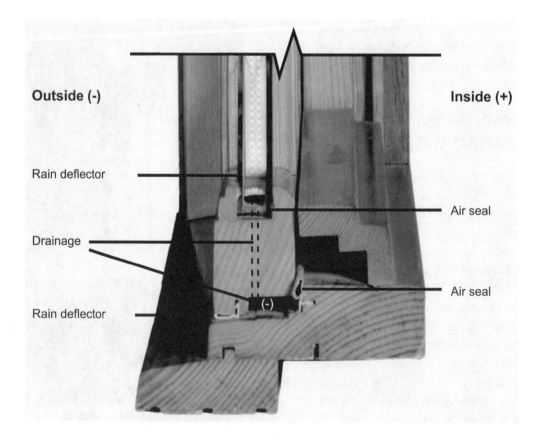

spacer bar and small holes are drilled into it to facilitate the absorption of moisture that gets into the air space. This is an important characteristic to look for when evaluating windows. A quality window should last for years, and any indication of condensation on the inner pane of the glazing is the sign of a poor-quality or defective window unit.

GLAZING-UNIT INNOVATIONS

Glazing-unit design has seen the greatest technical development in recent years. It is now possible to meet the requirements for heat gain, conservation, light transmission, and light direction at different latitudes. The design and orientation approach should optimize useful solar gains and minimize heat losses during winter. The glazed areas can, therefore, balance heating, cooling, and daylighting needs. Some unique glazing types are described next.

Multiple Glazing

All three types of heat losses discussed earlier in the chapter—conduction, convection, and radiation—occur across the glazing unit. Since glass is a poor thermal insulator, there are a number of simple ways to decrease heat loss. Double glazing (i.e., two panes of glass with an air gap in between) is the most commonly specified energy-efficient window type. This concept was extrapolated to create triple and even quadruple glazing. The R-value ranges from about R-1.1 (RSI 0.19) for single-paned windows, to R-1.8 (RSI 0.32) for double-paned windows, to R-3.3 (RSI 0.58) for triple-paned windows (Jones 2008). However, only conductive and convective heat losses are reduced, with no significant effect on radiative heat loss. Additional layers will not necessarily increase the value by the same ratio: one to two layers—50 percent reduction in energy loss; two to three layers—33 percent further reduction in energy loss; three to four layers—25 percent further reduction in energy loss. Triple- and quadruple-glazed windows are highly expensive, heavy, and cumbersome, making them impractical for home design (Jones 2008). The effects of various glazing types on thermal performance are shown in figure 7.13.

Low-Emissivity (ε) Glass

An alternative to multiple glazings that provides similar thermal resistance is to use double-paned glass with polyester films suspended between the panes. These films can also be coated with metallic low-emissivity coatings (Schaeffer 2005). The actual emission (in W/m^2) of an object is the amount of infrared radiation emitted by it, which is just one of the ways in which heat is transferred from a window to the outdoors. It is directly proportional to the object's temperature and emissivity. An object's emissivity, ε, is a unitless ratio of its actual emissions to its maximum possible emissions if it were a blackbody with an emissivity of 1. Standard glass has an emissivity of 0.84. In the interest of minimizing heat loss, therefore, one must use windows that have low emissivities. That is achieved

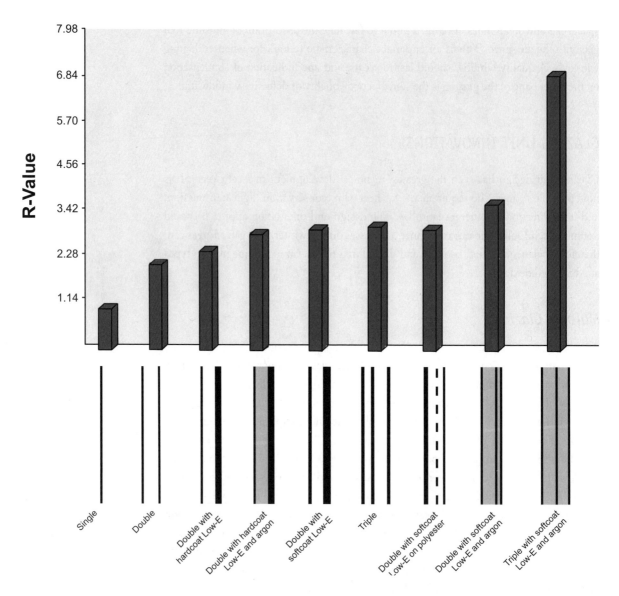

FIGURE 7.13 The effect of various glazing unit types on thermal performance.

by using glass with low-ε films and coatings. As for the casing and frame, low emissivities can be achieved for polished or galvanized metal surfaces too (Harvey 2006). Low emissivity also means low absorption, and any radiation not absorbed is reflected. When the inner side of the inner pane of glass is coated, infrared radiation is reflected back into the room. Low-ε coatings decrease radiation heat loss through glazing. The problem that remains is that of radiative heat transfer, both across the air space and through the glass to the interior. A variety of coatings can be applied at different parts of the window to control radiative heat transfer. These include tinted or reflective coatings, which are intended to reduce glare and solar heat gains, and low-ε coatings that allow most of the shorter-wavelength infrared radiation to pass through but reflect most of the larger-wavelength radiation back into the building, as illustrated in figure 7.14. The result is a thermal resistance close to that of a triple-glazed unit but not nearly as heavy, cumbersome, and expensive (Smith 2005).

The air in double-glazed windows can be replaced with heavier gases (gases with greater molecular weights) to further reduce conductive heat transfer. Argon, krypton, and xenon are the most commonly used commercially available gases in North America and Europe (Harvey 2006). The added advantage of using them is that, to avoid convection, their optimal thickness is narrow, making the windows thinner and lighter. To remain effective, though, these panes must be well sealed to prevent the gases from leaking out.

Vacuum Windows

Vacuum-sealed double-glazing units in which some or all of the air is extracted, have been developed and are continuously being improved. When the air between the panes is removed, conduction and convection are eliminated. Typically, the air gap is very thin, 0.006 in. (0.15 mm), and so the glazing thickness is only 0.24 to 0.32 in. (6 to 8 mm) in total, which makes a very thin window. There are a few challenges with this window type, though. It has a very energy-intensive manufacturing process to fuse the edges of

FIGURE 7.14 Differences between light and solar transmission through standard single, double, and low-ε glazing.

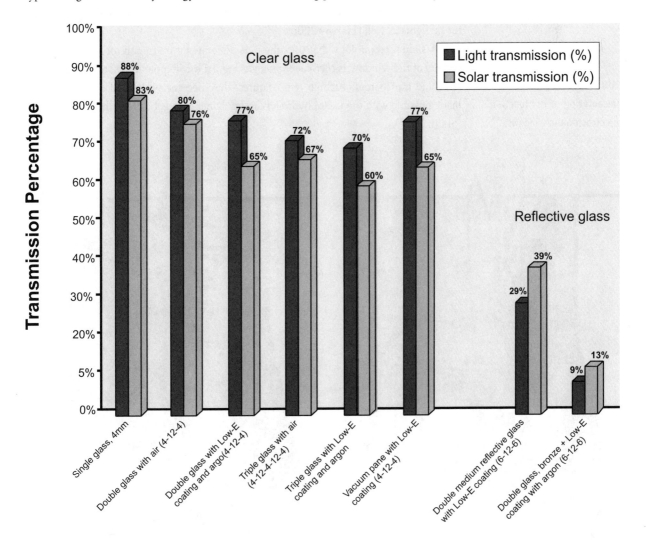

the panes together. It also requires finding a low-conductivity seal that will maintain such a vacuum for the typically 20-year life of a window. The large temperature difference between the outer and inner panes may cause significant thermal expansion and overstress the ridge edge seals. Commercially available vacuum-sealed glazing is a 0.24 in. (6 mm) thick window with a U-value that is half that of conventional double-glazed windows (Harvey 2006).

Electrochromic and Thermochromic Windows

A creative technological innovation is the *electrochromic window*, also called a *smart window* (fig. 7.15). These windows change from clear to dark and back again by means of a small voltage applied to layers of electrolyte, conductors, and films between the glass panes. This is a unique feature because one can achieve the best of both window types: transparent windows in the winter to both maximize solar heat gain and minimize heating costs, and opaque windows in the summer to minimize solar heat gain and cooling costs. The change of state happens in a few minutes. Although their cost is still prohibitive for most home buyers, it is steadily decreasing. This useful technology may be used for skylights as well (Harvey 2006).

A similar technology that uses the outside temperature to control and change the opacity of the window is *thermochromic glazing*. At low temperatures, the windows are clear and transparent. At high temperatures, they become white and opaque. This is made possible with the use of hydrogels and polymer blends between the panes of glass (Smith 2007).

FIGURE 7.15 Diagrammatic representation of the function of electrochromic windows.

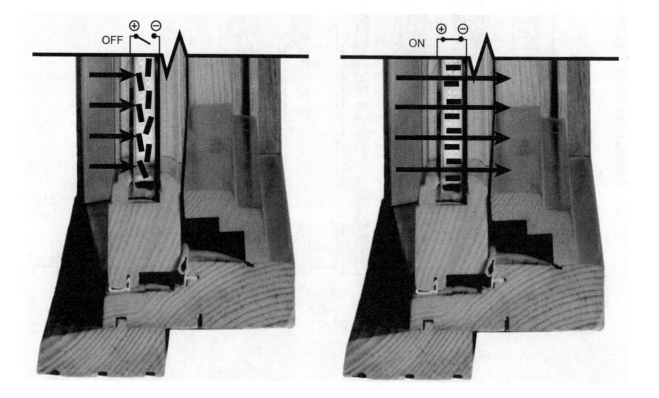

WINDOW INSTALLATION

The joint between the frame and the wall is the final but critical link in an energy-efficient envelope. The performance of this joint relies entirely on the installation procedure and sealant used. Generally, installation should provide an airtight seal while allowing for differential thermal and/or structural movement between the frame and the wall.

The airtight qualities of the joint can be ensured by using a backer rod and sealant. Batt insulation alone is not sufficient to stop air movement; the unit must be caulked (Efficient Windows Collaborative 2010). For smaller gaps, applying a silicone sealant is also recommended. Wider gaps should be filled with polyurethane. Expanding foam, shown being applied in figure 7.16, can also be effective, but care should be taken not to overfill the cavity joint. This may apply stress on the window frame, causing it to deform and bend, resulting in windows that are difficult to open.

The upper part of the window should not be shimmed, to allow for some movement. Sufficient tolerance should be provided in the rough opening of the structural frame, no less than 0.5 in. (12.7 mm) on the top and sides (Efficient Windows Collaborative 2010). The top flange should also be secured when using metal window frames in a manner that will allow for shrinkage. The transfer of loads to the window frame should also be avoided.

Prescott Passive House

Location: Kansas City, Kansas, USA

Design: Studio 804

Completion: 2010

Site area: 0.3 acres (0.279 hectares)

Total floor area: 1,700 sq ft (160 m²)

Number of floors: 3

FIGURE 7.17 The strategically located windows equipped with adjustable louvers permit maximum cross ventilation and passive solar gain. Used with permission.

Designed to meet LEED platinum and Passivhaus standards, the project aims to achieve 90 percent energy savings in heating and cooling requirement. The cost-efficient passive strategies, such as high-performance windows, louvers, super insulation, southern orientation, and open plan, equip the house with an airtight thermal envelope to maintain a stable interior temperature.

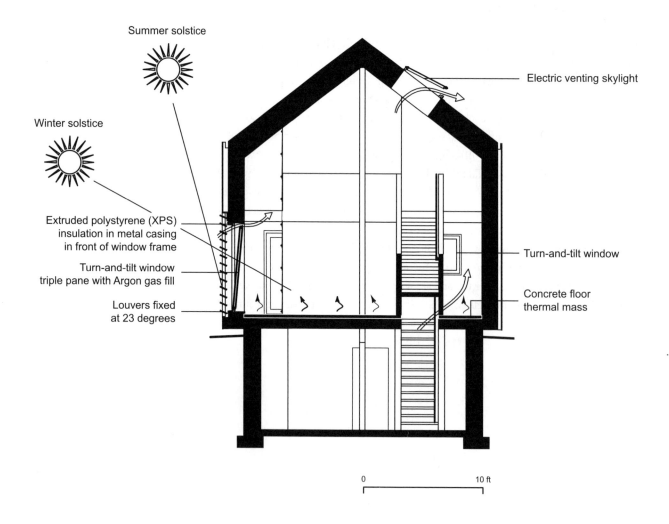

Summer solstice

Winter solstice

Electric venting skylight

Extruded polystyrene (XPS) insulation in metal casing in front of window frame

Turn-and-tilt window triple pane with Argon gas fill

Louvers fixed at 23 degrees

Turn-and-tilt window

Concrete floor thermal mass

0   10 ft

The high-efficiency windows are strategically placed to allow maximum passive solar gain, natural cross ventilation, and minimum heat loss (fig. 7.17). On the southern facade, a long stretch of operable windows protected by adjustable louvers lets in ample light while promoting natural ventilation (figs. 7.18, 7.19). The louver blades can be adjusted to an optimal angle to protect the interior against direct sun exposure during summer and to allow heat gain during winter. On the north elevation, only a couple of electric venting skylights punctuate the envelope to discreetly prevent heat loss. The remote-controlled skylights provide an effective means for temperature and moisture control, as they encourage cooling and ventilation. All windows are triple glazed and filled with argon gas to achieve optimal energy efficiency. Extruded polystyrene foam insulates the metal casing in front of the window frame to eliminate air leaks and heat loss through conduction.

FIGURE 7.18 The extensive southern glazing consists of turn-and-tilt windows and adjustable louvers to allow maximum passive solar gains and natural ventilation. The exterior is covered in a charred Douglas fir rain screen, which gives an ultraviolet-protected dark finish to the house. Used with permission.

FIGURE 7.19 The outdoor deck on the east elevation shelters a carport, which is also accessible from the full-walkout basement. Used with permission.

FIGURE 7.20 Natural light
from the southern fenestration
floods the living area. Used
with permission.

FIGURE 7.21 The extensive
southern glazing provides
ample daylight throughout
the house. The open stairway
connects the main floor to
the loft, which is open to the
lower level. Used with permission.

The open interior layout allows the house to efficiently distribute the natural light, heat, and fresh air gained through the fenestrations (figs. 7.20, 7.21). On the double-height main floor, an open stairway connects the living area and the loft level containing the master bedroom and other open space that overlooks the level below. A frosted glass wall extends over two stories and screens the centrally located stacked bathrooms on the main and the upper levels, allowing in natural light gained through the extensive southern windows while providing privacy.

In conjunction with natural ventilation strategies, a heat recovery ventilator further reduces heating and cooling demand and enhances indoor air quality. It preheats the incoming air with extracted heat from the exhaust air or precools incoming air by extracting heat from it.

CHAPTER 8

Heating and Cooling Systems

Technological advancements that have been introduced since World War II have made contemporary homes more energy efficient. Since building envelopes are more airtight, there is an increased concern for indoor air quality (see chapter 9) and, with it, a need for mechanical ventilation. The selection of heating, ventilating, and air-conditioning equipment is made complex because of the wide variety of available systems. Choosing between a simple solution and an advanced alternative will depend on size of dwelling, configuration, grouping of units, and budget, among other factors. This chapter reviews various heating and cooling systems and examines their efficiency as well as their constraints. It is important to note, however, that prior to including mechanical systems, designers should do their utmost to consider natural means of ventilation that do not burden the environment and consume energy.

PRINCIPLES OF HEATING, VENTILATION, AND AIR-CONDITIONING (HVAC) SYSTEMS

A *heating, ventilation, and air-conditioning* system controls indoor climate. This means achieving comfortable temperature, optimum humidity levels, and clean air via heating, cooling, humidification, air purification, and ventilation. The proper choice of HVAC system depends on several factors: the size of the space that needs air control, the size of the indoor space available to house equipment, the type of energy needed to fuel it, and its efficiency and effectiveness. Each of these factors is illustrated in figure 8.1 and will be discussed next.

Proper Equipment Sizing

Proper sizing for heating and cooling does not require special equipment or construction techniques. It depends on the airtightness of the building envelope. Suitably sized equipment can save builders and homeowners money and create a more energy-efficient and comfortable home (Janis and Tao 2009). There are several advantages to installing properly sized HVAC systems. First, smaller systems usually cost less, and those savings often encourage people to upgrade to high-efficiency equipment. Second, properly

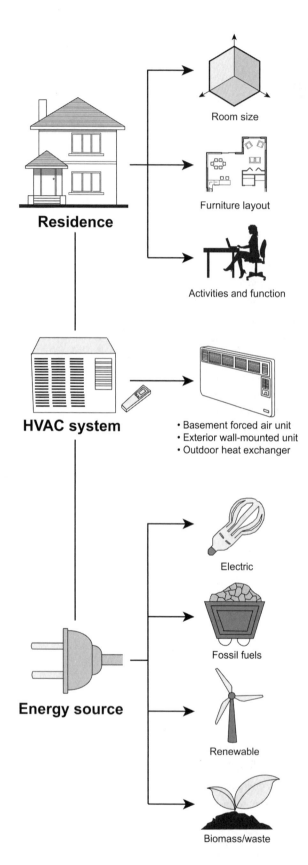

Residence
Room size

Furniture layout

Activities and function

HVAC system
- Basement forced air unit
- Exterior wall-mounted unit
- Outdoor heat exchanger

Energy source
Electric

Fossil fuels

Renewable

Biomass/waste

FIGURE 8.1 Tasks and considerations affecting the selection of HVAC systems.

sized equipment operates longer at maximum efficiency, as opposed to oversized equipment, which will run for a shorter period of time. Third, in warm, humid weather, HVAC systems remove moisture from the air, but oversized systems remove less moisture because of short cycling. Last, properly sized equipment will last longer, as it will start and stop less often. Longer run times allow air conditioners and furnaces to maintain consistent room temperatures and achieve more comfortable humidity levels. Undersized equipment will not heat or cool properly and will cost more to operate because of frequent on-off cycling. Selecting the right size is often more important than choosing a specific brand.

When overhauling an HVAC system, one needs to bear in mind several principles. Remodeling provides an opportunity to replace an existing system with a unit that offers optimal heating and cooling while using less energy. In fact, if the existing equipment is more than 10 years old, replacing it with a basic model can reduce utility bills significantly, as well as more effectively eliminate moisture and mildew problems.

Another consideration is that a system with variable speed will operate better. A system with a single-speed fan motor may heat or cool rooms too quickly. A variable-speed motor, on the other hand, automatically adjusts the flow of heated or cooled air to the desired comfort level (Stein and Reynolds 2000). Variable-speed systems typically run longer but at lower speeds, cutting operating costs and saving wear and tear on equipment. For that reason it is important to select the most practical efficiency rating, which can be found by consulting the manufacturer's manual for estimated annual cost savings.

Available Indoor Space

Different HVAC systems have different installation requirements. For instance, *central systems* such as forced air require some space in the house's basement and have to be attached to a network of conduits to force the air through the house. Such systems require pipe chases and wall sections that allow for the installation of ducts (Stein and Reynolds 2000). *Convection systems*, such as ductless heat pumps, electric baseboard heaters, and fan-assisted room heaters, are more flexibly located inside the house. It is recommended that electric baseboard heaters and fan-assisted room heaters be placed under windows when possible (House-Energy 2011). A ductless heat pump, on the other hand, is usually installed on an exterior wall close to the ceiling. Fortunately, it is not necessary to install the units on exposed walls if the implementation is planned prior to construction, which allows the builder to run the connecting pipes in the walls. Finally, *air-air heat pump* systems require an outdoor heat exchanger. In row house developments, for example, this might cause a problem because of the limited size of the lots on which the houses are built. Furthermore, although contemporary systems are much improved, such heat exchangers are considered noisy, which might be problematic where the units are attached.

Energy Sources, Efficiency, and Effectiveness

Another factor to consider when selecting an HVAC system is the type of available energy and whether using sustainable or renewable energy is an option. One must be aware of the cost of gas and electricity for the unit before installing any system, as the energy rates can greatly affect the life-cycle cost (Janis and Tao 2009). Up-front costs associated with more sophisticated equipment may be problematic in affordable housing, but an investment in more energy-efficient systems may reduce long-term heating and cooling costs.

Studying efficiency and effectiveness allows for the meaningful comparison of various HVAC methods. *Efficiency* represents the ability of a system to transform a power source into usable energy. It is a quantitative value usually provided by manufacturers. The standard measurement used to determine the efficiency of a system or an appliance is Btu (British thermal unit) divided by the power input in watt-hours. *Effectiveness*, on the other hand, measures how much of the energy produced is actually used to condition the environment. For example, because of reduced effectiveness, an old air conditioner will consume more energy than a new one to achieve the same temperature. The measurement units for effectiveness are generally similar to those for efficiency.

HEATING SYSTEMS

According to principles of physics, heat is transferred in a building in one or more of three ways, as discussed in chapter 7: convection, conduction, and radiation (fig. 8.2). In buildings, *convection* is the transfer of heat through the air and can be either natural or forced, depending on whether mechanical assistance is required. *Conduction* is the transfer of heat through a solid object, such as a wall or roof. *Radiation* is the transfer of heat, via electromagnetic radiation, such as the sun's rays traveling through the atmosphere to Earth or from a radiant heater (Kwok and Grondzik 2007). The various heating systems can be classified according to the energy they use, if any. If no external energy source is used to fuel the system, it is considered pure heat transfer and recovery. Some systems and their relation to the environment are outlined next.

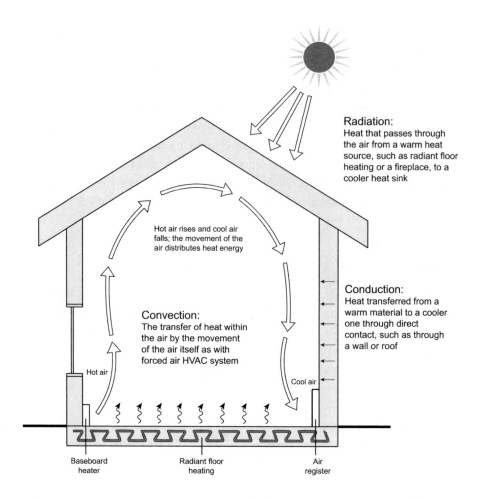

Radiation:
Heat that passes through the air from a warm heat source, such as radiant floor heating or a fireplace, to a cooler heat sink

Hot air rises and cool air falls; the movement of the air distributes heat energy

Conduction:
Heat transferred from a warm material to a cooler one through direct contact, such as through a wall or roof

Convection:
The transfer of heat within the air by the movement of the air itself as with forced air HVAC system

Hot air

Cool air

Baseboard heater

Radiant floor heating

Air register

FIGURE 8.2 Modes of heat transfer in an indoor space.

Solar Energy

Solar energy is transferred to and from Earth's surface by radiation as well as rainfall, snow, ice, and wind. It is a sustainable source that can be used to heat air or water in a low-tech and, for some systems (e.g., solar water heaters), low-cost manner. Solar energy collectors absorb both direct sunlight and diffuse radiation and therefore can still operate under cloudy conditions. Common installations can typically provide 28 kWh/ft^2 (300 kWh/m^2) of energy (Halliday 2008).

A *solar thermal system* contains components that collect, store, and distribute the sun's heat. The three main types are unglazed, flat-plate, and evacuated-tube solar collectors, which are illustrated in figure 8.3. *Unglazed collectors* consist of black plastic or metal pipes through which the fluid medium is circulated. They are very simple and relatively inexpensive, but they are best suited for places where the temperature required is below 86°F (30°C) (EAESL 2011).

Flat-plate collectors, the most widely used, consist of a flat insulated box through which the fluid medium circulates. They can produce temperatures up to 158°F (70°C) above the ambient temperature. A flat-plate system is composed of water-carrying copper pipes bonded to a copper absorber plate. The fluid is heated by the sun and transported to an insulated water tank, and then it is transferred to the domestic water system through

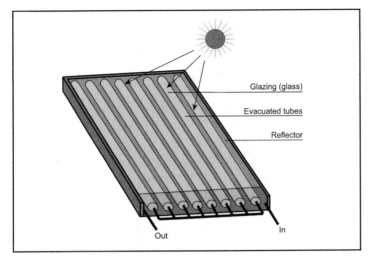

Glazing (glass)

Evacuated tubes

Reflector

Out   In

Evacuated tube

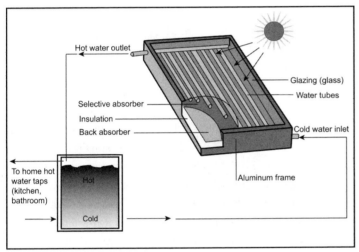

Hot water outlet

Glazing (glass)

Water tubes

Selective absorber

Insulation

Back absorber

Cold water inlet

To home hot
water taps
(kitchen,
bathroom)

Hot

Cold

Aluminum frame

Flat-plate

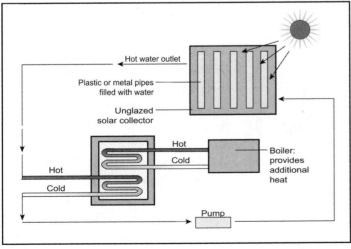

Hot water outlet

Plastic or metal pipes
filled with water

Unglazed
solar collector

Hot

Cold

Hot

Cold

Boiler:
provides
additional
heat

Pump

Unglazed

FIGURE 8.3 The three main types of solar collectors.

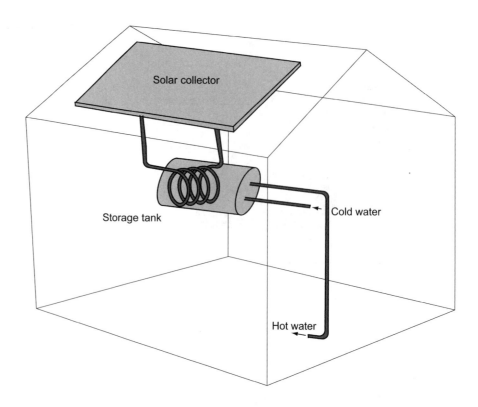

FIGURE 8.4 Solar thermal hot-water systems.

Solar collector

Storage tank

Cold water

Hot water

a heat exchanger. According to Strongman (2008), a flat-plate system is commonly made up of a flat panel of 32 to 43 sq ft (3 to 4 m²) on a south-facing roof, with the fluid medium flowing to a 44 gal (200 L) tank (figs. 8.4, 8.5). This should provide around 30 percent of an average household's hot-water needs, which may increase in summer months (Strongman 2008). A hot-water cylinder stores the heated water during the day so that it can be used after sunlight hours. The system can be mounted on any roof that will bear the load and is compatible with all boiler systems except combination boilers (Strongman 2008).

Evacuated tube collectors, shown in figure 8.6, consist of an array of glass tubes, each containing an absorber that collects solar energy and transfers it to the heat-transfer fluid. These collectors are more advanced that other systems and can produce temperatures of 212°F (100°C) or more above ambient. According to Strongman (2008), "they are comprised of glass pipes containing a small amount of antifreeze hermetically sealed within a small central copper pipe. When heated by the sun, this antifreeze converts to steam, which rises to the top of the tube, transfers its heat to a collector head and condenses back into liquid for the process to be repeated."

Solar collectors need to be mounted so as to catch the sun. A south-facing pitched roof is desired, as collectors generally face south and

FIGURE 8.5 A solar thermal hot-water system mounted on top of an apartment building.

are tilted at an angle to the horizontal that is roughly equal to the latitude of the site. In North America, this means a tilt of 35 to 65 degrees. Also, when choosing solar thermal systems, it is important to verify that shadows from surrounding buildings and trees will not obstruct sunlight falling on the collectors, especially in winter, when the sun's angle is low.

FIGURE 8.6 Evacuated-tube roof-mounted solar thermal system. Used with permission.

The distribution and storage parts of a solar heating system are similar to those of a conventional one. The distribution medium is usually based on either air or water. The heat storage unit will often be larger than in a nonsolar system because of the need to store heat during cloudy periods. A backup heat source such as wood, oil, or gas is usually necessary. In general, an average-size home requires about 43 sq ft (4 m^2) of solar collectors to provide about 20 percent of the domestic demand. Because of the clean nature of solar energy, the system is environmentally appropriate because it eliminates about 1.1 tons (1 tonne) of CO_2 per year. Solar collectors commonly have efficiencies of anywhere between 40 and 70 percent (Halliday 2008).

A good-quality, properly maintained system should last 15 to 20 years. A Guarantee of Solar Results (GSR) is often given by the manufacturer (OPET 2011). It is a commitment that the system will provide at least a preset amount of solar energy or the company will reimburse the cost of fuel to make up the difference, which protects the client against errors in design or installation.

In recent years, to encourage the proliferation of solar energy, governments began to offer incentives for the installation of solar systems and their use. Tax incentives or rental programs have been offered by some. Others, such as the Government of Ontario, Canada, purchase overproduced power for much more than the market rate.

Geothermal Systems

Geothermal heat pumps use the ground's ambient temperature as a heat source or sink to heat or cool the home. Loops of pipes containing liquids exchange energy from the ground to the building interior via forced air. The workings of a heat pump are outlined here. Ground cooling will be discussed in the Ground Cooling Systems section.

Ground-source heat pumps extract latent heat from the ground via a borehole or a network of underground pipes. According to Strongman (2008), new dwellings are the easiest places to use heat pumps because they can be buried either in the yard or under the structure before it is built. Strongman also recommends having a professional who specializes in geothermal systems carry out a site assessment prior to selection of the system. In straightforward cases, the installation can be completed in 2 days.

The heat from the ground is absorbed into a mix of water and antifreeze carried in the pipes and then converted, via the heat pump, into thermal energy for space heating and hot water. Technically this is not renewable energy if electricity is needed to power the pump. Yet, that electricity amounts to one-third of the total energy produced, so the excess could be considered renewable (Strongman 2008). The pump

FIGURE 8.7 Loops for geothermal heat pumps.

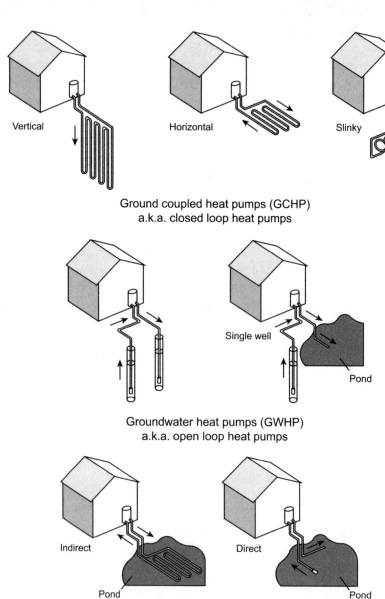

Vertical   Horizontal   Slinky

Ground coupled heat pumps (GCHP)
a.k.a. closed loop heat pumps

Single well   Pond

Groundwater heat pumps (GWHP)
a.k.a. open loop heat pumps

Indirect   Direct

Pond   Pond

Surface water heat pumps
a.k.a. lake or pond loop heat pumps

can also be powered by solar energy or another renewable energy form. According to the Geothermal Heat Pump Consortium, surveys conducted by utilities across the United States indicate that more than 95 percent of all geothermal customers would recommend the system to a family member or friend. Geothermal systems typically cost 30 to 60 percent less to operate than any other traditional residential or commercial system (Geotility 2009). One needs, however, to recognize that such systems require a large up-front investment. Several manufacturers suggest that cost recovery for such systems takes approximately 8 years. Figure 8.7 illustrates various pipe systems for geothermal heat pumps.

In summary, when selecting a mechanical heating system, one should consider factors such as cost, efficiency, and effectiveness. The selection will greatly depend on the type of house and the type of available energy, as well as local climate. Various heating systems and efficiency are summarized in figure 8.8.

FIGURE 8.8 Advantages and disadvantages of heating system alternatives.

Systems	Efficiency	Advantages	Disadvantages
Electrical			
Central	100%	High efficiency High air quality	High initial cost Central control Space requirements
Baseboard	100%	Very low initial cost Individual room control Silent Easy to install	Poor heat distribution Low effectiveness
Fan-assisted	100%	Low initial cost Good heat distribution Excellent thermostat control Individual room control Silent	Space restriction (furniture)
Heat pumps			
In general		Very high efficiency Low operation cost Environmentally friendly Reversible (heat and cool)	High initial system cost Auxiliary system (cold climate) Outside heat exchanger
Geothermal	COP* 4	Highest efficiency (COP)	Land requirement (soil) Central control
Air central	COP* 3.5	High efficiency	Central control
Ductless	COP* 3.5	Excellent thermostat control Individual room control	
Oil / gas			
Central	90%	High air quality High efficiency	High initial cost Fossil fuels Central control

Electricity-Based Systems

Sustainable *electrical HVAC systems* use electricity that has been generated using renewable and sustainable sources, such as domestic wind turbines, solar panels (fig. 8.9), biomass, and various types of waste, including agricultural, forestry, and municipal waste, and sewage. Biomass and waste technologies are further discussed below. Since all of the generated energy put in the electrical system is transformed into heat, except for the amount used by fans and other such devices, their gross efficiency is commonly rated at 100 percent. In electrical systems, a current is passed through a resistor that, in turn, generates heat. The three basic types of electrical systems, shown in figure 8.10, are forced-air, fan-assisted, and baseboard units.

The *electric furnace*, which is also known as a *forced-air electrical system*, is a central unit that distributes hot air through a network of ducts. Such systems function efficiently and effectively by forcing heat through different rooms of a dwelling (Stein and Reynolds 2000). However, systems with a heating capacity less than 10,000 W for small houses are hardly available, making the system's initial cost high.

The permanently mounted *baseboard heater* is probably the most common type of room heater. Ideally installed under windows, they have a 100 percent gross efficiency. When they are not installed under a window, air circulation may be compromised and efficiency reduced. Their effectiveness, however, is significantly compromised, since only a portion of the heat delivered is actually used to heat the air. Individual controls can be installed in the different rooms, allowing independent temperature control. When conventional thermostat and baseboard reaction is used, the time delay between temperature readings is long and often leads to wasted energy and very warm temperatures in the vicinity of the heater. Electric baseboard systems require a substantial amount of power to operate, but their low initial cost justifies their popularity (House-Energy 2011).

The *wall-mounted fan-assisted units* are growing in popularity. In addition to circulating the air for better effectiveness and comfort, some systems include a preheat device to reduce energy consumption. Indeed, the heating element (i.e., resistor) is kept at a "ready to heat" temperature to prevent the surge in electrical load that would result from heating a cold element. The fan-assisted units consume less energy than the standard baseboards described above because of forced convection, the preheat device, and the built-in electronic thermostat, which provides better temperature control. Like baseboard units, fan-assisted systems come in different sizes, shapes, and capacities according to the needed use.

FIGURE 8.9 Electricity-generating solar panels mounted on a building's side.

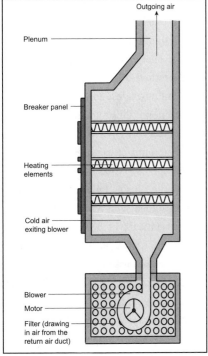

Electrical forced-air furnace

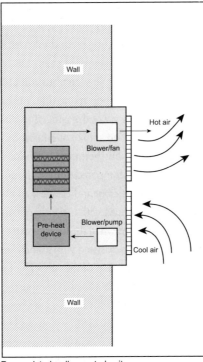

Fan-assisted wall-mounted units

FIGURE 8.10 The three basic electric systems are forced-air, fan-assisted, and baseboard units.

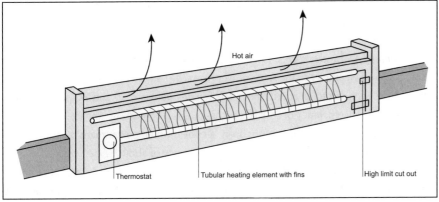

Electrical baseboard heaters

Fossil Fuel Combustion

According to Strongman (2008), *condensing boilers* are highly energy-efficient systems and are as easy to install as conventional boilers. They are available as floor-standing or wall-hung units in a variety of sizes, including models small enough to fit into a kitchen cupboard. They are, however, more costly than conventional systems. The combustion process generates gas by-products, including water vapor and carbon dioxide. In a conventional heating system, these gases are vented out of the house. A condensing system, illustrated in figure 8.11, cools the combustion gases, capturing the additional heat that is released from the gases and distributing it to the dwelling. It is advantageous to replace older conventional boilers that are operating inefficiently, at only 55 to 65 percent efficiency, with new ones. New noncondensing boilers are around 78 percent efficient, while new condensing boilers can be up to 92 percent efficient (Which? 2010).

The efficiency of gas- and oil-fired furnaces has significantly increased in the past few years. Notwithstanding their use of a renewable energy source, traditional wood boilers tend to have low combustion efficiency and produce a large amount of air pollutants, such as carbon monoxide, nitrogen oxides, sulfur oxides, and VOCs. The advantages of using a wood-gasification boiler, whose section is illustrated in figure 8.12, is that it has almost no smoke or emissions and therefore is a very environmentally friendly heating method. Furthermore, it produces very small amounts of wood-ash particulates, especially when compared with traditional stoves and boilers (Wood Energy 2008).

The most efficient and cleanest combustion of wood is obtained when the flame does not come into contact with fuel, other than that being consumed. This type of combustion is generally obtained when the flame is directed downward at the top of the fuel. An appropriate furnace design, assisted with a small fan, provides good airflow while inverting the flame so that it burns the top of the fuel. The fuel heats up, becomes gaseous, and rises into the flame, at which point its actual combustion takes place. The result is a controlled burn that starts at the top of the furnace and progresses downward, providing clean, efficient combustion with an efficiency of 90 percent and low emission levels similar to those of natural gas.

Advanced boilers can be programmed to work on standby mode until full heat is required, and they can be loaded with wood to last up to 24 hours, depending on capacity. Gasification wood boilers typically have a peak capacity of between 30 and 100 kW, making them suitable for domestic use. They can also be combined with fossil fuel–based heating systems.

Combined heat and power (CHP), or cogeneration, systems simultaneously produce usable heat and electricity in the same power plant (fig. 8.13). Thermal power plants that convert heat energy into electricity have efficiencies between 30 and 50 percent (Roth 2005). The overall efficiency of a CHP process is about 86 percent, and the energy is delivered as heat or electricity. By comparison, a conventional power plant combined with a conventional boiler would typically have an efficiency of about 57 percent.

In residential planning, CHP can also be used in the form of district or community heating. Small CHP systems, each consisting of an internal combustion engine burning gas or oil with an electrical output ranging from 25 to 1,000 kW, are the most common (WBCSD 2008). *District heating* is the common generation of heat for a group of buildings. It is usually most successful in dense, mixed-use developments. A wide range of fuels can be used effectively, including wood, sawdust, waste materials, and solar energy.

The economics of CHPs are very site and machine specific. They are governed by the site's energy demand, the plant's capital and maintenance costs, operating hours, and energy prices. For economic viability, a site should normally have an electricity load of at least 45 kW and a heat load of at least 120 kW. Simultaneous demands for heat and power should also be present for at least 4,500 hours a year, which is about a 50 percent load factor (Smith 2007).

CHP units capture and use the heat generated when fuel is burned to produce electricity. CHP technology can be applied on various scales, from a single home to a large industrial plant. Micro-CHP units are suitable for use in the home, replacing the con-

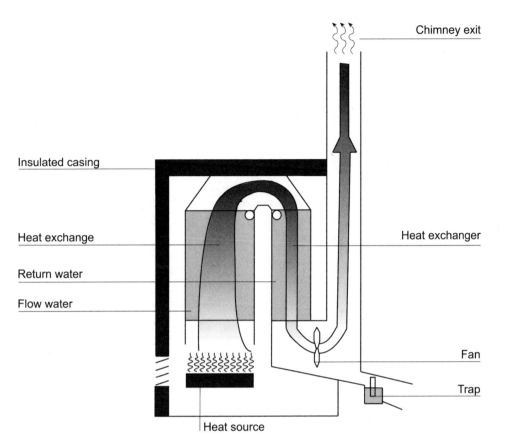

Chimney exit

Insulated casing

Heat exchange

Heat exchanger

Return water

Flow water

Fan

Trap

Heat source

FIGURE 8.11 Section through a condensing boiler system.

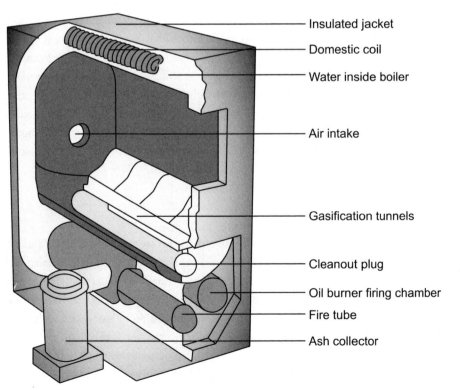

Insulated jacket

Domestic coil

Water inside boiler

Air intake

Gasification tunnels

Cleanout plug

Oil burner firing chamber

Fire tube

Ash collector

FIGURE 8.12 Section through a gasification wood boiler.

FIGURE 8.13 Diagrammatic
representation of a combined
heat and power (CHP) system
in a dwelling.

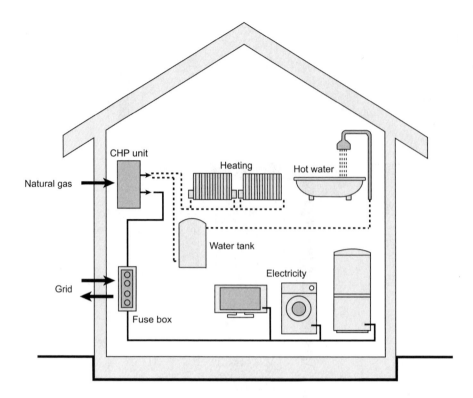

ventional boiler in a central heating system with a small gas engine that drives an electrical generator. This powers domestic lights and appliances, while the waste heat from the engine can heat both interior space and water (Kwok and Grondzik 2007).

One needs to bear in mind that the installation should be carried out by a trained and certified professional. Homes fitted with CHPs are usually also connected to the electricity grid and may retain backup boilers to ensure that they are never short of an energy supply during maintenance of the CHP plant or during periods of unusually high energy demands.

The maintenance of CHP systems is straightforward. The heating system within the CHP unit requires servicing similar to that for any residential boiler. The generator requires routine service every 1 to 2 years, or after 2,000 to 3,000 working hours (Smith 2005). The majority of these systems use natural gas for fuel, although CHPs are compatible with most forms of fuel, including biomass sources.

Biomass/Waste

According to Strongman (2008), home *biomass systems* "vary in complexity from a stand-alone stove that can heat a single room to a wood-pellet boiler with an automated fuel supply that can run a central-heating system or heat water." The fuel used in domestic applications is usually wood pellets, chips, or logs. Nonwood biomass fuel, such as animal waste, biodegradable products from the food-processing industry, and such high-energy crops as rape, sugar cane, and corn can also be used (fig. 8.14).

The ecological merit of biomass fuel is disputed by some, as it still pumps carbon dioxide into the atmosphere when it is burned. Still, the system is effectively carbon neutral, since the carbon dioxide released is equal to that absorbed by the plants during their lifetime, and a biomass boiler can save 6.6 to 7.7 tons (6 to 7 tonnes) of carbon dioxide a year compared with fossil fuel–generated electricity (Strongman 2008).

Qualified stove dealers can advise which appliance will suit the circumstances and can help install a safe and efficient system. Installation is straightforward, and the boilers are often compatible with existing radiators, pipe networks, and underfloor heating. Wood systems must be cleared of ashes, and a regular fuel supply is required, so they are most appropriate for homes with a wood supply and with plenty of storage space.

GROUND COOLING SYSTEMS

Soil temperature is affected by air temperature, moisture content, soil type, and vegetative cover. In Earth's top crust, the temperature ranges from 18°F to 26°F (–8°C to –3°C) for most sodded surfaces. At shallow depths—20 to 200 ft (6 to 61 m)—the mean ground temperature approaches the annual average air temperature plus 2°F (1.1°C), with no significant change from summer to winter. Ground cooling is, therefore, based on the concept that the ground temperature is lower than that of the outdoor air during the cooling season, and the building's heat may be stored in the ground, which has high thermal inertia and low conductivity (Schaeffer 2005).

The exchange of heat can take place through two principal methods: ground cooling or earth-to-air cooling. *Ground cooling* occurs when the building is designed with a portion of the envelope in direct contact with the ground (fig. 8.15). *Earth-to-air cooling* occurs where air that has been cooled by circulating underground is introduced into the building (Smith 2007).

A typical earth-to-air cooling system consists of one or more pipes of appropriate diameter and length buried in the ground horizontally. Ambient, or indoor, air is drawn through the pipe, usually by electric fans. The system of air circulation may be either an open or a closed loop. *Closed-loop systems* circulate a water-based solution through a loop system of underground pipes. As with geothermal heat pumps, there are three orientations for closed-loop systems: horizontal, vertical, or submerged in a pond of

FIGURE 8.14 Diagrammatic representation of a biomass system.

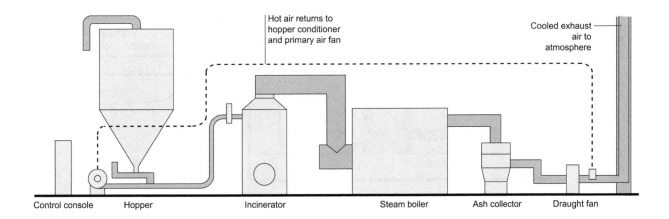

Control console   Hopper   Incinerator   Steam boiler   Ash collector   Draught fan

Hot air returns to hopper conditioner and primary air fan

Cooled exhaust air to atmosphere

water. *Open-loop systems* use an existing underground water well or surface water. In both cases, heat is transferred to or from the structure, regardless of outdoor temperature, to provide year-round heating and cooling (Water Furnace 2010). Earth-to-air cooling systems are simple and low cost, but the economics of ground cooling depends on the climate, the nature of the site, and the building.

HEAT TRANSFER/RECOVERY SYSTEMS

Domestic *heat-recovery systems* can be used to both heat and cool a dwelling. A system consists of two separate air-handling units: one collects and exhausts stale air from inside the building while the other draws in fresh air and distributes it (Strongman 2008) (fig. 8.16). Both airstreams pass through a heat-transfer module, and although the airstreams remain physically separate, heat from the exhaust air is transferred to the fresh incoming

FIGURE 8.15 Schematic representation of a ground cooling mode of a residential geothermal system.

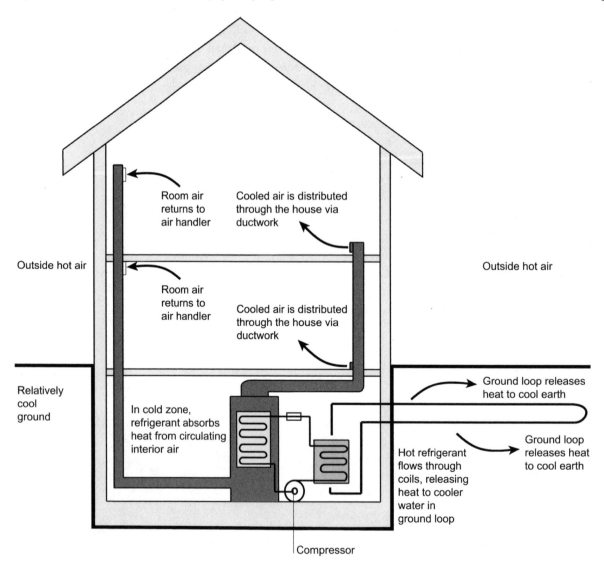

Room air returns to air handler

Cooled air is distributed through the house via ductwork

Outside hot air

Outside hot air

Room air returns to air handler

Cooled air is distributed through the house via ductwork

Relatively cool ground

In cold zone, refrigerant absorbs heat from circulating interior air

Ground loop releases heat to cool earth

Ground loop releases heat to cool earth

Hot refrigerant flows through coils, releasing heat to cooler water in ground loop

Compressor

air in the winter. In the summertime the air being exhausted cools incoming warmer air. The transfer reduces the energy needed to heat a house in the winter and cool it in the summer (Janis and Tao 2009; Strongman 2008).

While small wall-mounted heat-recovery systems are available, most are centralized, with the heat-recovery unit installed in the lofts or on a roof, such as the passive air shaft (fig. 8.17), and attached to a network of ducts (Janis and Tao 2009; Strongman 2008). A central panel controls the fan speed and the air temperature entering the building. For best results, the system should be serviced annually, by either the owner or a professional. The task involves cleaning or replacing the filters and vacuuming inside the ducts.

The main advantage of a heat-recovery system is its ability to improve interior air quality by removing pollutants and odors (Baker-Laporte et al. 2001). The system uses the heat energy generated by washing machines, showers, stoves, and necessary heat-producing activities and avoids the need for noisy extractor fans or unsightly trickle ventilators in windows. The disadvantage is that the fans in the system require energy to run, so it is less energy efficient than natural ventilation in the summer (Strongman 2008).

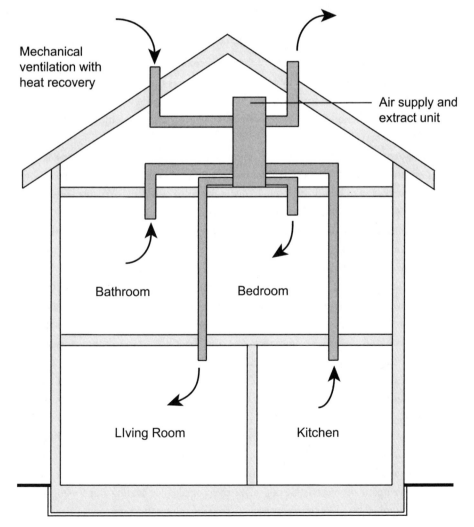

FIGURE 8.16 Diagrammatic representation of a heat-recovery system.

Mechanical ventilation with heat recovery

Air supply and extract unit

Bathroom

Bedroom

LIving Room

Kitchen

FIGURE 8.17 A passive air
shaft that in winter returns
cleaned hot air to the unit,
installed on a roof of an
apartment building. Used with
permission.

Radiant Heating/Cooling Systems

Radiant heating/cooling systems supply both heating and cooling in an energy-efficient manner by changing the temperature of the walls, ceiling, and/or floor of a space instead of heating and cooling the air. The radiant temperature is the average temperature of all the objects that surround the body. These systems work because the temperature experienced by the human body is approximately equal to the average radiant temperature in a room (Watson and Chapman 2002).

A radiant heating/cooling system generally consists of an array of water-carrying pipes or tubes installed in or behind the wall, ceiling, or floor of an interior space. The three main types of radiant heating/cooling systems are a concrete core, suspended radiant ceiling panels, and applied capillary tubes (McDonell 2007).

In concrete-core systems, the water circulates through plastic tubes imbedded in a slab of a concrete ceiling, wall, or floor. This allows the thermal mass of the slab to be used in smoothing out heating and cooling loads (Janis and Tao 2009). With suspended radiant ceiling panels, there is minimal thermal mass but a very swift response time. A panel encloses an electric heating element between two layers of insulation. Once turned on, the system can heat a space, and its effectiveness will depend on the number of panels used in relation to the area of the room. An applied-capillary-tube system consists of a fine grid of small-bore plastic tubes installed under wall or ceiling plaster or imbedded in gypsum board. The system provides an even surface temperature and has a heat-storage capacity intermediate between the other two types of systems. It is preferred for retrofit applications.

Unlike conventional wall-mounted-radiator systems, a radiant heating/cooling system will usually occupy a large part of the total surface area of a space, such as a ceiling or wall (Stein and Reynolds 2000). The actual change in water temperature necessary to improve the occupant's comfort is, therefore, relatively small. The heating and cooling load is generally supplied by a low-temperature boiler, an efficient refrigeration system, a passive cooling system, or a heat pump with a high coefficient of performance. Once installed, radiant systems disappear from view. Architectural integration requirements are limited to providing each room with the necessary unobstructed wall, floor, or ceiling surface.

Unlike air-conditioning systems, radiant systems do not detrimentally affect indoor air quality. They can significantly reduce the amount of mechanical ventilation needed to ensure comfort, and they reduce the amount of ductwork needed for a conventional HVAC system by about 80 percent (Keeler and Burke 2009). Radiant systems can be effectively used for residential buildings, with or without mechanical ventilation systems.

Radiant Barriers

Radiant barriers are commonly installed in the attic to reduce summer heat gain and winter heat loss, which in turn helps lower heating and cooling costs. The radiant barriers consist of a highly reflective material, such as aluminum foil, that reflects radiant heat from the sun rather than absorbing it (US DOE 2009).

When the sun heats a roof, a large portion of the heat travels by conduction through the roofing materials. The hot roofing materials then radiate their gained heat energy onto the cooler attic surfaces, including the air ducts and the attic floor. A radiant barrier on the underside of the roof reduces the radiant heat transfer to the other surfaces in the attic and, consequently, the heat transfer to the rooms below (US DOE 2009).

Underfloor Heating

High-tech plastic pipes containing water can be buried in a screed underneath the floor or can run just below the surface, as shown in figure 8.18. These underfloor heating systems are compatible with all floor finishes, can be installed throughout a house on any story, or can be combined with radiators fitted in other rooms. Because the system employs full lengths of piping without any joints, it is almost maintenance-free and has a life span of up to 100 years. Because heat is transferred to the entire floor area, water temperatures of 113°F to 149°F (45°C to 65°C) can achieve room temperatures of 77°F to 82°F (25°C to 28°C). Regular radiators would have to reach 176°F (80°C) to achieve a similar room temperature (Strongman 2008). If the system is installed alongside a condensing boiler, energy savings of up to 40 percent can be made. Even with a standard boiler, a 15 percent energy savings is common.

FIGURE 8.18 Installation of an underfloor heating system.

English Residence

Location: Orleans, Massachusetts, USA

Design: ZeroEnergy Design

Completion: 2009

Site area: 1.42 acres (0.575 hectares)

Total floor area: 2,000 sq ft (186 m²)

Number of floors: 2

English Residence is a LEED gold–certified home that combines a high-performance building envelope, energy-efficient systems and appliances, and a solar thermal system to achieve low energy consumption. The building envelope was constructed to reach a high insulation value and to minimize thermal bridging and air infiltration. The walls and roof combine open- and closed-cell spray foam with additional rigid insulation to counteract heat loss due to thermal bridging. The open-cell spray foam insulation expands up to 150 times its original size and is highly efficient in preventing air leaks and heat loss. Because of its lasting flexibility, the insulation does not break and allow air infiltration during the natural expansion and contraction of the wood studs. The closed-cell spray insulation, having a higher rigidity and thermal value, effectively prevents mold growth and interior condensation.

The design integrates an Energy Star–qualified gas furnace with a hydro-air system that operates at variable speed. The radiant floors evenly distribute heat while providing optimum comfort. Radiant-heating systems promote healthy indoor air quality by eliminating the discomfort of allergen and noise production often associated with forced-air systems. The house is also pre-plumbed for the future use of a solar thermal system to deliver hot water.

To optimize the home's efficiency in heat distribution, an HVAC zoning control system was installed. The multistage equipment establishes four different temperature zones in the house. Each interior zone is monitored by programmable thermostats that control the temperature according to a variety of schedules set for the week. The heat-recovery ventilator further prevents the need for excessive heating and cooling by preheating or precooling the incoming fresh air. Along with the ventilator, the whole-house allergen-filtration system ensures optimum indoor air quality.

Besides mechanical systems, the house makes use of passive means to maintain a stable interior temperature. It was designed to allow maximum natural cross ventilation through strategic placement of awning and casement windows and the open floor plan that maximizes air circulation (figs. 8.19, 8.20). The window overhang above the southern glazed facade shades against the sun during summer while letting in its warmth during winter (fig. 8.21). On the rooftop terrace, a roof garden yields passive cooling to mitigate the urban heat island effect while acting as additional insulation to help maintain a constant interior temperature (fig. 8.22).

FIGURE 8.19 To achieve optimal air quality, the house incorporates a whole-house ventilation and allergen-filtration system, finishes that emit low or no VOCs, radiant heating, and hard floor surfaces with bamboo flooring. Used with permission.

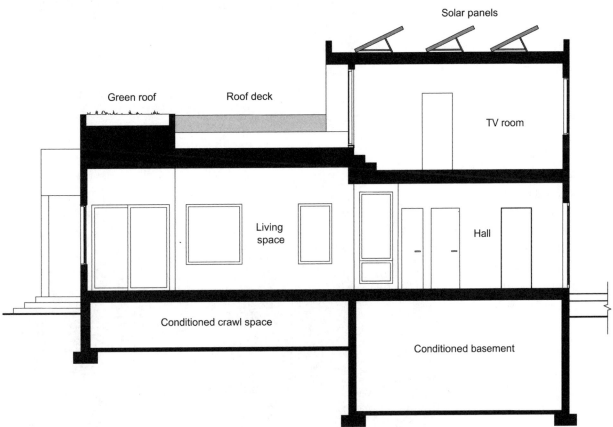

FIGURE 8.20 The strategic location of the windows permits maximum cross ventilation throughout the house. Used with permission.

FIGURE 8.21 The roof overhangs and deciduous trees shade the dwelling from the penetrating sun during summer while admitting its warmth during winter. Used with permission.

FIGURE 8.22 The rooftop deck incorporates a garden designed with native and drought-tolerant plants, and the upper roof supports solar panels. The solar panels generate 30 percent of the home's electricity demand and harness the sun's heat to provide hot water. Used with permission.

CHAPTER 9

Healthy Indoor Environments

I ndoor air quality (IAQ) is of paramount importance in ensuring the health and comfort of occupants. Lack of daylight, poor ventilation, excessive noise, or noxious compounds emitted from building materials can have lasting consequences on health and may result in allergies, stress, and/or the transmission of communicable diseases. Comfort is a complex issue affected by factors such as type of activity, clothing, age, and gender as well as air temperature, air movement, radiant temperature, humidity, noise, light, and odors. This chapter examines these aspects and suggests alternative design strategies and products that can reduce harmful emissions while ameliorating comfort.

BUILDINGS AND COMFORT

Building materials have undergone significant changes in the past half century, many of which have led to efficient and cost-effective alternatives. The introduction of composite wood products, stain-resistant synthetic carpets, thermally efficient rigid insulation boards, cleaning agents, and furnishings, for instance, have broadened the design options. Many of these products, however, emit odors and, in some cases, toxic compounds into the air. These elements are commonly emitted at a room temperature of 70°F (21°C) (Nugon-Baudon 2008). If effective ventilation is not provided, the concentration of harmful pollutants can compromise the physical and psychological well-being of the occupants, as well as reduce their levels of productivity. Several new green products that consider IAQ, some of which have been described in chapter 6, have been introduced in recent years. In addition, the LEED system provides guidance and sets criteria for IAQ management. Those criteria refer to storage of building products away from possible moisture damage, replacement of filtration components that have been used during construction on HVAC systems, and a "flush-out" to clean the indoor air at the project's end.

The health issues related to poor IAQ have become a topic of great concern. In the 1970s, the energy crisis precipitated the development of thermally insulated "airtight" buildings that helped reduce energy consumption. Lack of proper ventilation in some of these buildings, however, created poor IAQ conditions. A study done in Toronto,

Canada, showed that in 20 percent of the analyzed dwellings built in the 1960s and 1970s, numerous respiratory problems were caused by polluted indoor air and poor IAQ (CMHC 2010; Bas 2004). According to a World Health Organization report (WHO 2010), indoor air pollution is responsible for 2.7 percent of the global transmission of disease. The report also estimated that up to 30 percent of all new and remodeled buildings worldwide may have problems with IAQ.

Conditions inside a building affect not only its occupants' health but also their level of comfort, which is affected by thermal, visual, acoustic, and indoor-air quality, illustrated in figure 9.1. Occupant-related aspects include their activity, clothing, age, and gender. Indoor environment factors include air speed, radiant temperature, relative humidity, air movement, noise, light, and odors (Winchip 2007).

Designers modify the external natural environment by providing comfortable shelter and by moderating indoor climate. An important consideration of theirs will be how the site, the building's form, and the human body interact to achieve suitable levels of comfort. Since comfort is subjective, architects need to consider conditions that are acceptable to a majority of users. Another important aspect that affects the occupants' comfort

FIGURE 9.1 Comfort is the outcome of the relationship between indoors, outdoors, and occupant-related factors.

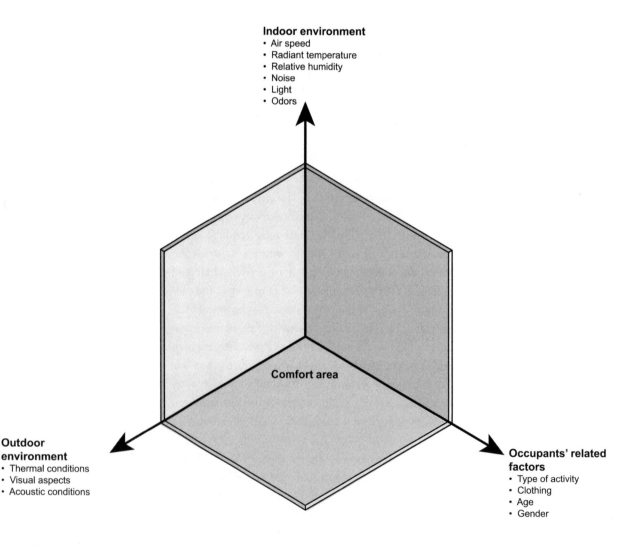

Indoor environment
- Air speed
- Radiant temperature
- Relative humidity
- Noise
- Light
- Odors

Comfort area

Outdoor environment
- Thermal conditions
- Visual aspects
- Acoustic conditions

Occupants' related factors
- Type of activity
- Clothing
- Age
- Gender

is the relation between a dwelling and the environment as a result of its siting, a subject that was discussed in chapter 2.

Over the years, various governmental and nongovernmental organizations have developed standards to guide the design and construction of healthy interior environments, which will be discussed below. The objective of these standards is to highlight important issues and strategies that promote alternative products with few or no harmful emissions.

INDOOR AIR QUALITY

More than any other environmental issue, indoor air pollution directly affects health and, by implication, comfort and productivity. It is common knowledge that health effects of indoor air pollution include allergies and asthma, infectious diseases, cancer, and other genetic damage. The series of widespread and chronic effects on occupants' health due to the poor indoor air quality of a building are referred to as *sick building syndrome*, which serves to describe a physical environment that is unhealthy for its inhabitants (Bas 2004). Indoor air quality is determined by the quality of the air outside the building that is taken in through the ventilation system, pollutant emissions within the building, the ventilation rate, the efficiency of filtration, and the standard of maintenance of mechanical systems.

According to Craig et al. 2004, people spend 80 to 90 percent of their lives indoors. The impact of constant exposure to low-level emissions from the wide variety of materials commonly found in buildings is still unknown. Most of these pollutants originate in the building itself. With an increase in the use of solvents, interior finishes emitting VOCs, and cleaning agents, indoor air pollution has become a serious concern. In fact, a 2005 Health Canada study supports the notion that interior environments are up to five times more polluted than the outdoors.

Making buildings more airtight to conserve energy also affects air quality. There is less incidental, unplanned ventilation, and dust emission concentrations in the air are increased. One view is that lower ventilation rates create unhealthy conditions. Another is that the increase in indoor pollutant sources is the real problem. Common causes for sick building syndrome include poor building design, poor maintenance, and poor operation of the structure's ventilation system. The ventilation system, in particular, is often found to be the main culprit because it can secretly harbor a buildup of pollutants within the building over time, resulting in an indoor environment whose air quality is actually much lower than that of the outdoor air, even in a heavily polluted city center with its clouds of vehicle exhaust and other pollutants (Environmental Illness Resource 2010). Furthermore, in underventilated spaces, mold spores and house dust mites thrive and VOCs reach higher concentrations. It is also well established that a healthy indoor environment will be achieved only if artificial and mechanical systems are correctly installed, fully commissioned to ensure that they operate as intended, and properly maintained. These factors increase the need for care in the specification of materials and in the design of ventilation systems.

Four main approaches might be used to control indoor air pollutants: removing the source of pollution from the building, controlling pollutant emissions at the source, expelling the pollutants from the building through ventilation measures, and commissioning the heating, ventilation, and air-conditioning (HVAC) systems and the filtration systems.

While many causes and effects of poor indoor air quality are known, designing for a healthy environment is not a simple task. Many of the issues involved in IAQ are not exact sciences. Although sources of pollutants can be identified, there is rarely enough information to evaluate the exact impact of design decisions on the occupants. Not enough is known about the effects of pollutants on long-term human health or about the quantities of harmful pollutants emitted from materials within buildings. Furthermore, there are many strongly interrelated factors that determine IAQ.

The process of designing for IAQ is based mostly on identifying and avoiding materials that are known to be strong sources of odors, irritants, or toxins and on ensuring that adequate measures are taken to provide sufficient ventilation to occupied spaces. These principles will be outlined next.

Ventilation

Efficient ventilation dilutes pollutant concentration and removes pollutants. The amount of ventilation required depends on pollutant source strength, types of contaminants, and occupant and space characteristics. Increasing the rate of fresh air intake alone, however, does not guarantee that a healthy indoor air quality will result. Attention must therefore be given to the design, installation, operation, and maintenance of the entire HVAC system or a system of baseboard heating complemented with a heat-recovery ventilator. Even with high ventilation rates, buildings may suffer from poor IAQ if there is an uneven distribution of air or an insufficient exhaust mechanism (fig. 9.2). There are several factors that merit careful consideration, as they are common causes of indoor air problems (Bas 2004).

The dilution of indoor pollutants is predominantly achieved by increasing the rate at which outdoor air is supplied to the building. When the outdoor air quality is poor, proper filtration is needed before the air is let in. Any air that is brought in needs to be heated and/or conditioned to provide comfortable thermal and humidity conditions, which in turn requires energy. Minimum ventilation rates should not be determined solely by the thermal conditioning needs of a building. They should also be determined by humidity and airflow (Keeler and Burke 2009). Some systems operate at reduced or interrupted flow during certain portions of the day, as is the case with variable air cleanliness and distribution.

Uneven air distribution may result in variable temperature and humidity conditions in different parts of the building. Not only would this compromise the overall indoor air quality, but it may result in the occupants interfering with the operation of the mechanical ventilation system. Uncomfortable drafts, for instance, may tempt the users of a space to block the air registers if they emit unwanted hot or cold air, or people may be encouraged to open operable windows under undesired

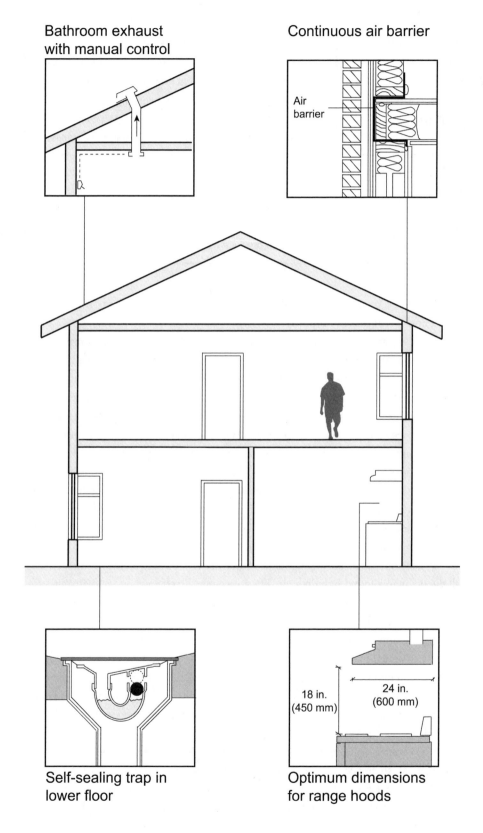

Bathroom exhaust with manual control

Continuous air barrier

Air barrier

FIGURE 9.2 Ventilation strategies to improve indoor air quality in a dwelling.

Self-sealing trap in lower floor

Optimum dimensions for range hoods

18 in. (450 mm)

24 in. (600 mm)

FIGURE 9.3 Types of air cleaners and their characteristics.

Type	Characteristics
Mechanical filters	• Flat or pleated; Effective at removing particles • Flat filters are effective at removing large particles • Pleated filters, such as high-efficiency particulate air filters (HEPA), collect the smaller, respirable particles
Electronic air cleaners	• Use electronic charge to remove airborne particles • May also produce ozone, a lung irritant
Ion generators	• Use electronic charge to remove airborne particles • May also produce ozone, a lung irritant

circumstances, creating additional indoor environment challenges such as condensation and uncontrolled humidity.

The placement of supply and return registers too close to one another may lead to uneven fresh air distribution and inefficient removal of contaminants. At the building's exterior, air supply vents that are installed too close to the exhaust vents may redirect contaminated air back into the building. Similarly, the placement of supply vents near other sources of outdoor air pollution, such as loading docks, parking lots, heavy traffic areas, chimneys, trash collection sites, and smoking areas, can provide a pathway for contaminants to enter the building's ventilation system (Winchip 2007).

Improper maintenance of a mechanical system can cause the system to become a source of harmful pollutants. Lack of periodic cleaning may result in clogging and subsequently reduce or eliminate airflow. Particular attention should be given to the possible accumulation of water, which may foster harmful biological growth, such as of fungi and bacteria, that can be distributed throughout the building.

While air cleaners are an important part of any HVAC system, they cannot remove all the pollutants found in indoor air. They are generally effective in removing airborne particles, but special filter systems are required to remove specific contaminants (Engineering Edge 2010).

An important way to ensure that mechanical ventilation systems not only are accurately designed but also reduce the amount of unsafe incoming particles is to comply with the minimum efficiency reporting value (MERV). This standard was developed to evaluate the filtration and removal efficiency of each grille. The values range from 1 to 16, from the worst to the best, respectively (ASHRAE 2010). Characteristics of several types of air cleaners are listed in figure 9.3.

It is possible, for example, to reduce gaseous pollutants if the cleaner contains special material, such as activated charcoal or other absorbent products (Aller Air 2009). While these materials are usually effective in removing specific pollutants, none is expected to remove all gaseous substances typically found in indoor air. As is the case with all filters, they require periodic cleaning and filter replacement to function properly.

MATERIALS AND IAQ

In many cases, the selection of healthy building materials involves a trade-off between constraining environmental aspects. Particleboard, for example, made mostly from sawdust, is attractive because it reduces the need for solid sawn lumber. The binders used in its manufacturing, however, are toxic (PWGSC 2009). The exercise becomes one of finding the right balance between replacement needs and toxic emissions.

The process is complicated because there are no simple rules to follow. There is also a common misconception that natural is better. Compounds like arsenic, lead, formaldehyde, and asbestos are naturally occurring substances used in products and equipment, yet they are much more toxic than many synthetic substitutes. Furthermore, natural materials are usually susceptible to quick degradation and require treatment and/or protection with compounds that may emit toxic substances. Carpets made of wool, for instance, require protection to control pests. Some natural fibers are also less stain resistant and may require industrial solvents for cleaning that are sources of contamination in themselves (Baker-Laporte et al. 2001).

While many of these factors either are not quantifiable or have unknown implications, IAQ can still be improved through careful material selection based on understanding of two important aspects. The first is the mechanism by which pollutants are released into the air. The second has to do with the emissions characteristics of the end products made from these materials. Emissions from building materials are produced at all phases of a building's life cycle. Most emissions can be anticipated through careful consideration during design. They can originate from three sources: the product itself, the surrounding air, and materials used to install, clean, and maintain the products, some of which are shown in figure 9.4.

Emissions can be either wet or dry. Wet emissions are usually solvents, water-based primers, paints, sealants, adhesives, and caulks. Some may be emitted from solvents used to clean tools during application. Emissions usually reach their highest level while the material is drying, which may take a few hours or days. Many products may continue to emit substances at lower concentrations for weeks, months, and even years after application.

FIGURE 9.4 Potential sources of emissions in the dwelling's interior.

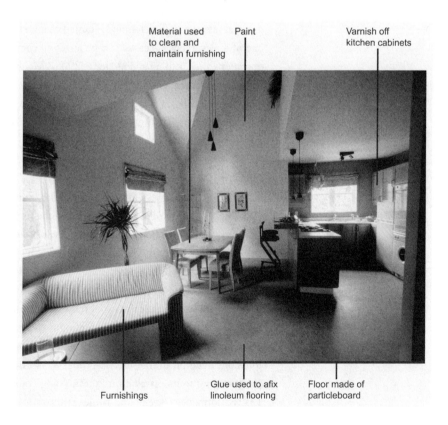

Material used to clean and maintain furnishing

Paint

Varnish off kitchen cabinets

Furnishings

Glue used to afix linoleum flooring

Floor made of particleboard

Dry emissions come from products that do not involve an on-site wet process but emit harmful substances nevertheless. Solvents that were used during the manufacturing process are emitted, usually in an initial outburst, when the product is first exposed. This is most noticeable if the product was packaged soon after its manufacture, which did not leave the volatile substances enough time to evaporate. The most familiar of these dry emissions are responsible for "new car smell" and "new carpet smell" (Yudelson 2007). Other examples of dry products emissions include those that come from carpets backed with styrene butadiene rubber (SBR) latex and composite wood products, such as particleboard, made with formaldehyde-based resins. Recent research and development of carpets, which was described in chapter 6, also saw the introduction of alternative adhesives and undercarpet products with no harm to indoor air quality.

Building surfaces may also emit substances and particles that they have absorbed from the surrounding air. While all surfaces adsorb molecules of chemical substances and compounds from the surrounding air to which they are exposed, some processes are reversible while others are permanent. The degree to which a substance is adsorbed depends on the chemical characteristics of the compound and on the area and the texture of the surface, which is also known as *sink material*. The sink material's loading is directly proportional to the concentration of pollutants in the air. It can store pollutants during periods of high concentration and emit them later when the concentration is low (Haghighat and Huang 2003).

Substances used to maintain building surfaces and equipment can also be strong sources of pollutants. Although these materials are not generally part of the original construction, their use is determined to a large extent by decisions made at the design stage. Proper material selection will determine required cleaning agents and maintenance needs and the rate of replacement necessary, so it can significantly reduce emissions from maintenance operations and cleaning agents (Jones 2008). Maintenance products that have strong odors or irritating constituents should be avoided where possible. Also, standard guidelines like those from Green Seal and GREENGUARD have been developed to direct and encourage the use of cleaning and maintenance products that are safe and free of noxious emissions.

Selection Criteria of Healthy Materials

Some products such as carpets, particleboard, and other manufactured wood products are subject to standard testing procedures, the results of which can be compared. Manufacturers of these products that do not disclose full emission test reports should be considered with skepticism, if considered at all. The reports are commonly displayed on the manufacturer's website or are submitted with bidding documents to clients. In a case where testing is not common or standardized, the manufacturer should disclose the product's contents and a description of the manufacturing processes and treatments that are likely to affect its emissions. The willingness of manufacturers to take steps to improve a product's performance in terms of reducing harmful emissions should also be taken into consideration in the selection process. For instance, pretreatment and aeration of a product prior to its installation in a building could significantly improve that product's IAQ performance (Keeler and Burke 2009).

It should also be mentioned that considerations for good IAQ are not limited to construction. Many furnishings are made of particleboard products or have lacquered finishes that have high levels of emissions, sometimes for lengthy periods (Hegger et al. 2006). While furniture selection is usually beyond the responsibility of either the architect or the builder, it might be useful to include suggestions in an owner manual, along with recommendations for cleaning products and maintenance of ventilating equipment.

The most harmful indoor contaminants emitted from building materials can usually be traced back to a few chemical components. Most harmful emissions originate from adhesives, products that require polymerization or foam expansion, vinyl products, particularly those with plasticizers, and maintenance products such as waxes and cleaning agents. These materials are listed in figure 9.5.

FIGURE 9.5 Sources and duration of emission of indoor air pollutants.

Principle pollutants	Building product	Timing/duration of emission
Formaldehyde	Hardwood, plywood, particleboard and other glue-bonded wood products Some coatings and sealants may contain in lower concentrations	Highest emissions when new or recently applied; may continue for up to a year in lower amounts; emissions increase with temperatures and humidity
Toluene, Xylene hexane, aliphatic hydrocarbons 4-Phenylcyclo-hexane	Styrene Butadien Rubber (SB-R) sealants; Butyl Rubber (BR) or solvent based acrylic sealants	Time may vary from few to many hours depending on drying time
	Styrene Butadiene (SB) latex backed carpets	Low emissions, but may persist due to the high sink potential of carpeting
Volatile Organic Compounds (VOCs)	Vinyl tile and sheet flooring	Decrease substantially after 24 hours if well ventilated; lower emissions can continue for years
	Traditional multi-purpose carpet adhesives, both organic solvent and water based	Highest for the first 3-6 weeks; may persist depending on potential of floor material
	Latex (water or organic solvent-based) and acrylic paints; fiberglass and mineral wool insulation	During application and drying; lower emission may persist for months

The use of adhesives in building materials is one of the biggest challenges associated with poor IAQ. Multipurpose adhesives used for carpeting and sheet or tile flooring initially emit VOCs at very high rates. Adhesives used as binders in composite wood products like particleboard and plywood are major sources of formaldehyde in homes, but not all glue-bonded products emit harmful levels of pollutants. Products that contain phenol formaldehyde instead of urea formaldehyde–based adhesives emit negligible amounts of formaldehyde that do not pose a threat to IAQ. Exterior-grade, waterproof composite wood products, like softwood plywood and waferboard, are a few examples. Binders and fire retardants used in insulation products like fiberglass, mineral wool, or cellulose also emit smaller amounts of VOCs, but it is unlikely that the indoor air will be affected significantly as a result (Baker-Laporte et al. 2001).

Adhesive manufacturers have also developed "low-" and "zero-emission" adhesives, which can substantially reduce the amount of noxious compounds being released into the surrounding air. One can significantly reduce pollutants by specifying products made with low- or zero-emission adhesives or by sealing the product to keep the VOCs from being released. Particleboard furniture and cabinets covered with laminate on all sides, for instance, can keep emissions down to acceptable levels (Salthammer and Uhde 2009).

Alternatively, these materials can be replaced altogether with solid sawn lumber components. Carpets can be laid using the *tackless strip method*, which requires little or no gluing. Flooring products made from PVC, such as vinyl tile and sheets, have very high VOC emissions, particularly in the first 24 hours following installation. Although tiles contain fewer plasticizers than sheet materials and have fewer emissions, their impact on IAQ can still be substantial (Hegger et al. 2006). The effect is compounded with the use of multipurpose adhesives. Figure 9.6 summarizes various carpet chemicals and their emissions.

Carpets backed with SB latex emit styrene and 4-phenylcyclohexene (4-PCH), the cause of the "new carpet smell." Although the level of emissions is usually low, they may persist for a long time because of the high sink potential of carpets (Katsoiyannis et al. 2008). Unless other building materials and furnishings have a high sink potential, sufficient ventilation during application and drying can significantly reduce the potential impact on IAQ.

The effect of maintenance products such as cleaning agents and waxes should not be underestimated. The frequent use of these products may result in constant emissions that can seriously affect IAQ, particularly with furniture and fabrics present, which have a high sink capacity. In addition to VOCs, some building materials emit small particles that can be harmful if inhaled over prolonged periods. Fibers from fiberglass or mineral wool insulation, for instance, are suspected carcinogens. Installation of these products should take place only under well-ventilated conditions (Wilson 2009). A well-sealed envelope can keep the insulation from being disturbed by air currents, keeping most of these pollutants out of the living spaces.

While building materials can be a major source of indoor air pollution, there are several other contaminants from other sources listed in figure 9.7. Combustion gases from unvented furnaces and appliances, radon gas from soil, and particulates such as dust and pollen can seriously affect occupant comfort and health, particularly in sensitive individuals.

STANDARD	GUIDELINES*	
Green Label Plus **	Target pollutant	Maximum emissions ($\mu gm^2/hr$)
Carpet program	Acetaldehyde	130
	Benzene	55
	Caprolactam	130
	2-Ethylhexanoic Acid	46
	Formaldehyde	30
	1-Methyl-2-pyrrolidinone	300
	Naphthalene	8.2
	Nonanal	24
	Octanal	13
	4-Phenylcyclohexene	50
	Styrene	410
	Toluene	280
	Vinyl acetate	190
Adhesive program	Acetaldehyde	130
	Benzothiazole	30
	2-Ethyl-1-Hexanol	300
	Formaldehyde	30
	Isooctylacrylate	690
	Methyl biphenyl	95
	1-Methyl-2-pyrrolidinone	300
	Naphthalene	8.2
	Phenol	190
	4-Phenylcyclohexene (4PCH)	50
	Styrene	410
	Toluene	280
	Vinyl acetate	190
	Vinyl cyclohexene	85
	Xylenes (m-, o-, p-)	65
	TVOC	8000

* Based on a 24-hour test of emissions
** Carpet and Rug Institute website, n.d. (http://www.carpet-rug.org/pdf_word_docs/
071028_Carpet_GLP_Criteria.PDF)

FIGURE 9.6 Environmental aspects of various carpets and adhesive programs.

Type of pollutant	Examples	Effect on occupant health	Source of Contamination
Biological Growth			
Fungi	Mold, mildew	Allergic reaction and aggravation of asthma symptoms in high concentrations; irreversible lung damage (with inhalation of mold spores)	High humidity levels caused by washing, bathing, cooking, unvented clothes dryers, etc.
Chemicals			
Inorganic gases	Carbon monoxide	Reduce endurance, worsen symptoms of heart disease, nausea, headache, dizziness; causes death in very high concentrations	Gas stoves, kerosene heaters, tobacco smoke, vehicle exhausts
	Carbon dioxide	Unlikely to affect health in low quantities that are generally found in houses	People, gas stoves, furnaces, kerosene heaters, combustion devices
	Nitrogen dioxide	Breathing difficulty in high concentrations; respiratory illness with prolonged exposure	Mainly outdoor sources, unless sulphur-containing fuels are burned indoors in unvented appliances
	Chlorine	Irritation in susceptible occupants	Household cleaning and laundry products; municipal water sources
	Ammonia	Irritation in susceptible occupants	Household cleaning products
	Ozone	Coughing; chest discomfort; nose, throat and windpipe irritation	Electrostatic air cleaners, arcing electric motors, photocopiers, outside air
Volatile Organic Compounds (VOCs)	Formaldehyde and other aldehydes, hydrocarbons, alcohols, phenols, ketones	Unpleasant odors; eye, nose and throat irritation; central nervous system depressant; possible carcinogens; prolonged exposure may cause sensitization	Building materials; furniture, carpets, synthetic floor coverings, wallpapers; household products, beddings, toiletries, etc.; tobacco smoke; gas stoves; space heaters; pesticides
Particulates			
Biological particles	Viruses, bacteria, spores, pollen, cell debris, dust mites	Few health problems at levels normally found in houses; high concentrations of pollen grains may cause allergic reactions or aggravate asthma symptoms; bacterial growth in stagnant water may cause serious disease	Stagnant water, dust, water droplets
Non-biological particles	Dust, smoke, etc.	Effects may vary from mild discomfort to lung cancer	Tobacco smoke, wood stoves, open fireplaces, combustion operations; construction materials
	Fiber	Temporary eye and skin irritation; lung disease with prolonged exposure; glass fibers may be carcinogenic; asbestos cause lung cancer	Construction materials; fiberglass and mineral wool insulation

FIGURE 9.7 Types, effects, and sources of indoor air pollutants.

THERMAL COMFORT

Thermal comfort is achieved by creating a balance between body heat and heat loss to the surroundings. The balance depends on seven parameters: the individual's metabolism, clothing, skin temperature, air temperature, relative humidity, surface or radiant temperature of the elements in the room, and air speed (Winchip 2007). Some of these factors are shown in figure 9.8. The last four parameters are related to the design process in which aspects such as body weight or direct sunlight will have to be considered. The reader can also consult the sections on insulation in chapter 5.

The *ambient air temperature* affects body heat loss by convection and the evaporation of perspiration. *Relative humidity* is a measure of the moisture in the air and affects heat loss by controlling how much evaporation is possible (Kwok and Grondzik 2007). It has been demonstrated that a range between 30 and 60 percent is acceptable to generate a comfortable thermal sensation, which may vary, however, depending on seasonal conditions (Bas 2004). *Mean radiant temperature* is the average surface temperature of the elements enclosing a space. It influences both the heat lost by radiation from the body and the heat lost by conduction when the body is in contact with other surfaces. Poorly insulated buildings have cold internal surfaces in the winter, requiring higher air temperatures to compensate. An increase in the mean radiant temperature implies that comfort conditions can be achieved at lower air temperatures, and a reduction of 1.8°F (1°C) in air temperature may reduce energy consumption by up to 10 percent (Harvey 2006). Insulation, therefore, saves energy not only by reducing actual building heat loss but also by reducing air temperatures. *Air speed* does not decrease the temperature but

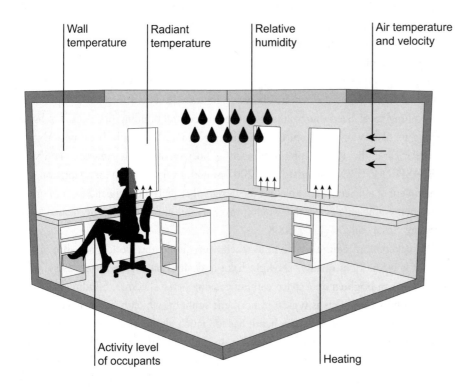

Wall temperature | Radiant temperature | Relative humidity | Air temperature and velocity

Activity level of occupants | Heating

FIGURE 9.8 Thermal comfort is affected by factors that have to be considered during design.

causes a cooling sensation through heat loss by convection and increased evaporation. Typical airflow velocities in residential buildings are 13 ft/s (4 m/s) in the main duct and 10 ft/s (3 m/s) in the branch ducts (Harvey 2006). Figure 9.9 summarizes some design strategies for improving indoor thermal comfort.

Finally, it is important to highlight that technical standards should be applied to avoid uncomfortable situations. The American Society of Heating, Refrigerating and Air-Conditioning Engineers (ASHRAE) has created a set of standards for thermal comfort for North America. ASHRAE 55-2004 sets guidelines that help design, install, and operate air-conditioning devices as well as humidifier/dehumidifier systems (ASHRAE 2010). This standard not only establishes limits for temperature and relative humidity under regular conditions but also addresses strategies for dealing with special circumstances in the building.

VISUAL COMFORT

Healthy indoor environments can also be affected by the visual quality of the interior and the external views. Color schemes, lighting, and outdoor views can generate connections between the exterior and the occupant and improve psychological well-being and mood, resulting in raised levels of productivity (fig. 9.10). In contrast, poor lighting can cause eye strain, fatigue, headaches, irritability, and psychological discomfort, as well as lack of concentration, errors, accidents, and low productivity. Comfortable lighting conditions depend on quantity, distribution, and quality of light (Jones 2008). The light source may be natural or artificial or a combination of both, but daylight has a distinct advantage. Almost all spaces need artificial lighting after dark, while other areas might need it during daylight hours. Where this is the case, the artificial light spectrum should be as close as possible to that of natural light.

Lighting requirements for the specific occupants and activities are established through a variety of factors that are shown in figure 9.11. This stresses the importance of consulting specialized sources that regulate and control building practices. For lighting, the regulatory agencies are the American National Standards Institute (ANSI), ASHRAE, and the Illuminating Engineering Society of North America (IESNA). ANSI/ASHRAE/IESNA standard 90.1-2007 provides valuable data for adaptation and development of efficient alternatives for the design of artificial lighting and for the correct use of energy-efficient devices that will improve the building's energy performance while providing visual comfort (Jones 2008).

Visual comfort requires daylight to reach every living and work space. But not all sunlight is of the right quality. Daylight has the desired quality because it is soft and diffused. It can brighten up a space without causing harsh shadows, blinding glares, or unwanted heat gain. This is typical of northern sunlight, which has a pale, cool white color. Direct sunlight, on the other hand, has too much glare, brightness, and heat. It is a warm yellow color and generally is avoided through shading devices (Winchip 2007). Visual comfort can be evaluated by assigning it a *visual comfort probability* value. This value indicates how much glare is likely to be produced from a specific light source and

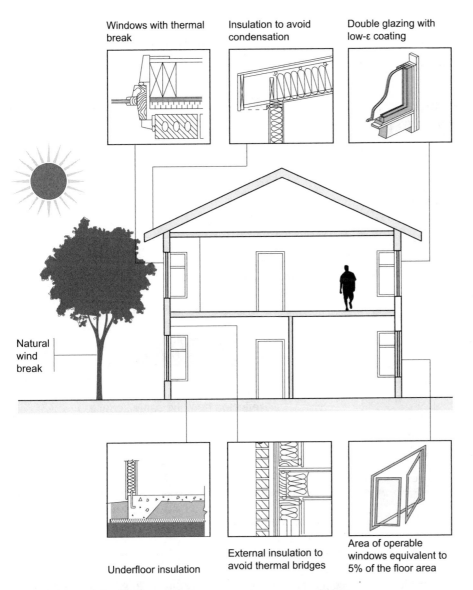

Windows with thermal break

Insulation to avoid condensation

Double glazing with low-ε coating

FIGURE 9.9 Strategies for improving indoor thermal comfort.

Natural wind break

Underfloor insulation

External insulation to avoid thermal bridges

Area of operable windows equivalent to 5% of the floor area

FIGURE 9.10 Color schemes, lighting, and views can improve psychological well-being and mood. Used with permission.

FIGURE 9.11 Factors
used in studying light-
ing requirements and
their definitions.

Factors	Definitions
Luminance (Candela/m²)	The amount of light reflected from a surface
Illuminance (Lux/m²)	The amount of light falling on a surface
Contrast (Factor between 0-1)	The relationship between the brightness of an object and its background
Reflectance (Expressed in percentage)	The ratio of light falling on a surface to the light reflected from the same surface
Foot candle (Lux)	The *illuminance* at a point on a surface which is one (1) foot from, and perpendicular to, a uniform point source of one candela

is dependent on the room dimensions and user tasks (Jones 2008). Daylight provides excellent quality in terms of direction, color appearance, and color rendering. People prefer and enjoy daylight and the views that come with them. Figure 9.12 provides basic strategies to increase visual comfort in the home.

Daylighting is also directly beneficial to health. The absence of daylight, usually in late autumn, has been found to be a cause for a disorder known as seasonal affective disorder (SAD), bone disease due to vitamin D deficiency, and disturbances of sleep and concentration, also known as the winter blues. This condition is associated with depression, which makes it difficult to diagnose, since these symptoms can also be associated with other diseases (CMHA 2010). This means that people living or working under poor daylight conditions may develop symptoms of this illness regardless of season. Links, which were described in Live-Work Dwellings in chapter 3, have been made between occupants' satisfaction and productivity and the quality of natural light.

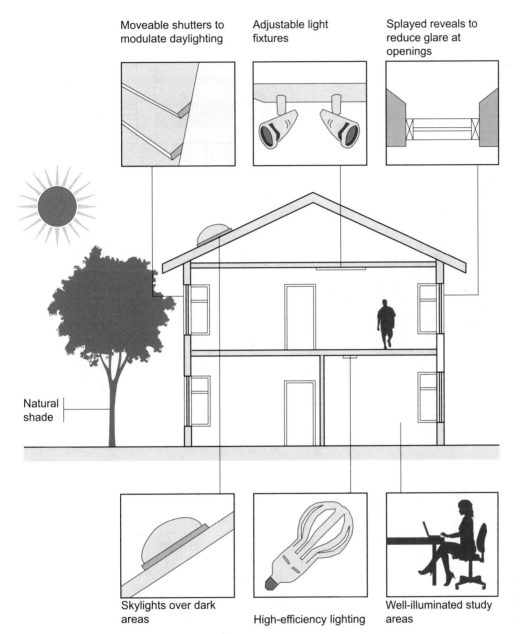

Moveable shutters to modulate daylighting

Adjustable light fixtures

Splayed reveals to reduce glare at openings

Natural shade

Skylights over dark areas

High-efficiency lighting

Well-illuminated study areas

FIGURE 9.12 Strategies to increase indoor visual comfort.

ACOUSTIC QUALITY

Although acoustic quality is not a primary issue in sustainable dwellings, a designer needs to consider the consequences of noise. Natural ventilation, for example, may imply open windows or openings between interior spaces, which may let in obtrusive noise or cause loss of acoustic privacy. If carpeting or other absorbent floor finishes are eliminated to allow the structure to act as a thermal store, other measures may have to be taken to reduce transmission of impact noise and provide enough sound absorption in occupied spaces (GreenBuilding 2010). Standard environmental parameters include acceptable noise levels and limits.

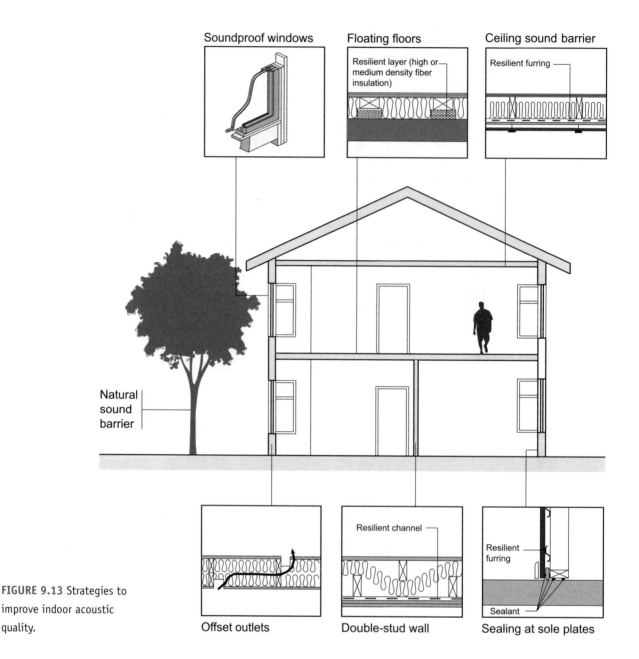

Soundproof windows

Floating floors

Resilient layer (high or medium density fiber insulation)

Ceiling sound barrier

Resilient furring

Natural sound barrier

Offset outlets

Double-stud wall

Resilient channel

Sealing at sole plates

Resilient furring

Sealant

FIGURE 9.13 Strategies to improve indoor acoustic quality.

In general, sources of noise discomfort vary according to external or internal influences. External sources include traffic noise. Internal sources may be loud or disruptive noises created by routine daily activities, impacts on hard interior surfaces, or utilities (e.g., mechanical ventilation). Exposure to excessive noise levels can produce stress-related illness and hearing loss (CCOHS 2008). Design strategies for improved acoustics quality in dwellings are illustrated in figure 9.13.

18th Avenue South

Location: Seattle, Washington, USA

Design: Dwell Development

Completion: 2009

Site area: 0.152 acres (0.062 hectares)

Total floor area: 1,684 sq ft (156 m²)

Number of floors: 3

This urban infill development consists of four detached, single-family homes constructed with an emphasis on resource conservation, energy efficiency, sound material choices, community integration, and a healthy indoor environment (figs. 9.14, 9.15).

The high-performance building envelope insulated with EcoBatt ensures that a stable interior temperature is maintained while effectively preventing moisture and mold accumulation. Certified by GREENGUARD, EcoBatt insulation is free of toxic chemicals and artificial colors and is highly resistant to microbial growth and insects. The airtight assembly also incorporates high-efficiency windows, which achieve a high insulation value even during temperature extremes.

The *whole-house radiant heating* system provides superior thermal comfort and helps maintain a healthy indoor air quality by avoiding the discomfort of allergen production often associated with forced-air systems. To accommodate different thermal levels in the house, the heating system supports separate temperature zones for sleeping and living areas. The sealed combustion equipment prevents adverse effects on indoor air quality by drawing only external air for combustion and venting out exhaust gases.

FIGURE 9.14 The site incorporates xeriscaping techniques with gravel and drought-tolerant grasses along with limited plants and turf grass. Pervious surfaces and a rainwater retention system provide all of the site's irrigation needs. Used with permission.

FIGURE 9.15 The project incorporates a wide range of locally produced materials such as cedar siding, lumber, and concrete. Used with permission.

Third floor

Second floor

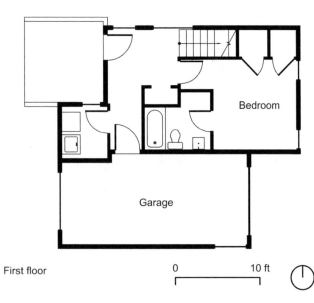

First floor

0   10 ft

FIGURE 9.16 The ground floor accommodates an attached sealed garage with exhaust fan to ensure acceptable indoor air quality. The open-plan floor layout promotes spatial flexibility and ameliorates natural light and ventilation. Used with permission.

FIGURE 9.17 Hardwood flooring and radiant heating provide optimal air quality and thermal comfort as they evenly distribute heat without producing allergens. Used with permission.

FIGURE 9.18 The kitchen cabinets were coated with formaldehyde-free products, and all interior walls are painted with paint low in VOCs. Used with permission.

The strategically placed operable windows provide natural ventilation and updraft cooling throughout the house. While two units have no garages, the other two each contain a small sealed garage with an exhaust fan to protect indoor air quality (fig. 9.16).

The interior finishes were carefully chosen to ensure a long-lasting healthy indoor environment. Wood flooring, ceramic tiles, and sealed concrete offer better alternatives to carpet flooring by effectively safeguarding against allergens and mold growth (fig. 9.17). To avoid harmful emissions, all cabinetry and trim were coated with formaldehyde-free products and interior walls were finished with paint low in VOCs (fig. 9.18).

CHAPTER 10

Water Efficiency

Droughts and water shortages have been exacerbated by a changing climate. Furthermore, in recent years, domestic sewage from treatment plants has been discharged into bodies of water, creating large-scale contamination. Water efficiency has since become necessary as awareness has grown and governments have tightened regulations. While the industrial sector consumes a great deal of water, domestic consumption accounts for nearly half of all municipal water use. Water-efficiency methods not only benefit the environment but save money. Water efficiency, as a result, makes simple economic and environmental sense. This chapter examines sources of water consumption in dwellings and suggests various strategies for its efficient management.

FIGURE 10.1 Estimated average daily domestic water use per capita in several countries in 1999.

A NEED FOR CONSERVATION

Potable water is essential to all living beings, yet, according to Green Living Tips (2009), it is not consumed in equal quantities around the world. For example, in the United States the average daily water consumption per capita in 2008 was 152 gallons (575 L), compared with 21.1 gallons (80 L) in China and 9.24 gallons (35 L) in Haiti (fig. 10.1). Costs of providing water purification and sewage treatment are on the rise as more and more interventions are needed to ensure that water is safe to drink and that wastewater is sufficiently treated. These cost increases are expected to accelerate with the need to construct new plants and upgrade water and wastewater infrastructures to meet demand. Moreover, public resistance to rising taxes and a growing demand for other community services have made the reconstruction of these facilities more challenging. This has

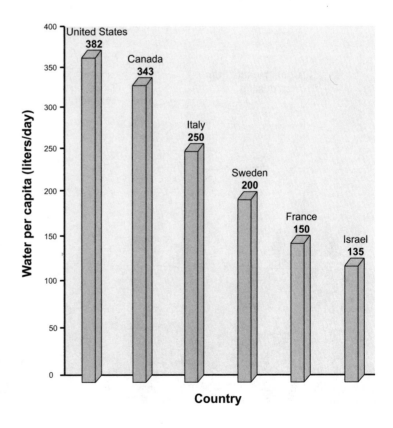

resulted in a deferral of necessary upgrades and a growing backlog of maintenance and replacement needs.

Acute shortage of potable water, a result of several years of severe droughts in the southwestern and western parts of the United States, brought to the forefront an urgent need to conserve water and to put in place formal regulations and bylaws for its implementation.

Reduced flow from homes would likely result in less-diluted effluent, which would help treatment plants to operate more efficiently. Since operating costs are proportional to the volume of treated wastewater, reductions can extend the life of facilities significantly. Changing common practices would translate into savings to the community and its inhabitants and benefit the environment at large. A good portion of the water that is used in the garden, for example, can come from rainwater and recycled gray water that are stored for later use, a process that will be elaborated on below.

COMPONENTS OF A WATER SYSTEM

Mains water is a term used to describe the principal supply of potable water from a distribution system. This water is treated, filtered, ozonated, and chlorinated to meet standard quality regulations of color, taste, and total dissolved solids. Most cities obtain their mains water from a combination of surface water and groundwater. Groundwater is usually pumped from wells or drilled boreholes and collected into aquifers. It might be contaminated by human processes such as agricultural crop dusting, spills from factories, sewage overflow, contaminated soil leaching, and road salting during winter, as

FIGURE 10.2 Possible sources of groundwater contamination.

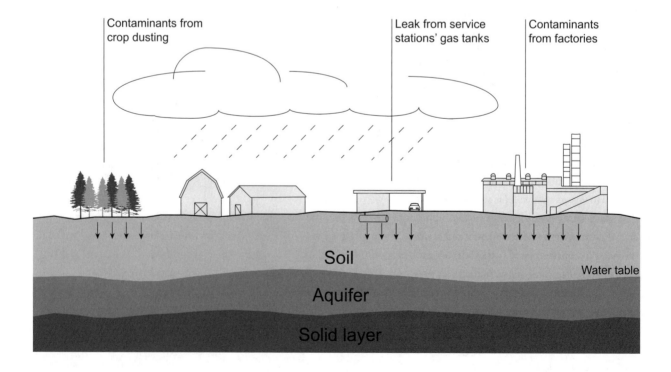

Contaminants from crop dusting

Leak from service stations' gas tanks

Contaminants from factories

Soil

Water table

Aquifer

Solid layer

shown in figure 10.2 (Thomas 2005). *Gray water* is wastewater from all domestic uses except for the toilet. It includes the discharge from kitchen and bathroom sinks, baths and showers, dishwashers, and washing machines. *Surface water* includes rainfall runoff as well as small bodies of water such as ponds, springs, and streams. *Black water* refers to the wastewater leaving the toilet and any water that is combined with it in the foul drain leading to the sewer system (Ireland 2007).

The three main parts of any water system are a source, a storage area, and a delivery system. It is necessary to study each part to find out how water is obtained, delivered, and potentially conserved.

Sources of potable water are wells, springs, ponds, creeks, captured rainwater, recycled and purified gray water, and reservoirs from dammed lakes. Well water is more commonly used in rural areas and tends to be cleaner than surface waters. Surface waters such as springs, streams, and ponds are susceptible to contamination from both wild and farm animals, as well as herbicides and pesticides. Therefore, wells will typically require less energy for purification than surface waters (Schaeffer 2005).

Water storage is needed during dry spells, to create and provide water pressure, and to maintain cleanliness of purified potable water. Storage needs to be insulated to avoid freezing during winter. Water is stored either at its source, such as a well, or more commonly in urban areas in elevated or pressurized tanks, which can be underground or covered aboveground. Their common construction materials are polypropylene, fiberglass, and concrete or ferro-cement. *Pressure tanks* store the water under pressure so that the tap is constantly pressurized. Finally, the delivery mechanism is the pump used to push the water up to a storage tank to pressurize it (Schaeffer 2005).

STRATEGIES FOR WATER EFFICIENCY

Levels of freshwater available depend on the amount of rainfall and local hydrology and geology. If consumers use more water than the natural system can supply, it may lead to the lowering of the water table and possible negative effects on water quality. This can have harmful consequences for agricultural production, wildlife, and the environment, reducing flowing rivers to muddy puddles.

According to Thomas (2005), to sustain a reasonable quality of living requires 26 gallons (100 L) per person per day. In reality, the average consumption ranges from 1.4 gallons (5.4 L), which is barely enough to live on in parts of the world with low rainfall during the dry season, to 73 gallons (278 L) per person per day in the United Kingdom and even 152 gallons (575 L) per person per day in the United States. Much of this extra use is carelessly wasteful. For example, losses from a tap dripping in the United Kingdom at 30 drops per minute add up to 66 gallons (250 L) of water per month (Green Living Tips 2009).

There is often a misconception that conserving water will inconvenience consumers. A toilet flush in a well-designed and efficient fixture, though, can be just as convenient and effective as a conventional toilet flush, because the smaller amount of water is concentrated in a brief, carefully engineered pulse with a much higher peak-flow rate. This can save 3.6 gallons (6 L) per flush (Friedman 2007). Also, water from a low-flow showerhead

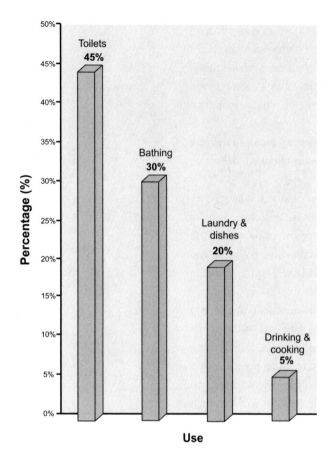

Percentage (%)

Toilets
45%

Bathing
30%

Laundry &
dishes
20%

Drinking &
cooking
5%

Use

FIGURE 10.3 Breakdown of domestic water use.

is often stronger and more pleasant than the flow from a conventional one. Flow delivered by low-flow faucet aerators can be powerful and more effective for washing hands and dishes. The service delivered and the user experience with an efficient device are often the same as or better than with a less-efficient fixture, with a relatively small cost difference between them (Schaeffer 2005).

During summer months, outdoor use causes domestic water consumption to increase sharply. Replacing conventional landscapes with species that consume less water could significantly reduce outdoor use, as discussed in chapter 12.

Indoors, the bathroom and the kitchen account for the lion's share of all domestic use, as shown in figure 10.3. Efforts for water conservation should therefore target sinks, toilets, and showerheads. Aerators for faucets, for example, can offer an inexpensive way to save water, and homeowners seeking even higher efficiency can obtain water-efficient appliances (Schaeffer 2005). These strategies are described next.

WATER-SAVING TECHNOLOGIES

When considering the purchase of new water-related gadgets and appliances, one should examine existing water-related systems for their effectiveness. Highly efficient showers, toilets, and taps may use 50 percent or less of the water that standard models use. In the calculation of savings from water-efficient appliances, the reduction in energy needed to heat water should be taken into account as well as the savings on paid metered water.

Toilets

Water conservation in toilets is measured by the volume of water per flush. Installation of a *low-flush toilet*, which most major toilet manufacturers now market, would reduce the flow to about 3 gallons (13 L) per flush. Purposely designed ultra-low-volume toilets with innovative features and improved design can further reduce consumption to 1.6 to 1.8 gallons (6 to 7 L) per flush or less, instead of the conventional 5 to 9 gallons (15.7 to 40.5 L) per flush (Kwok and Grondzik 2007). This can reduce water consumption by toilets by 70 percent and total indoor water use by 28 percent (Harvey 2006). These toilets use various technologies to achieve efficient flushing, the most common being the use of a well-engineered tank-and-bowl system. The wash-down performance of these fixtures is at least as good as that of conventional toilets, while they provide significant water savings.

Existing toilets may be retrofitted with low-tech devices such as simple do-it-yourself bricks in bags or bottles filled with water to displace some of the water in the tank and, therefore, reduce the quantity used in each flush. This, however, may reduce the effectiveness of the flush. The use of low-flush equipment will also put less pressure on a septic tank system because of the lower volume of water it will take in (Schaeffer 2005).

Dual-flush toilets have two water-level options so the user can decide what volume of flush is needed. The mechanism is shown in figure 10.4 (Harvey 2006). A dual-flush toilet will use 0.5 to 0.6 gallon (2 to 3 L) on a half flush and 1 to 1.5 gallons (4 to 6 L) on a full flush, compared with 3 gallons (13 L) of water for a low-flush toilet (Strongman 2008). Dual-flush toilets are now obligatory in some countries that experience water shortages, such as Australia.

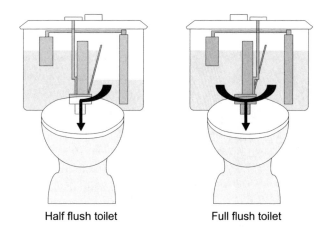

Half flush toilet   Full flush toilet

FIGURE 10.4 Schematic sections of dual-flush toilet mechanisms.

Compost Toilet

A *compost toilet* could also be installed when appropriate, instead of flushing away waste. The added benefit of this simple technology is the rich compost obtained at the end of the process, which can return nutrients to the soil that would otherwise end up in rivers. Compost toilets need no water and depend upon bacterial action to break down the waste, as shown in figure 10.5.

Showerheads

Showers commonly use less water than baths, depending on the duration of the shower, flow rate, and pressure of the shower. A typical shower uses 5 to 10 gallons (20 to 40 L) of water per minute, compared with 30.5 gallons (140 L) for a full bath (Strongman 2008; Sassi 2006). In the

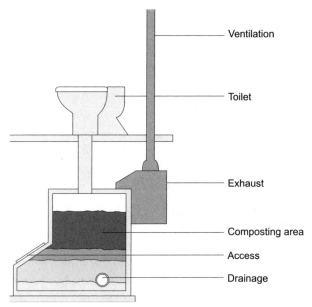

FIGURE 10.5 Section through a compost toilet.

past, the use of various types of flow restrictors resulted in poor performance in terms of user satisfaction. There is, however, a wide range of water-efficient showerheads on the market that have been engineered to provide flows that may be even more pleasant than those from conventional fixtures but that use only 2 gallons (9.5 L) per minute or less. According to Strongman (2008), "low-flow showerheads come in two types: aerating and non-aerating. Aerating is the most popular, as it draws air bubbles into the water to give a fuller shower spray with steady pressure." *Aerating low-flow showerheads* are self-cleaning, as the air bubbles eliminate any buildup of mold or calcium. Whereas in aerating showerheads the temperature may drop because of the mix with air, *non-aerating low-flow showerheads* maintain a steady water temperature. Maintaining a proper water pressure will also contribute to water efficiency. Yet, an even greater advantage of low-flow showerheads is the money saved by reducing the energy used to heat water. A low-flow showerhead is shown in figure 10.6.

FIGURE 10.6 A manually adjusted water-efficient showerhead.

FIGURE 10.7 A mixer tap with aerator.

Faucets and Taps

A worthwhile economic investment in water efficiency can be made in aerators for faucets. Some faucets include built-in aerators, although attachments are available for conventional faucets as well. For a small amount of money, an aerator can reduce the excessive flow from a conventional faucet of 3.6 gallons (13.5 L) per minute by more than 50 percent. In bathrooms the flow can be reduced to 0.5 gallon (2 L) per minute. In the kitchen, where more water pressure and volume are required, a reduction to 1.6 to 2.4 gallons (6 to 9 L) per minute would still be sufficient while reducing consumption by about a fourth (Harvey 2006). Aeration valves may be retrofitted on existing taps to significantly reduce consumption to around 1.8 gallons (6.8 L) per minute (Schaeffer 2005). The appropriate aerator must be selected according to the intended use, to give the desired water flow and preferred temperature.

For domestic usage, the key to water-saving taps is careful operation. Shutoff valves and levers may be fitted to allow water to be turned off mid operation while maintaining comfortable temperature, which is more convenient than turning both hot and cold individually off and on again in quick succession. There are many types of taps that are more efficient than conventional models. In general, it is more economic to run a *mixer tap*, shown in figure 10.7, with a reduced water flow. Mixer taps require less cleaning, because soap- and dirt-covered hands do not have to touch them. Reduced-flow taps cut water consumption, leading to savings on water and heating bills. Some eco-taps have lever controls fitted with water brakes that keep the water flow to a moderate level. Other taps have sensors that switch them off automatically when there is nothing underneath (Fuad-Luke 2004). Including efficient fixtures in the design of a dwelling can result in saving significant amounts of water, as shown in figure 10.8.

Appliances

Further savings in both water and energy can be achieved by using efficient appliances. Both dishwashers and clothes washers that economize these two resources are now widely available. Such appliances may be more expensive, but when the cost of water and energy are examined, the savings make them very attractive options. Their operating costs and the associated payback period can result in significant savings over their lifetimes, as argued by programs such as EnerGuide. A qualified clothes washer uses about half the 40 gallons (151 L) per load used by a conventional machine, and it removes more water during the spin cycle, which reduces drying time (Schaeffer 2005). Water-efficient dishwashers are also available. The new models not only reduce energy consumption but can save some 1,300 gallons (4,921 L) over the lifetime of the appliance.

ADDITIONAL WATER-SAVING METHODS

There are additional advanced water-saving measures and products, including pressure-reducing valves, water and gray-water reuse, and cisterns for rainwater collection and use.

FIGURE 10.8 Water consumption comparison between a conventional home and a home using water-efficient fixtures shows that a substantial amount of water can be saved.

Basement   Ground floor   Upper floor

	Fixture	Conventional fixture	Water-efficent fixture	Water Savings
Basement	Toilet	5.2 gal (20 l) / flush	1.6 gal (6 l) / flush	3.6 gal (14 l) / flush
	Shower	5.2 gal (20 l) / min	2.5 gal (9.5 l) / min	2.8 gal (10.5 l) / min
	Bathroom faucet	3.6 gal (13.5 l) / min	0.5 gal (2 l) / min	3.1 gal (11.5 l) / min
	Washing machine (w)	60 gal (225 l) / load	46 gal (175 l) / load	14 gal (50 l) / load
	Laundry faucet	3.6 gal (13.5 l) / min	2 gal (7.5 l) / min	1.6 gal (6 l) / min
Ground floor	Kitchen faucet	3.6 gal (13.5 l) / min	2 gal (7.5 l) / min	1.6 gal (6 l) / min
	Dishwasher (dw)	9.7 gal (37 l) / load	5.5 gal (21 l) / load	4.2 gal (16 l) / load
	Toilet	5.2 gal (20 l) / flush	1.6 gal (6 l) / flush	3.6 gal (14 l) / flush
	Bathroom faucet	3.6 gal (13.5 l) / min	0.5 gal (2 l) / min	3.1 gal (11.5 l) / min
Upper floor	Toilet	5.2 gal (20 l) / flush	1.6 gal (6 l) / flush	3.6 gal (14 l) / flush
	Shower	5.2 gal (20 l) / min	2.5 gal (9.5 l) / min	2.8 gal (10.5 l) / min
	Bathroom faucet	3.6 gal (13.5 l) / min	0.5 gal (2 l) / min	3.1 gal (11.5 l) / min

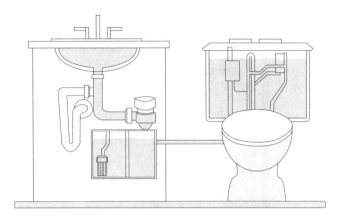

FIGURE 10.9 Directing gray water from a sink to the toilet is common in countries that experience water shortages.

Pressure-Reducing Valves

It is not uncommon to find water distribution systems operating at twice the necessary pressure. Excess water pressure generally leads to wasted water in sinks and showers. Special valves installed in the water main can effectively and economically reduce household water pressure and, as a result, consumption (WaterSense 2010).

Gray-Water Harvesting and Recycling

While use of gray water for various purposes, such as flushing toilets, is being explored, most municipalities have restrictions on its use, for health reasons. In some countries, such as Australia, directing gray water from the sink to the toilet, however, is common, as illustrated in figure 10.9. A setback, however, is that significant changes in plumbing systems are required to accommodate this reuse. Even gray water, which can be used for outdoor watering, would most likely require some type of treatment. Gray water from the bath and shower are relatively easier to filter and purify than gray water from the kitchen, which may contain food waste, fats, and other organic matter (Thomas 2005).

Rainwater Capture

Diverting and using rainwater off-site, *rainwater capture and harvesting*, has attracted the attention of environmentalists and sustainability promoters seeking to reuse this water resource. A method of rainwater management called the Mulden-Rogolen system collects rainwater from public areas and rooftops and uses it for flushing toilets or releases it into nearby ponds and wetlands. The purpose is to incorporate local water ecology into the landscape without disturbing it (Low et al. 2005). During site and dwelling design, one of the objectives can be to retain or properly redirect rainwater so that most of it will be put to good use (Thomas 2005).

FIGURE 10.10 A tank for purification of rainwater using sand and rocks.

Rainwater could theoretically be used for drinking as well, but this would require extensive filtration and purification. Such a system would collect the rainwater from the roof, filter it through sand, as shown in figure 10.10, and pump it to large storage tanks where particles would have time to settle to the bottom. It would then pass the water through a 5 μm filter, to remove any particles that hadn't settled, and then pass it through a carbon filter to eliminate any dissolved chemicals. Next, ultraviolet

Lid
Distribution pipes
Sand
Rocks
Lower drain
Liner

light would be used to kill bacteria and neutralize viruses in the water, and finally the water would flow out the taps (Smith 2005).

Rainwater is usually cleaner than gray water and is less prone to contamination. However, it can be contaminated by dust as well as atmospheric gases that can make it acidic. Rainwater collection systems can be integrated in neighborhood planning. A group of dwellings, for example, can collect and recycle rainwater from roofs and store it in large underground storage tanks for various later uses (Thomas 2005).

Cisterns

One inch (25.4 mm) of rainfall can provide approximately 0.5 gallons of water per sq ft (20 L per m²) of catchment area. A *cistern* used to collect and store this water can capture as much as 75 percent of the annual rainfall on the catchment (Keeler and Burke 2009). Many current plumbing codes do not allow nonpotable, nonmunicipal sources to feed a dwelling, as mentioned above. Even when indoor nonpotable uses are permitted, costs are high because of the size of the system and the amount of extra plumbing required. Though cisterns may be somewhat attractive for outdoor watering purposes, the use of water-saving landscaping is a more cost-efficient and environmentally sound option (see chapter 12). A diagram of a rainwater collection and harvesting system is shown in figure 10.11.

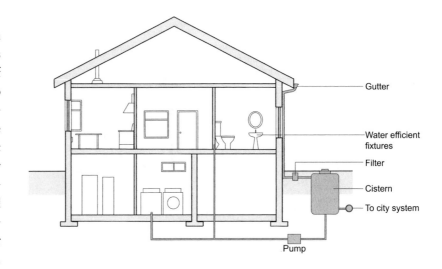

FIGURE 10.11 Diagrammatic illustration of rainwater collection and harvesting system.

CONSUMER HABITS

Minimizing water use depends not only on fixtures consumers could purchase but also on their attitude toward water efficiency. As noted earlier, water conservation at home makes economic and environmental sense. Choosing showers instead of baths, for instance, will help conserve water, as will turning off the faucet while brushing one's teeth or washing dishes. Water that would be wasted from a running tap while users are waiting for it to warm up can be collected for watering plants. Also, dishwashers and washing machines should run only when they are full, and on the shortest effective cycle.

Further smart strategies could be thought of to conserve water. Refrigerating drinking water, for example, avoids having to run the tap while waiting for cold water to flow, and insulating hot water pipes prevents running the tap while waiting for hot water. Finally, to conserve while watering the yard and to give plants the maximum benefit, it is best to water out of direct sunlight and in the evening, which will cut down on water loss due to evaporation, and to avoid sprinklers, which use water indiscriminately (WaterSense 2010). Some water-saving tips are illustrated in figure 10.12.

A sustainable-housing project called BedZED in the United Kingdom achieved its 58 percent reduction of water use by carrying out a number of strategies. These included using water-efficient washing machines and taps, smaller baths, and dual-flush toilets. Also, visible water meters were placed in the kitchens, which allowed users to easily check how much water they were using at any given time. It was found that the first step to changing any behavior is awareness. The second is the ability to measure the change quantitatively (Low et al. 2005).

FIGURE 10.12 Water-saving tips—usage often depends on attitude and behavioral changes.

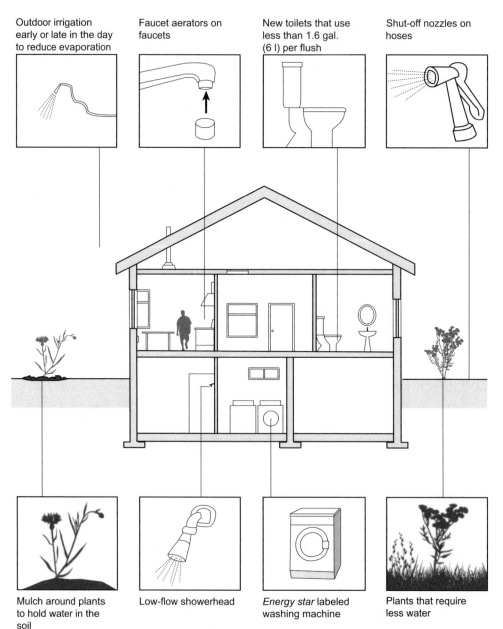

Outdoor irrigation early or late in the day to reduce evaporation

Faucet aerators on faucets

New toilets that use less than 1.6 gal. (6 l) per flush

Shut-off nozzles on hoses

Mulch around plants to hold water in the soil

Low-flow showerhead

Energy star labeled washing machine

Plants that require less water

Solar Umbrella

Location: Venice, California, USA

Design: Pugh + Scarpa Architects

Completion: 2005

Site area: 0.094 acres (0.038 hectares)

Total floor area: 1,790 sq ft (166 m²)

Number of floors: 2

Solar Umbrella was designed to rely as little as possible on external utilities. The dwelling is a conversion of an existing bungalow (figs. 10.13 to 10.15). Situated near the seashore, the house responsibly integrates a water conservation system that manages 90 percent of precipitation on-site through sustainable landscaping and irrigation, water recycling, and water-saving fixtures and appliances.

Over 65 percent of the site is landscaped or permeably paved, which significantly mitigates water runoff and the urban heat island effect. Through the incorporation of drought-resistant native plants and gravel, landscaping requires little irrigation. Water is

Second floor

First floor

0   10 ft

1   Study
2   Closet
3   Bedroom
4   Dining room
5   Kitchen
6   Living room
7   Utility closet
8   Laundry
9   Fish pond
10 Wading pool
11 Patio
12 Roof

FIGURE 10.13 The siting takes advantage of the southern orientation to optimize passive solar gains. Used with permission.

FIGURE 10.14 The solar
panels, which create a canopy
over the rooftop patio, supply
95 percent of the building's
electricity demand. Used with
permission.

further conserved through a drip irrigation system with seasonal adjustments that allow water to trickle directly to plant roots without flooding the surface. The hardscapes consist of gravel and decomposed granite in place of impermeable materials such as concrete and stone (fig. 10.16). As permeable paving maximizes the ground area for water absorption, it helps replenish groundwater supplies and reduce storm-water runoff.

The water recycling system collects storm water and rainwater for indoor and outdoor uses. Eighty percent of the storm water from the roof is collected through a large scupper and stored in an underground cistern. Rainwater is collected and stored on-site in a fish pond–wading pool complex installed with an automatic overflow recirculation pump (fig. 10.17).

The incorporation of energy-efficient and water-conserving appliances and plumbing fixtures significantly reduces indoor water consumption. The dishwasher and the front-loading washing machine, for example, have been selected for their high water-conserving efficiency. Low-flow faucets, showerheads, and toilets have been installed throughout the house.

FIGURE 10.15 The stair to the upper level facilitates airflow and creates natural convection. The open plan and the extensive windows maximize daylight and cross ventilation throughout. Used with permission.

FIGURE 10.16 The site is landscaped with drought-tolerant plants and paved with gravel and decomposed granite for a permeable driveway. Used with permission.

FIGURE 10.17 The wading pool seen from the south features an automatic overflow recirculation pump to mitigate rainwater runoff and offers passive cooling during warm summer days. Used with permission.

CHAPTER 11

Green Roofs

Green roofs are the integration of plants and their supporting structures in a building's roof. A green roof can provide habitat for local flora and fauna, help manage storm water, reduce the heating demand in winter and the cooling load in summer, create usable space, and enhance the aesthetic value and comfort of a dwelling. Because roofs represent approximately 40 to 50 percent of the surfaces in urban areas, green roofs have an important role in drainage and, as a result, water management as well (Lawlor et al. 2006) This chapter classifies green roofs and examines their benefits, construction principles, and applications. The past few years saw an increased interest by designers and property developers in green roofs. They form part of most buildings that claim to be built to high environmental standards. In fact, when a green roof is installed on 50 percent or more of the roof's surface, it guarantees 2 points and can contribute 7 additional points toward LEED certification—almost 20 percent of the required points for a project to be LEED certified.

CLASSIFICATION OF GREEN ROOFS

A *green roof* or *eco-roof* extends the idea of what is traditionally called a rooftop garden, where planting is done in planters. Both are shown in figure 11.1. A *brown roof* is also mentioned here to distinguish roofs that are not intentionally planted but are filled

FIGURE 11.1 Green roofs (*a*) differ from roof-top gardens (*b*) in their integration of planting and supporting structures with the building construction.

FIGURE 11.2 Brown roofs are distinguished from green roofs in their self-colonization by flora and fauna, as was imaginatively preserved in New York City's High Line.

with layers of various materials that would otherwise be wasted in landfill, such as gravel, brick rubble, crushed concrete, and subsoils. Even an accidental brown roof, like a brownfield, can foster valuable ecosystems for plants and insects through self-colonization, as shown in figure 11.2 (Mauritius EcoBuilding 2008).

Green roofs are generally found on flat surfaces of buildings, but there is a type of green roof that is pitched. The pitched green roof originated in Iceland, where sod roofs (fig. 11.3) and sod walls have been used for thermal reasons for centuries. From there the concept spread throughout the Scandinavian countries (GreenRoofs 2010). Slopes of up to 35 degrees are possible, though some systems mandate no more than 20 degrees to prevent soil slippage and slump, which will be discussed here (Kwok and Grondzik 2007).

Pitched green roofs are typically simpler to design than flat ones. The pitch allows rainfall and excess water to drain more easily, as illustrated in figure 11.4, and this reduces the risk of leakage. Sloped green roofs therefore need less waterproofing and usually do not need installed drainage systems, thereby saving materials and labor costs (Mauritius EcoBuilding 2008). Another reason pitched roof design is simplified is that they are harder to access and use for diverse activities and planting than flat green roofs are. The pitched green roof is often on the lower end of the scale in terms of maintenance, which is an important way to classify green roofs.

There are three common levels of maintenance and upkeep: extensive, semi-intensive, and intensive (fig. 11.5). These systems also vary in cost, depth of soil, and types of plants they can support (Lawlor et al. 2006). Figure 11.6. shows examples of extensive, semi-intensive, and intensive flat green roofs

FIGURE 11.3 A structure with a sod roof.

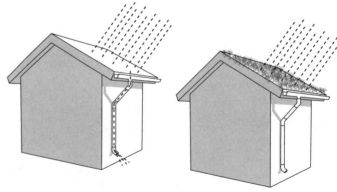

FIGURE 11.4 Pitched green roofs have simpler designs compared with flat ones because they have better drainage.

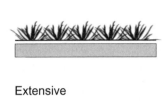

Extensive

Semi-intensive

Intensive

 Plants & mulch

 Growing media

☐ Integrated irrigation & drainage mat

■ Waterproof protection

■ Waterproofing

▥ Substrate

FIGURE 11.5 Extensive, semi-intensive, and intensive roofs vary in the depth of planting medium and the amount of maintenance required.

Extensive green roofs typically require minimal maintenance, are lightweight and inexpensive, and have little plant diversity. The plants are grown in a mixture of sand, gravel, crushed brick, LECA (light expanded clay aggregate), perlite, peat, organic matter, and some soil (Peck and Kuhn 2008). This mixture is usually between 2 and 6 in. (5 and 15 cm) deep, and full saturation will cause an increase in weight of 16 to 35 lb/ sq ft (78.1 to 169.4 kg/m²) (Peck and Kuhn 2008; Lawlor et al. 2006). Once the plants take root, maintenance is needed only twice annually for weeding and safety inspections. These plants are typically indigenous and hardy enough to withstand extreme climate conditions (GreenRoofs 2010).

Semi-intensive green roofs have the same low- or no-input practice as extensive ones and similarly use lightweight substrates and modern construction technologies, but they have slightly deeper layers of growing medium, about 4 to 8 in. (10 to 20 cm), and therefore enable a wider and more diverse range of plants to be grown (Dunnett and Kingsbury 2008). Since the growing medium is thicker, this type of roof requires a slightly higher level of maintenance in the form of tending to the vegetation.

An *intensive green roof* is similar to a traditional garden. It can support diverse vegetation, is labor intensive, has deeper soils and heavier weight, costs more, and requires irrigation, fertilizing, and additional maintenance. The substrate here is predominantly soil and can range in depth from 8 to 24 in. (20 to 60 cm), which allows trees, shrubs,

FIGURE 11.6 Extensive (*a*), semi-intensive (*b*), and intensive (*c*) green roofs. Used with permission.

and a more diverse ecosystem to grow and which can weigh over 61 lb/sq ft (300 kg/m²) (Peck and Kuhn 2008; BCIT 2009). Also, because the roof is accessible to people, it requires additional features such as railings, lighting, access, and egress (BCIT 2009; Dunnett and Kingsbury 2008). When trees are planted, they need to be protected from, and anchored against, strong winds, which is a concern at high elevations. It is important to note that the weight of the substrate increases when it is fully saturated and makes up 60 to 70 percent of the total weight of the roof (Optigreen 2011).

It is feasible to combine extensive and intensive techniques on accessible roofs, with larger herbaceous and woody plant material in strategically placed containers or planters to create sustainable gardens.

ADVANTAGES OF GREEN ROOFS

Motivations for the integration of a green roof in residential design are rooted in social, economic, environmental, and cultural aspects, which affect both a single user and the community at large.

Personal Benefits

A rooftop garden can be used to grow fruits, vegetables, herbs, and flowers, particularly in high-density urban areas where conventional garden space may be limited. Many herb species perform best in free-draining soils in the sunny conditions found on most rooftops.

The substrate and vegetation also help insulate the building from outside noise. Soil has been found to absorb and block lower frequencies, while plant life blocks the higher ones (Mauritius EcoBuilding 2008). A green roof with a soil layer of up to 8 in. (20 cm) can reduce noise pollution by up to 50 decibels (LiveRoof 2010).

Furthermore, planted roofs could slow down the spread of fire to and from the building, particularly when the growing medium is saturated. On the other hand, very dry vegetation on a roof can pose a fire hazard. Where fire is a concern, integrating firebreaks such as gravel or concrete pavers at regular intervals as well as using fire-retardant plants with high water content, such as sedums, is advised (Mauritius EcoBuilding 2008).

Green roofs offer thermal insulation that is superior to conventional interior insulation. A green roof prevents heat from escaping out the top in cold climates and prevents heat from penetrating through the roof in summertime. The insulation values can be increased by using a low-density soil with a high moisture content and large, leafy plants. An 8 in. (20 cm) substrate with an additional 8 in. (20 cm) layer of grass has an equivalent insulation value of 6 in. (15 cm) of mineral wool, as shown in figure 11.7 (Peck and Kuhn 2008).

Reductions of up to 90 percent in passive solar gain can be achieved when using green roofs. Indoor temperatures have been shown to be 6°F to 8°F (3°C to 4°C) lower under a green roof when outdoor temperatures are between 77°F and 86°F (25°C and 30°C). An Environment Canada study shows that a typical one-story building in Toronto with a grass roof and 4 in. (10 cm) of substrate brought about a 25 percent reduction in summer cooling needs, compared with an unvegetated roof (Dunnett and Kingsbury 2008).

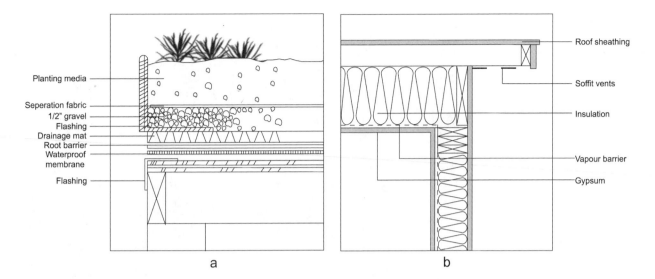

Planting media
Seperation fabric
1/2" gravel
Flashing
Drainage mat
Root barrier
Waterproof
membrane
Flashing

Roof sheathing
Soffit vents
Insulation
Vapour barrier
Gypsum

a

b

When green roofs are constructed properly such that the likelihood of leaks and damp penetration to the house is minimized, they can last longer than conventional roofs, which will result in obvious cost benefits. In fact, studies have shown that green roofs may last two to three times longer than conventional ones and will require less maintenance (Mauritius EcoBuilding 2008). Without "greening," flat roofs are 50 percent more susceptible to damage after 5 years than slightly sloped roofs, as a result of water collecting and pooling.

Plants can shield the roof from the elements, preventing component degradation by the sun's ultraviolet (UV) radiation and preventing cracks caused by dry winds, and it can reduce contraction and expansion due to temperature fluctuations by up to 90 percent (LiveRoof 2010).

Finally, green roofs can offer pleasant roofscape views, eliminating the unsightly expanse of dark asphalt and gravel. Even where roofs are inaccessible but clearly visible, attractive planting can be beneficial. The therapeutic effects of having green plants and nature around one are known to be considerable and include stress reduction, lowered blood pressure, relief from muscle tension, and increase in overall positive feelings (LiveRoof 2010; Sassi 2006).

FIGURE 11.7 Comparison between intensive green roof (*a*) and conventionally constructed and insulated flat one (*b*).

Community Benefits

When the load-bearing capacity is sufficient, green roofs can provide outdoor recreational areas for several dwelling units in neighborhoods, which is especially important for those with little ground-level space. In an apartment block development, for instance, casual activities such as clothes drying, barbecuing, and exercising can take place on the roof. It has the advantage of controlled access, thereby being a safer place for community activities (fig. 11.8).

The enhancement of biodiversity through the use of green roofs is closely linked to the choice of plant species and the habitat or vegetation type used. Extensive roofs are not designed to be walked on and are, therefore, isolated and can provide undisturbed

FIGURE 11.8 In Vancouver's Olympic building, which was converted for use by seniors, a green roof was designed to function as a community gathering place. Used with permission.

habitat for flora and fauna such as butterflies, insects, and birds. Green roofs can also be the place where community gardens or urban agriculture can be located, as shown in figure 11.9.

A green roof not only affects the home's indoor thermal conditions, it also influences the climate of the city by reducing the urban heat island effect. Heat island effect is caused by a large, hard surface area that absorbs, reflects, and reradiates the sun's heat. This in turn leads to air currents, dust, smog, and microclimate changes. Green roofs mitigate this phenomenon by cooling, slowing down currents, and filtering out air pollutants and dust (Peck and Kuhn 2008).

Rainfall on land covered with vegetation is different from rainfall on the hard surface of built-up areas. The vast majority of precipitation on a green roof is absorbed by plants, and through them the water is transpired back to the atmosphere. On manufactured hard surfaces (e.g., asphalt, concrete, roof tiles), on the other hand, water cannot be absorbed and runs off, through drainage systems, into rivers. The main aim of conventional drainage systems is to remove a maximum amount of water from an area as quickly as possible to prevent flash flooding. As a result, around 75 percent of rainfall on urban areas is lost as surface runoff, compared with around 5 percent for a forested area (Dunnett and Kingsbury 2008).

Green roofs can reduce the amount of water leaving a site, through either retention or detention. Rainwater can be captured and reused for irrigation or domestic purposes (see chapter 10). This reduces pressure on urban drainage systems while allowing groundwater to be replenished, providing areas of habitat and wetlands as amenities, reducing flood risk, and lowering infrastructure cost.

FIGURE 11.9 Use of a green roof as a community garden for urban agriculture was initiated at McGill University in Montreal, Canada, by Prof. Vikram Bhatt.

Green roofs can help to improve air quality. As air passes over the plants, fine airborne particles can settle onto leaf and stem surfaces. This material will then be washed off into the soil by the rain. Trees and larger vegetation can also absorb gaseous pollutants in their tissues.

CONSTRUCTION PRINCIPLES AND COMPONENTS

Despite the many benefits of green roofs, their construction poses a challenge. Careful attention needs to be paid to various factors, outlined here, that affect the roof's performance.

Structural Capacity

The intensive and extensive types already discussed have different structural requirements because of differences in weight. Lightweight extensive systems with substrate depths of 2 to 6 in. (5 to 15 cm), for instance, increase the load on a roof by 14 to 35 lb/sq ft (70 to 170 kg/m^2). Each country, region, or city has its own building standard for the minimum capacity of a roof. In Ontario, Canada, for example, roofs must be designed to support a load of at least 40 lb/sq ft (195 kg/m^2) (Peck and Kuhn 2008). This takes into account a typical winter snow load of 22 lb/sq ft (107 kg/m^2). It then leaves 18 lb/sq ft (88 kg/m^2) spare capacity—enough for a simple extensive system (Dunnett and Kingsbury 2008). In calculating load, it must be noted that the weight of green-roof materials will vary greatly depending on how compacted and how moist they are (Portland Online 2006).

Slippage, Wind Uplifts, and Irrigation

One construction consideration for a pitched green roof is slippage. The maximum possible slope is controlled by the friction coefficient between the two most slippery materials. Virtually no green roofs avoid having a fabric-membrane or membrane-membrane interface—for example, at root barriers and sheet drains. These are the planes along which slope movement will occur. For slopes steeper than 2:12 (9.5 degrees), it is unwise to design green roofs without additional slope stabilization measures. Figure 11.10 illustrates two sloped green-roof designs. Slipping and slumping can be countered by the use of horizontal strapping, laths, battens, or grids, as shown in figure 11.11. When these methods are used, green roofs can readily be constructed on pitches up to 7:12 (35 degrees), which is the angle of repose for most granular materials. To build on steeper pitches, it is necessary to use special media mixes and devices (Dunnett and Kingsbury 2008).

Roofs need to be able to withstand high wind uplift due to their exposed conditions. A strip of gravel, stones, or pavers around the roof's edge can prevent wind damage. Such strips are also often used as vegetation barriers, preventing plants from damaging the edges where the waterproofing layer rises above the surface of the growing medium.

Finally, irrigation for green roofs should be designed and controlled, ideally to include rainwater storage and recycling systems. Four main irrigation methods are used on green roofs: surface spray with traditional sprinklers, drip and tube, capillary, and standing-water systems. Figure 11.12 illustrates these methods. In general, traditional surface spray is less recommended because it wastes water and can cause surface rooting (GreenRoofs 2010).

Components of Green Roofs

Green roofs can be constructed over any type of deck, whether steel, wood, or concrete, as long as the structural considerations already discussed are met. Layering components in a green roof for residential use are the same regardless of the material used in the construction of the structure. These components (fig. 11.13) have to satisfy requirements for weatherproofing, protecting the roof surface from root penetration and damage, drainage, and the support and growth of the vegetation layer (Werthmann 2007).

A *weatherproof membrane* consists of a built-up roof and its single-ply and fluid-applied membranes. *Built-up roofs* are common and are usually composed of waterproof conventional asphalt (also called bitumen) roofing and felt or bituminized fabrics. These roofing materials generally have a life span

FIGURE 11.10 Green roofs can be designed with various slopes. Steeper slopes will be subject to greater moisture stress and require different designs to control slippage.

Pitched roof up to 20 degrees

Pitched roof up to 35 degrees with a slippage-preventing measure

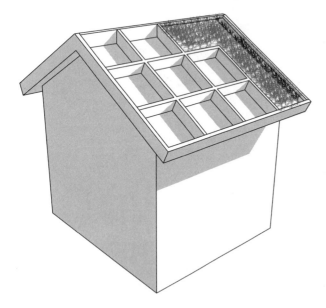

FIGURE 11.11 Wooden grid on a sloped roof provides further stabilization as well as a template for planting.

FIGURE 11.12 Various irrigation methods for green roofs.

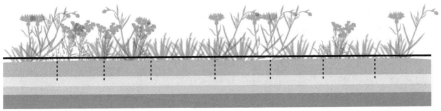

Traditional sprinkler

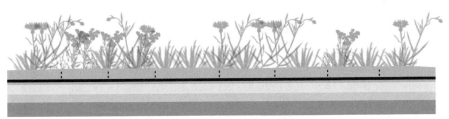

Irrigation by drip tube

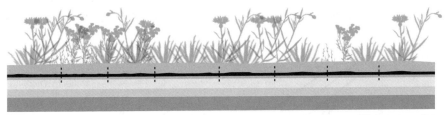

Capillary method using moisture absorbing mat

Stationary water

of 15 to 20 years and are susceptible to degradation from temperature extremes and ultraviolet radiation, both of which cause cracking and leakage, although a layer of substrate and vegetation will reduce this. A conventional asphalt/felt built-up roof is not recommended as a base for a green roof (Cantor 2008). There are other types of built-up roofing systems that are more robust and entirely different in material and performance. However, if an asphalt/felt built-up roof is the base for a green roof, a waterproof membrane is required, as illustrated in figure 11.14. Equally important is these roofs' susceptibility to plant root growth. A root-protection barrier must, therefore, always be used with a waterproof membrane.

Single-ply roof membranes are rolled sheets of inorganic plastic or synthetic rubber material that are overlapped at the joints and sealed with heat. They are also available

FIGURE 11.13 The various components of green roofs.

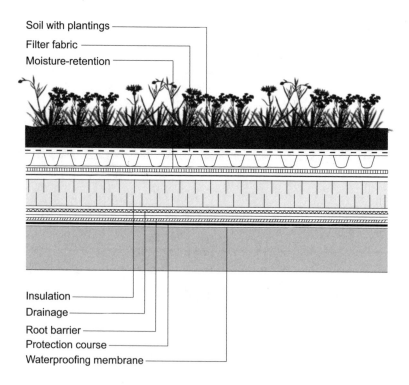

Soil with plantings
Filter fabric
Moisture-retention

Insulation
Drainage
Root barrier
Protection course
Waterproofing membrane

as tiles (sometimes made of recycled rubber). These membranes can be very effective if properly applied. The seams or bonds between the sheets and tiles can, however, be weak points that may be exploited by plant roots and can cause leaks. Sealing material can be susceptible to degradation from UV rays, therefore it is essential that all parts of the liner are protected from sunlight. Fluid-applied membranes, available in hot or cold liquid form, are sprayed or painted onto the surface of the roof and form a complete seal

FIGURE 11.14 Waterproof membranes of built-up roofs are commonly asphalt or tar.

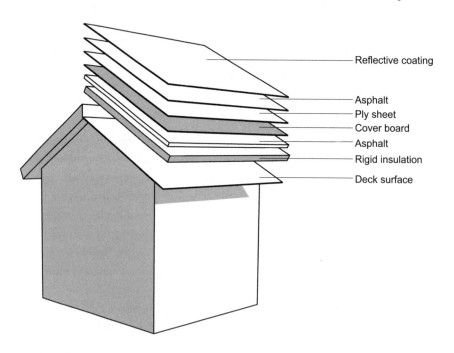

Reflective coating
Asphalt
Ply sheet
Cover board
Asphalt
Rigid insulation
Deck surface

when set, eliminating joint problems. They are easier than single-ply membranes to apply to vertical or irregularly shaped surfaces (Werthmann 2007).

A *root protection barrier* is extremely important. If the membrane upon which a green roof is to be installed contains asphalt or any other organic material, it is crucial that a continuous separation be maintained between the membrane and the plant layer because the membrane will be susceptible to root penetration and the activity of microorganisms—these organic oil-based materials are not root proof. If the roof is not completely flat, then any puddles of water can be bases of plant growth on a roof—again there must be protection from root damage. Plants particularly known to have aggressive roots that can penetrate the membranes are bamboo, lupines, and blackberry (BCIT 2009).

A *drainage layer* is necessary to protect the waterproof roof membrane. The function of the drainage layer is to remove excess water or underflow as quickly as possible to prevent saturation. Roofs require a slope of at least 2 percent and a drainage layer to drain properly. It is important to place the drains at the lowest point halfway between structural supports. Regular maintenance of the drains is necessary to prevent any clogs or blockage that might cause water accumulation (BCIT 2009). Also, one needs to avoid using vine plants on the edge of a green roof, because these might grow into the gutters and block the drainage path.

Because green-roof vegetation, particularly of the extensive-roof type, is selected to be drought resistant and tolerant of dry, free-draining soils, prolonged soil saturation is likely to cause plant failure, rotting, and sour and anaerobic conditions, and the roof may also lose its thermal-insulating properties. Drainage can be achieved in several ways, especially for roofs with a slope of less than 5 degrees, which require more specialized techniques. Additional information on proper drainage methods can be found at the National Roofing Contractors Association (NRCA) or in American Society for Testing and Materials (ASTM) manuals.

Combining a drainage layer with a water-storage layer below it not only reduces runoff, by 11 to 17 percent compared with roofs without such a layer, but also provides a reservoir for plants to draw upon in dry weather (Dunnett and Kingsbury 2008).

The last layer for green roofs is the *growing medium* or *substrate*, which absorbs and retains water while providing free-draining properties. Specifications for materials used in the substrate layer should be determined by experts.

When all functional layers of green roofs are properly applied, planting can begin. Specification of plants on green roofs can be determined using various sources. These sources can range from a local green-roof landscape designer who is familiar with native vegetation to national organizations such as the US Green Building Council (USGBC) or the Canadian Green Roofs for Healthy Cities (GRHC) coalition.

In general, there are four main approaches to establishing vegetation on green roofs: direct application of seed or cuttings, planting of pot-grown plants or plugs, laying of pregrown vegetation mats including turf, and spontaneous colonization. Plants on these roof gardens should be native plants and sustainable, that is, able to be grown without the need for feeding or for regular and prolonged irrigation unless recycled water is being used (Cantor 2008). On the other hand, accessibility to the roof and its appearance are also of interest to architects, and they will be affected by the type of plants chosen.

Euclid Avenue House

Location: Toronto, Ontario, Canada

Design: Levitt Goodman Architects

Completion: 2005

Site area: 2.4 acres (0.22 hectares)

Total floor area: 2,400 sq ft (223 m²)

Number of floors: 2.5

FIGURE 11.15 The green roof enhances the aesthetic values of the dwelling as well as the urban residential fabric. Used with permission.

Built on a narrow infill lot in downtown Toronto, this compact home features three levels of green roofs that cover its entire roof area (figs. 11.15 to 11.17). As a significant component of the building's sustainability strategy, the green roofs actively promote energy conservation, storm-water retention, and a healthier indoor environment while enhancing the aesthetic values of the home and the urban residential fabric.

The second story was offset to accommodate the skylight and the intensive green roof that surrounds the master bedroom. Planted at window level are hostas, native grasses, sedums, and lavender, which are accessible from the bedroom (fig. 11.18). Natural cross ventilation and fresh breezes filtered through the garden plants eliminate the need for mechanical air-conditioning and help enhance indoor air quality. On the upper story, the extensive green roof is covered with a variety of heat- and drought-resistant sedums

FIGURE 11.16 Three green-roof levels lower the environmental footprint of the house. Used with permission.

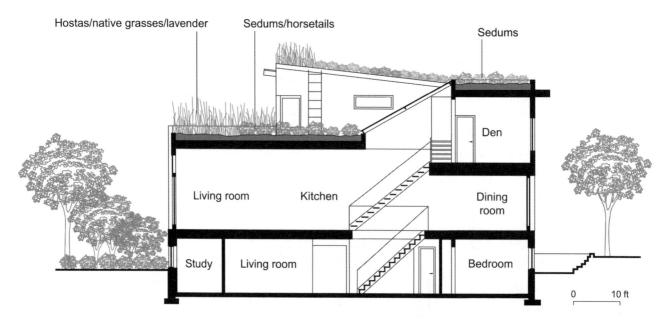

Hostas/native grasses/lavender   Sedums/horsetails   Sedums

Den

Living room   Kitchen   Dining room

Study   Living room   Bedroom

0   10 ft

FIGURE 11.17 A section illustrating the three green-roof levels. Used with permission.

FIGURE 11.18 The lush roof garden on the second level wraps around the master bedroom. Used with permission.

and serves to promote biodiversity (fig. 11.19). Additionally, the yards in front and back on the ground level incorporate storm-water management and xeriscaping techniques with native plant ground covers.

The additional permeable area provides a surface for natural storm-water management and mitigates the urban heat island effect. The green roofs also help reduce noise pollution and moderate internal temperature by acting as an extra sound- and thermal-insulation layer.

FIGURE 11.19 The extensive green roof on the top level is vegetated with a variety of sedums. Used with permission.

CHAPTER 12

Edible Landscaping and Xeriscaping

Conventional landscaping with grass, shrubs, and trees requires excessive amounts of water, maintenance, and chemicals, which result in resource depletion, energy consumption, pollution, and contamination. Because of a growing public and professional awareness, alternative practices such as edible landscaping and xeriscaping are taking hold in residences. These alternatives can significantly reduce adverse effects on the environment while maintaining aesthetic value. The principles behind these methods and their applications are discussed in this chapter.

DWELLING LANDSCAPES AND CONSUMPTION

A typical North American residential landscape often includes flora that is unsuitable to local climatic conditions. This was not always the case. Prior to the mid-nineteenth century the majority of the world's population resided in rural areas, and residential land was used to grow fruits and vegetables for household consumption. Yet, as gardening gained popularity with the upper classes and farming became associated with the poor, decorative plants slowly took over residential yards (Sacramento Hunger Commission 2005). Currently, yards are filled with foreign and newly introduced plants and vegetation that have adverse environmental ramifications, including increased water, chemical, and energy use, as described here.

Water Consumption

Most contemporary residential yards are covered with grass, which requires a great deal of watering since the water needs of lawn grasses are not aligned with the annual rainfall patterns in most areas. Furthermore, shrubs, trees, and plants grown in conventional yards all require irrigation. An average North American dwelling consumes approximately 236 gallons (895 L) of water per day to maintain the yard. When that amount is multiplied by the 113 million households in the United States, it results in 27.8 billion gallons (1.01×10^{11} L) of water per average day, with higher volumes during the hot and dry summer months (Friedman 2007).

Maintaining landscapes also accounts for a large portion of municipal water use through irrigation of parks. Outdoor water conservation is an important environmental consideration that must be addressed sustainably. As discussed in chapter 10, water shortages, a result of severe droughts in many parts of the world, make the need to conserve water an urgent matter.

Chemical Use

Approximately 1 million tons (9×10^5 tonnes) of fertilizer, a by-product of the petrochemical industry, are used each year on home lawns (NJ DEP 2008). Fertilizers, pesticides, and herbicides pollute groundwater when they are applied to turf and nonturf landscapes. Groundwater contamination is particularly harmful since contaminants can remain in the water system for a long time. In the United States, 49 percent of all households use groundwater as their main source of drinking water (Texas Groundwater Protection Committee 2006). Since a typical North American lawn commonly requires fertilizers and irrigation to foster healthy appearance and rapid growth, groundwater pollution is common. Inorganic fertilizers, for example, often leach nitrogen and chemicals into the water table (Owens 2008) and contaminate the soil and air. This is particularly apparent with sandy soils and heavily irrigated plantings. Fertilizers can also make their way into lakes and streams through storm sewers in runoff. When this occurs, soil, water, and air quality can be compromised locally and regionally. When fertilizers reach lakes and streams, they can lower the dissolved-oxygen level and release ammonia, which is toxic to fish. A reduction in the household use of fertilizers, pesticides, and herbicides can aid in lessening this environmental damage since 17 percent of all commercial fertilizers and 40 percent of all pesticides are used on residential lawns and gardens.

Energy Consumption

Species planted on a typical North American lawn require more energy from lawn mowing than indigenous flora suited for the regional climate. While wild plants can grow with little watering and maintenance, conventional lawns and imported trees and shrubs require a great deal of maintenance. In the United States, maintaining the lawn of a single household will consume on average 5 gallons (19 L) of gasoline per year (Perry 2009). Lawn mowing consumes roughly 200 million gallons (9.09×10^8 L) of gasoline per year nationally, emitting 11 times more air pollution per hour than a new car. Gas-consuming lawn maintenance equipment is known to contribute 5 percent of all air pollution in the United States (TCEQ 2010). According to LaMonica (2008), running a lawn mower for an hour pollutes as much as 34 hours of driving a car.

In recent years the US Environmental Protection Agency passed stricter regulations regarding air pollutants, which resulted in new equipment requirements for lawn maintenance equipment. *Catalytic converters* on mowers and boats will eliminate 600,000 tons (5.4×10^5 tonnes) of hydrocarbons, 130,000 tons (1.2×10^5 tonnes) of nitrogen oxides, 5,500 tons (5×10^3 tonnes) of particulate matter, and 1.5 million tons (1.4×10^6 tonnes) of carbon monoxide annually. They will cut gasoline consumption by 190 million gallons (720×10^6 L) yearly as well (Crowley et al. 2008). Energy use and air pollution could be reduced by alternative residential landscapes—with flora that do not require extensive maintenance and that consume little to no energy.

ALTERNATIVES TO CONVENTIONAL LANDSCAPES

Two alternative cultivated landscapes, edible landscapes and xeriscapes, have become increasingly popular because of their ability to reduce water and energy consumption, chemical use, and pollution as well as to produce food. Wild lawns, which are patches of land left unattended, are another type of landscape of note. Although the suburban landscape is still dominated by conventional turf lawns, the attractive benefits of edible landscapes and xeriscaping are gaining the interest of developers and homeowners alike. The principle behind edible landscaping is to utilize regional plants for a dual purpose: appearance and food production (De la Salle and Holland 2010). Instead of spending water, energy, and chemicals on both their dwelling's landscape and the food they consume, homeowners can create an attractive garden while growing food by using edible landscaping.

The main focus of xeriscaping is to minimize irrigation through indigenous and native plant species selection and an integrated approach to design and maintenance. When these principles are followed, a reduction in water, energy, and chemical consumption will be the result. The following sections will examine the principles behind each alternative.

EDIBLE LANDSCAPES

The benefits of *edible landscapes*, in contrast to conventional lawns, extend far beyond the reduction of water use, energy, and chemicals. They also provide shade, curb appeal, and a sense of community and promote health and leisure (Sacramento Hunger Commission 2005; Kourik 2004). Many North Americans reside in a "food desert" and buy their food in ubiquitous large retail outlets, to which they drive a long distance. Not only has the food they consume been treated with chemicals and been selected based on ease of picking and shelf life, it has also been transported roughly 1,500 environmentally damaging miles (2,410 km) and is 7 to 14 days old by the time it reaches the grocery store, so it

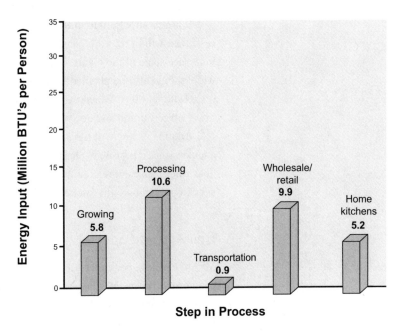

FIGURE 12.1 Energy input, measured in Btu, invested in growing, processing, transporting, and consuming food bought at the grocery store.

has lost a great deal of its nutritional value (Sacramento Hunger Commission 2005). Various chemicals such as methoxychlor, dieldrin, and heptachlor are used to make agricultural practices easier and the product more durable (Kourik 2004). Both dieldrin and heptachlor are suspected to cause cancer, and while the daily intake may be acceptable for some adults, it can cause health damage to children. According to Kourik (2004), the estimated consumption of fossil fuel due to the purchase of grocery store food alone is roughly 32.4 million Btu per person annually, as shown in figure 12.1. Not only do edible landscapes avoid or minimize the need for transportation, but maintaining edible landscapes does not require gasoline-consuming machinery. It can also be a leisurely pastime activity promoting community and family togetherness. There are several important principles of sustainable edible landscapes, which will be discussed next.

Aesthetics and Maintenance

In a multiunit project the developer needs to ensure that necessary maintenance is kept sensibly low for an edible landscape to have a chance of survival. Priority will, sometimes, have to be given to function, such as irrigation, over form to ensure success. Function, however, can often be blended with aesthetics to produce a low-maintenance and visually pleasing garden (Gerlach 2009).

An average-size lot of 1,200 to 2,400 sq ft (111 to 223 m²) should be composed of no more than 50 percent edible plants, and the other portion should be planted with carefree, low-maintenance ornamental shrubs, as illustrated in figure 12.2. When this amount is exceeded, it becomes time consuming and practically difficult to maintain the yard. When the landscaped area exceeds 2,400 sq ft (223 m²), the maximum coverage by the edible plants should decrease to 20 percent.

It is also important to initially plant only low-maintenance species to aid in the successful growth of the edible landscape. As the garden grows, the occupants may choose to replace some of the plants with others. Permanent paths, 2.5 to 3 ft (0.76 to 0.91 m) wide, should also be planned from the outset to allow barrier-free and wheelbarrow access (Kourik 2004). When the yard is sloped, one needs to plan for the transportation of heavy objects uphill and downhill.

Another example of functional aesthetics includes keeping the vegetable area rectangular, since it is visually pleasing and also an effective shape for hosing and harvesting. To further increase the potential success of the edible landscape, the garden should be sited in proximity to the kitchen (Kourik 2004).

Well-Adapted Species

When selecting species for edible landscapes, it is important to choose those that are well adapted to the climate. The plants need to have soil, water, and sunlight requirements that can easily be met. This reduces not only maintenance but also water and fertilizer consumption. For example, one can choose easier-to-maintain productive dwarf fruit trees with soil, water, and sunlight requirements similar to those of full-size ones. For cold, dry northern climates with only one growing season, examples of well-adapted edible plants are bunch-

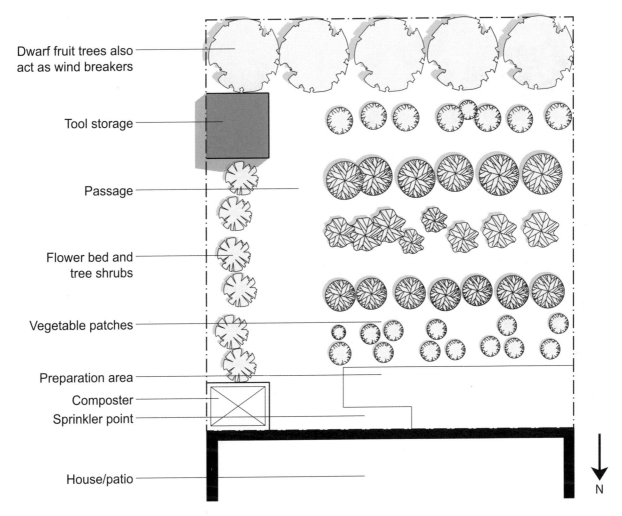

Dwarf fruit trees also
act as wind breakers

Tool storage

Passage

Flower bed and
tree shrubs

Vegetable patches

Preparation area

Composter

Sprinkler point

House/patio

N

FIGURE 12.2 Possible layout for the arrangement of plants in a yard with edible landscape.

berries, mountain sorrel, tomatoes, alpine bistort, and bearberries (About.com 2010). In warmer southern climates there can be two outdoor growing seasons for edible plants such as watercress, ground-cherries, and sunflowers (About.com 2010).

During the months when plants cannot grow outdoors in cold climates, some, such as musa bananas, pineapples, guavas, tomatoes, chives, mint, and oregano, can be cultivated indoors. While indoor plants can be placed outside in the summer, they are still indoor plants and, for the most part, do not have access to rainfall, thereby increasing water consumption. It is therefore important that the selected indoor plants have minimal water requirements.

Maintenance Zones

Following the selection of plant species, they should be divided into zones of similar water usage and fertilizer needs to foster healthy and successful growth as well as reduce maintenance. Since both excessive and inadequate maintenance and watering can harm a plant, defining zones will help ensure their productive life. Fruit and nut trees should, for example, be zoned together for easy care and also to avoid inhibiting the healthy

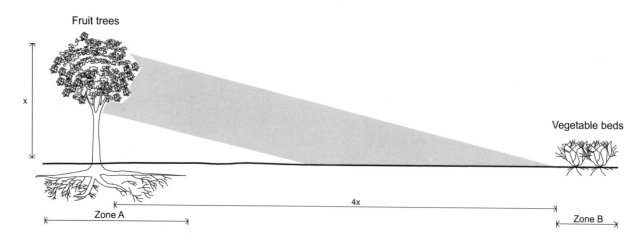

Fruit trees

Vegetable beds

x

4x

Zone A

Zone B

FIGURE 12.3 To avoid the expansion of tree roots and casting of shadows into vegetable beds, fruit trees should be kept a fair distance from them.

growth of neighboring plants that might receive unsuitable amounts of watering or fertilization otherwise. Additionally, vegetables can be zoned into a single bed. It can also be beneficial to place certain zones close to one another. For instance, zones of herbs and perennial flowers can attract helpful insects, which can positively affect vegetable beds placed nearby. On the other hand, placing fruit and nut trees too close to vegetable beds can jeopardize the health of both, since the trees may cast shadows and their roots may invade the vegetable beds, while the watering and fertilizing of the vegetables may weaken the trees. It is, therefore, suggested that fruit and nut trees be placed at least four times their mature height from the perimeter of a vegetable bed, as illustrated in figure 12.3 (Kourik 2004). The placement of defined zones will vary largely, depending on the needs of the species in each zone.

Soil

Amending soil refers to a process whereby soil that is not suitable for gardening is removed or is mixed with additives such as mulch that enrich its growing ability. Amendment can significantly reduce irrigation requirements since it improves the soil's water-holding capacity. The practice is particularly effective during planting and can reduce water consumption significantly. Amendment can be combined with composting, not only to alleviate landfill waste but also to ameliorate the soil's quality. The amended soil can be placed in wooden boxes, as shown in figure 12.4. While soil amendment during planting can benefit flora, the increase in available nutrients can adversely affect water relations by increasing leaf area and decreasing root growth, inhibiting the plant's ability to deliver water to its crown. Soil amendment, therefore, must not be done excessively (About.com 2010).

Shape the Wind

Just as vegetation can act as a windbreak for dwellings, it can be planted to shield edible plants from harsh winter winds and enhance the beneficial outcome of summer breezes. Since edible plants generally represent less than half of all plants in the garden, the nonproductive ones can be used as windbreaks. In the *windchill factor* phenomenon, illus-

FIGURE 12.4 A wooden box filled with amended soil can be constructed to improve the growing process.

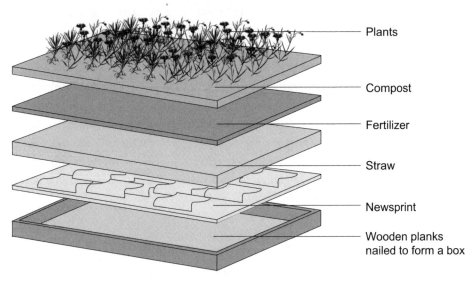

Plants

Compost

Fertilizer

Straw

Newsprint

Wooden planks nailed to form a box

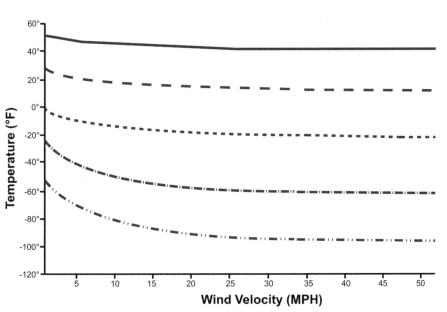

FIGURE 12.5 The planting of a windbreak counteracts the effect of the windchill factor. Low effective temperature, a result of increased wind velocity, can damage vegetable beds.

trated in figure 12.5, the effective temperature decreases with increases in wind velocity. Therefore, decreasing wind speed can protect edible plants from harmful cold temperatures. Additionally, windbreaks create habitats for wildlife, protect the soil from wind and water erosion, and offer privacy (Kourik 2004). On the other hand, summer breezes can be channeled toward the edible plants, and windbreaks can filter dust from the air and raise soil and air temperatures, fostering earlier growth in spring and bigger yields.

Land Form and Water

Natural site drainage needs to be integrated with the edible plant zones and considered simultaneously with windbreak placement to ensure a successful design. Since some areas will receive more water than others, the various watering requirements can be fulfilled based on the natural drainage. Zones for plants with high water needs can be placed in lower elevations, where the water is likely to drain, while plants that consume little water can be placed uphill, as illustrated in figure 12.6.

Any method that can collect rainwater or slow its drainage should be implemented. Mulch from compost, for instance, slows runoff and fosters soaking, which reduces secondary water consumption requirements (Kourik 2004). The use of swales, berms, dry wells, and barrels can also help retain some of the rainwater that may otherwise become runoff, as shown in figure 12.7. Deep-rooted plants are also vital for the health of edible landscapes. They foster deep cultivation by loosening heavy soils and adding organic matter, which allows water to be stored deeper.

FIGURE 12.6 In a sloping terrain, plants that consume little water can be placed atop while those with higher water needs can be planted at the bottom, where rainwater will collect.

Dwelling and Landscape

Just as windbreaks can be oriented to benefit both the plant and the dwelling, as discussed in chapter 2, several other aspects of edible landscape can be integrated to further benefit both. The eaves of a dwelling, for instance, can reduce frost and produce a microclimate suitable for small plants that would otherwise be unsuitable to the local climate

Plants with high water demand

Plants with low water demand

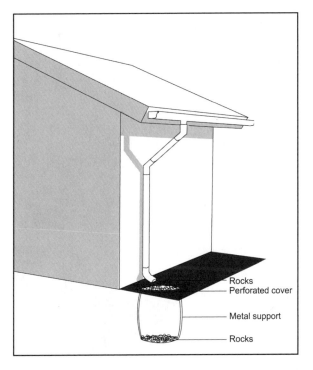
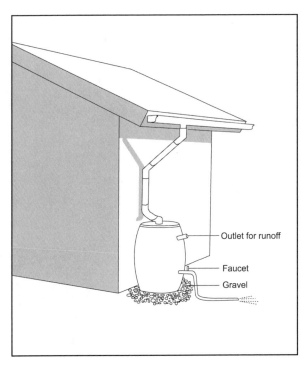

Rocks
Perforated cover

Metal support

Rocks

Outlet for runoff

Faucet
Gravel

FIGURE 12.7 A drywell to collect rainwater can be excavated near a downspout, or a barrel can be placed there.

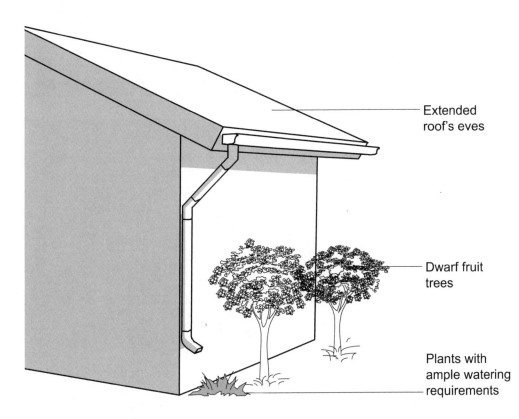

Extended roof's eves

Dwarf fruit trees

Plants with ample watering requirements

FIGURE 12.8 Dwarf fruit trees that need frost protection can be planted near a wall. Plants that require ample watering can be placed near the roof's gutter downspout.

FIGURE 12.9 Edible landscapes can be planted vertically, be part of a green roof, or grow in a solarium.

FIGURE 12.10 Enlarged indoor window sills can offer a place on which to rest edible plants in pots.

FIGURE 12.11 A community garden is tended by the residents of the nearby housing development in Montreal, Canada.

(Kourik 2004). Additionally, plants that require a great deal of water, such as asparagus, blackberries, water chestnuts, and strawberries, can be placed near the roof's gutter downspout, which funnels water to a smaller area, as illustrated in figure 12.8.

The design of each home and its edible garden will be unique, and it is the responsibility of the designer to identify areas that can benefit both. In cold climates, a garden can be planted in a glass solarium to provide semi-outdoor seating, heat, and humidity for the dwelling and to produce food during the winter months. Vertical planting can also be used, and edible plants can be part of a green roof, as shown in figure 12.9. Enlarged indoor windowsills can offer a place to rest edible plants in pots, as shown in figure 12.10. During wintertime, herbs, for example, can supplement the dinner menu.

Communal Edible Landscapes

Edible landscapes can also be developed on a large urban scale. The initiator can be the project's developer, the municipality through a network of community gardens, also known as *urban agriculture*, or the residents themselves. A large swath of land is then cultivated in common, as shown in figure 12.11.

The Kennedy Estates edible landscape project in Sacramento, California, developed a communal garden on the site of an existing dwelling complex in a shared outdoor area. It is commonly a more difficult and costly practice than incorporating an edible landscape from the outset. To ensure success after the initial planting, the community was surveyed and educated on the subject (Sacramento Hunger Commission 2005). The main goals of the residents were to increase the site's curb appeal while growing afford-

FIGURE 12.12 Aesthetically pleasing gardens can be planted using sustainable principles of xeriscaping (*a*) rather than conventional landscaping (*b*).

able produce by blending aesthetics and function. The developers selected plant species based on the community's interest and regional climatic conditions. The design began by zoning plants of similar water use and maintenance, amending soil, and shaping wind and water as well as integrating dwelling and landscape.

XERISCAPING

Similar to edible landscapes, xeriscaping can provide many sustainable benefits when compared with conventional lawns. *Xeriscaping* focuses on minimizing irrigation, energy consumption, and chemical use and, as a result, reduces soil contamination. The basic principles behind xeriscaping revolve around comprehensive plant species selection and the integration of maintenance and design. Water deficits affect almost all processes in plants, so plants should be selected that match local climate and water conditions. This will foster well-adapted, pest- and disease-resistant plants. According to Klimchuk (2008), studies have shown that while conventional Kentucky bluegrass lawns require 17 gallons of water per square foot (699 L per m^2), for example, the same lawn under xeriscaping principles consumes only 2.9 gal per sq ft (119 L per m^2). In many climatic conditions, this reduction can render outdoor irrigation, or water supply in addition to rainfall, obsolete. Furthermore, the principles of xeriscaping ensure that aesthetic values are not compromised during the conservation process, as shown in figure 12.12.

As with edible landscaping, applying several principles can aid in creating successful xeriscapes, and these will be discussed next.

Size of Turf Area

Although grass is not an ideal choice because of its heavy water requirements, some part of a yard will unavoidably be turf because of human activity needs. If a yard of 3,770 sq ft (350 m^2), for example, were planted with either regional shrub beds or trees, it would consume significantly less water per year than conventional lawns. The shrubs would

Deeper stronger roots

- Handle water stress well

- Require more irrigation

- Can handle long intervals between watering periods

Shallow weak roots

- Are at risk during drought

- Require more water

- Require short irrigation cycles

FIGURE 12.13 Plants with deeper roots will handle water stress better.

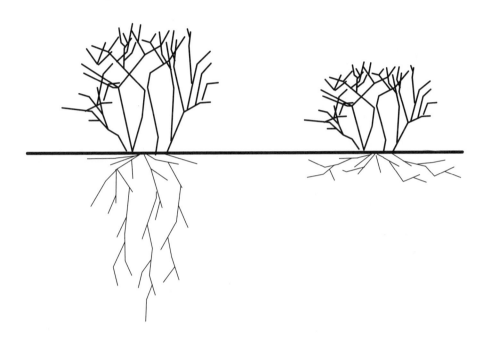

consume 8,850 gallons (4.025×10^4 L), and the trees would need 15,400 gallons (7×10^4 L). In contrast, 44,000 gallons (2×10^5 L) of water would be consumed by a turf lawn of the same size (Gleick 2010). The species of grass, as well as the size of the lawn, must be selected with thorough consideration.

Suitable Plant Material

When selecting plant species for xeriscaping, it is important to remember that the ultimate goal is to reduce irrigation. The plants should, therefore, require minimal water and preferably survive on rainwater alone. These plants are typically native species since those are the ones that have evolved and adapted to the local climatic restrictions. At times, however, site conditions can vary so vastly from regional conditions that they can render native plants unsuitable for the purpose of xeriscaping.

As a rule of thumb, deep-rooted mature trees and shrubs are able to handle water stresses, such as droughts, while newly transplanted flora cannot, as illustrated in figure 12.13. There will be an establishment period of 2 to 3 years during which even a well-adapted species will require additional watering while it roots itself (Trumbore and Gaudinski 2003).

Water-Use Zones

As with edible landscapes, creating water-use zones can help make water use by xeriscapes more efficient. The zones can be divided into four levels of irrigation requirements based on frequency and type of human activity, aesthetic requirements, and site constraints, such as slope, drainage, shade, and wind conditions. The principal water-use zone has high levels of human impact and water and energy use, while the secondary zone has high aesthetic requirements but needs less maintenance. Generally, areas that are located far away from the dwelling are easier to xeriscape since they are not being used for human activities and are not as visible. While the front yard has aesthetic requirements, human activity does not generally take place there but rather in the backyard. The immediate front yard is, therefore, typically a secondary zone while

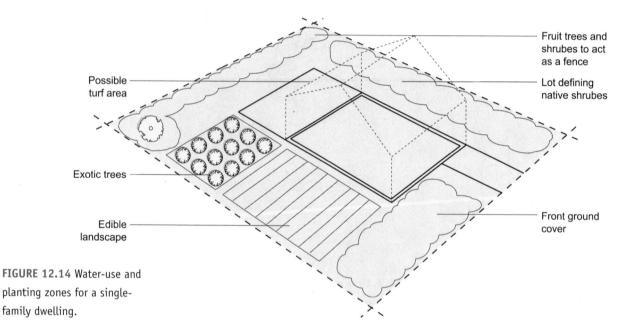

Possible turf area

Exotic trees

Edible landscape

Fruit trees and shrubes to act as a fence

Lot defining native shrubes

Front ground cover

FIGURE 12.14 Water-use and planting zones for a single-family dwelling.

the backyard remains the principal one, as illustrated in figure 12.14. Principal water-use zones can additionally be defined by areas of shade since evaporation is reduced in shaded places, further reducing water loss (Hassanain et al. 2003).

Mulch and Soil

Mulches are ideal for xeriscaping since they can reduce soil temperature, minimize evaporation of soil moisture, eliminate weed growth, reduce soil compaction, and slow erosion. Bark chips and shredded tree mulch are the preferable types since they are effective in reducing water loss (fig. 12.15). Furthermore, mulch decomposes to provide fertile soil. Smith and Rakow (1992) suggest a mulch depth of 1.5 in. (3.8 cm) because a deeper layer can result in oxygen loss.

Amending the soil is beneficial to xeriscaping as it is to edible landscaping. During planting, soil amendment can significantly improve the soil's water-holding capacity,

which in turn will reduce water requirements. It is, however, still important to recall that fertilization, commonly done annually, can increase leaf area and decrease root growth, which adversely affects water retention and inhibits the plant's ability to deliver water to its crown. Soil amendment must, therefore, be done in moderation and should generally be completed during planting.

Irrigation Systems and Rainwater Collection

Since soil is often unable to retain water, a great deal of irrigation water evaporates or runs off. Furthermore, conventional sprinklers and hoses have high evaporation rates, and more of the water is lost before actually reaching the lawn. Instead, soaking hoses and micro- or drip-irrigation systems should be employed. Since drip irrigation is costly, it is often a less attractive option to homeowners than sprinklers. Fortunately, in most climates appropriate species selection and the application of the principles mentioned here will result in a landscape that requires little or no irrigation (CMHC 2010).

Ross Street House

Location: Madison, Wisconsin, USA

Design: Richard Wittschiebe Hand

Completion: 2009

Site area: 0.153 acres (0.062 hectares)

Total floor area: 2,700 sq ft (251 m²)

Ross Street House, a LEED platinum–rated residence, incorporates a sustainable landscape design that conserves water and energy and maximizes functionality while providing a green sanctuary for the inhabitants and the surrounding wildlife.

The garden areas, classified as rain garden, vegetable garden, and butterfly garden, occupy the front and back yards (figs. 12.16 to 12.18). Landscaped with native plants acclimatized to the site-specific conditions, the gardens respect and maintain the existing ecosystem and require no fertilization or irrigation. The need for irrigation is further minimized through the absence of turf and the incorporation of drought-tolerant prairie plants in areas of strong sun exposure.

The house utilizes an integrated design for its water conservation systems. The rain garden, landscaped with perennials tolerant to wide moisture fluctuations, collects and absorbs storm water that has permeated through the bioswales and the pervious pavers (fig. 12.19). Through this process, the site proactively returns surface water to the ground and replenishes the groundwater supply. Furthermore, a rainwater collection and storage system captures water from the roofs into a 650 gallon (2.461×10^3 L) cistern to provide landscape irrigation.

FIGURE 12.16 To minimize pavement area, a strip driveway and flagstone steppers were incorporated in the landscape design. [used with permission]

FIGURE 12.17 The rear garden provides a green sanctuary for the inhabitants and the surrounding wildlife.
[used with permission]

FIGURE 12.18 Flagstone steppers offer a pleasant walk through the rear garden.
[used with permission]

During the excavation and construction process, the site was actively protected to minimize damage and disturbance to its surroundings. With the installation of a silt fence and erosion-control methods, soil sedimentation of the neighboring lots was avoided. The existing trees were preserved and protected in a fenced protection zone where they were guarded from root compaction and impairment of trunk and branches. To maximize the house's efficiency in storm-water management, the pavement area was reduced through the incorporation of flagstone steppers and a strip driveway with a xeriscaped swale in between strips.

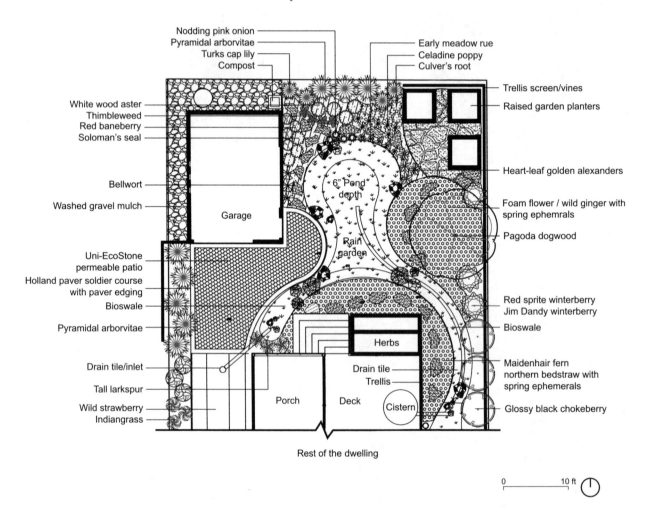

FIGURE 12.19 The backyard is landscaped with diverse native plants and features an integrated water recycling system. [used with permission]

CHAPTER 13

Waste Management and Disposal

L andfilling is the most common contemporary waste management method. Unfortunately, it is not one that can be sustained long term as we run out of viable sites and landfills continue to fill up much faster than anticipated. Landfilling also poses challenges that urgently need to be addressed. Leachate from landfill sites contaminates soil and groundwater, and the associated odors cause health concerns and discomfort among nearby residents. Furthermore, the emitted greenhouse gases are adding to the environmental damage. These effects can be alleviated if waste generation is reduced. Since dwellings are a leading generator of waste, this chapter focuses on finding sustainable ways to reduce the amount of waste created or to divert it to beneficial practices such as composting and recycling.

WASTE GENERATION

Waste generation and its disposal have been societal concerns since antiquity. Often, the accumulated waste was the cause of widespread epidemics, since it was rarely treated. With successive generations, those responsible for public health began to pay attention to waste in all its various forms, and its collection became an important task of all municipalities. *Municipal waste* is defined as any waste that is collected locally from residences, commercial and industrial enterprises, and public spaces (OECD 2004). In North America around 30 percent of all municipal waste is generated by the residential sector. As a result of the steady rise in the standard of living and increased consumption, domestic waste has been increasing. The average amount of municipal waste per capita generated annually by 17 of the world's most developed countries is 1,345 lb (610 kg). The smallest waste producer has been Japan, at 882 lb (400 kg) per capita. Developed countries generally produce substantially more waste than the developing world. In 2003, Mexico, for instance, produced 661 lb (300 kg) of waste per capita, whereas Canada produced more than three times as much—2,183 lb (990 kg) per capita (Environment Canada 2006). In the developed world, household waste has a relatively consistent composition, shown in figure 13.1.

Waste management can be expensive. Most midsize and large municipalities spend a significant portion of their annual budgets to collect, transport, and dispose of waste (Sta-

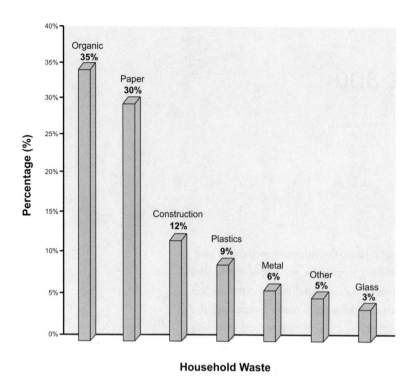

Organic
35%

Paper
30%

Construction
12%

Plastics
9%

Metal
6%

Other
5%

Glass
3%

Percentage (%)

Household Waste

tistics Canada 2005). In small towns and rural areas where formal municipal collection does not exist, residents are required to bring their waste to a local landfill and pay based on its weight. It is more than obvious that waste management is a pivotal issue that can affect the financial resilience and public health of all countries and that it needs to be dealt with sustainably. While the level of waste generated differs from country to country and even between households, it is hard to avoid creating any waste at all. The issue is not elimination but rather reduction and proper disposal (UNEP/GRID-Arendal 2002).

POSTCONSUMER WASTE MANAGEMENT OPTIONS

FIGURE 13.1 General composition of household waste in the developed world.

When residential waste is discarded, it will eventually go through one of five postconsumer waste management processes. From least to most sustainable, they are landfilling, incineration, anaerobic digestion, recycling, and composting. To understand how to design a dwelling and a community that fosters sustainable waste management, the environmental impact of each process must first be understood.

Landfilling

Because of the steady increase in waste generation, *landfills* around the world are filling up at a rapid rate, and new ones need to be created. Studies suggest that in the United States approximately 70 percent of all municipal waste ends up dumped and buried in landfills. Yet, resistance by residents to having landfills located near their communities is limiting the options for developing new ones (Nayab 2010).

Siting is one of several concerns associated with landfilling. The generation of leachate and emission of greenhouse gases (GHGs) are two important additional concerns. Leachate is a mixture of water and dissolved solids that may contain toxic polluting components in large amounts (Statistics Canada 2005). It is produced when water passes through the waste pile and collects at the bottom of the landfill. Leachate can seep through the ground and even into surface water, where it contaminates surrounding soil and potable water. Liners can be used to prevent leachate from reaching groundwater, as shown in figure 13.2. Unfortunately, liners are a fairly recent invention, and it is difficult to incorporate them into older landfills (Zero Waste America 2010).

Landfills produce GHGs, mostly carbon dioxide and methane, as well as small amounts of ammonia and sulfides and trace amounts of VOCs, such as toluene, vinyl

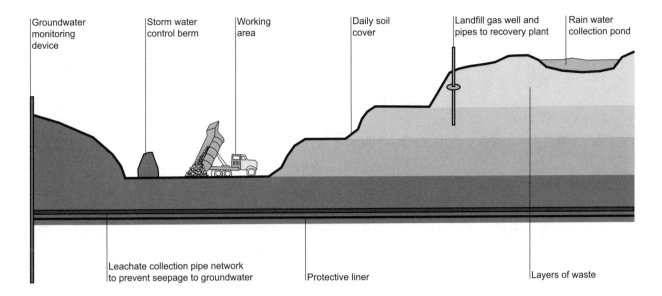

Groundwater monitoring device

Storm water control berm

Working area

Daily soil cover

Landfill gas well and pipes to recovery plant

Rain water collection pond

Leachate collection pipe network to prevent seepage to groundwater

Protective liner

Layers of waste

chloride, and benzene. Landfills contributed 3 percent of all GHGs produced by Canada in 2002, for a total of 23.8 megatons (21.6 megatonnes) (Statistics Canada 2005; Environment Canada 2006). These gases are produced during decomposition of organic waste. In a landfill pile that contains sufficient oxygen, carbon dioxide is the main gas released. When the oxygen in the pile has been depleted, methane is also produced. The amount and ratio of gases produced through decomposition vary depending on temperature, moisture content, and time.

Since vehicles are needed to transport the waste from urban areas to landfills and within the landfill itself, even more GHGs are produced. Studies have shown that the equipment used on-site for landfills generates about 8.7 lb CO_2 equivalents per ton (4 kg CO_2 equivalents per tonne) of waste landfilled (ICF Consulting 2005). Unfortunately, statistics regarding GHG emissions from vehicles transporting waste between municipalities and landfill sites are unavailable. It can, however, be assumed that since greater distances are now required for travel between municipalities and landfills located away from communities, emissions from trucks are also on the rise. Recently several North American municipalities have begun transforming their old landfills into parks. One of the most notable examples of such undertakings is Freshkills Park in New York City, formerly the world's largest landfill.

Incineration

Incinerators can produce energy from the combustion of solid waste, which can be used to heat buildings or generate electricity. The energy, however, is only useful when it is produced from waste with a high heating value that burns without requiring additional fuel. Ironically, many highly combustible materials that would make good fuel for incinerators, such as paper and plastic, are also recyclable and are likely to be diverted to recycling plants instead of reaching incinerators (Statistics Canada 2005). Incineration is a popular method of waste management near highly populated cities in Asia and Eu-

FIGURE 13.2 Components of modern landfills are meant to reduce environmental harm by incorporating various means of protection.

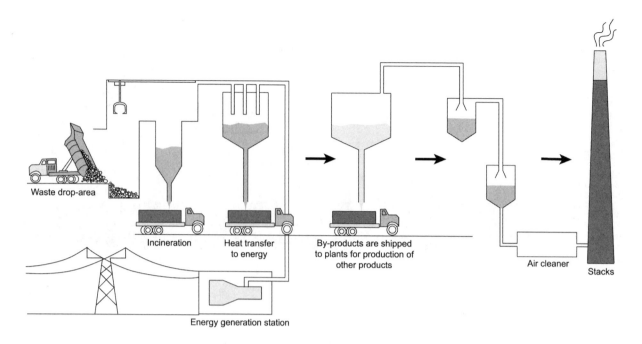

Waste drop-area

Incineration

Heat transfer to energy

By-products are shipped to plants for production of other products

Air cleaner

Stacks

Energy generation station

FIGURE 13.3 Incineration plants convert waste to energy and produce by-products for other industries.

rope, where landfill space is at a premium. New incineration methods, some of which have been introduced in Scandinavian countries, have mastered energy production by developing advanced filters that catch most polluting agents.

During incineration, the products of combustion pass through a pollution abatement system intended to retain particles and gases that cause air pollution and to prevent them from ever being released into the atmosphere, as shown in figure 13.3. Unfortunately, these systems are not always fully effective, and many pollutants are still being released. Sulfur dioxide and nitrogen oxides, for instance, are released and contribute to acid rain; nitrogen oxides react with volatile organic compounds in the presence of sunlight and form ground-level ozone, also known as smog; and carbon dioxide contributes to global warming (Jones 2008).

The metals and other contaminants captured by the pollution abatement system, as well as leftover ash from the incineration process and the wastewater generated from the gas treatment processes, must also be disposed of. The ash produced may or may not be contaminated. If it is, it must be disposed of carefully to prevent further harm to the environment. When it is not contaminated, it may be diverted to other uses such as the manufacture of concrete or brick.

Anaerobic Digestion

In *anaerobic digestion*, methane (CH_4) is purposely produced, collected, and burned for its energy value. Methane is produced by microorganisms breaking down biodegradable materials in the absence of oxygen (fig. 13.4). Although anaerobic digestion produces fewer gas emissions than landfilling, greenhouse gases are still emitted since the methane conversion and the gas collection system are never 100 percent efficient. The waste left over from digestion is not toxic or contaminated and therefore can be used as compost and tilled into soils (DeBruyn and Hilborn 2010).

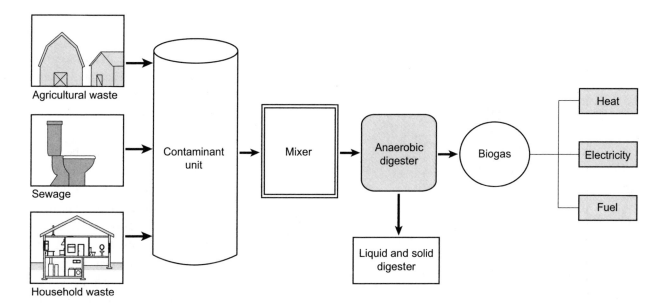

Recycling

Recycling involves the transformation of waste into other usable products. Although recycling requires transportation, which consumes energy and produces gas emissions, its advantage is reducing the amount of raw materials needed to make new products, and as a result it reduces air pollution and solid waste that would otherwise have been generated, as discussed in chapter 6. Using recycled materials rather than virgin ones during the manufacturing process not only avoids unnecessary greenhouse gas emissions but also reduces energy consumption, as shown in figure 13.5. For instance, when recycled aluminum instead of virgin bauxite is used to produce aluminum, energy consumption can be reduced by 95 percent (Statistics Canada 2005). Recycling, however, can produce dust particles, wastewater, emissions, and process residues. Fortunately, the levels of waste and pollutants are lower than for landfilling the same materials (Ecoworld 2007).

Recent years have seen a significant increase in the number of building and household products made of recycled materials. Decking boards made of recycled plastic, insulation made of recycled newsprint, and driveway pavers made of old tires are only a few of the most notable products (Meisel 2010).

Composting

Composting is the biodegradation of organic matter by bacteria or other organisms in the presence of oxygen. When organic matter decomposes aerobically, most of its end products are carbon dioxide and water, while its remaining solid mass can be used as fertilizer in soil. Since compostable materials originate directly or indirectly from trees or other plants, the carbon dioxide emitted from composting is not considered a pollutant but rather biogenic carbon dioxide (ICF Consulting 2005). Some methane, however, may be produced in composting as a result of anaerobic decomposition occurring when the center of the compost pile lacks oxygen. Fortunately methane is likely to be oxidized to carbon dioxide

FIGURE 13.4 Anaerobic digestion, which happens in stages inside airtight containers, produces biogas. Different kinds of microorganisms are responsible for the processes that characterize the different stages.

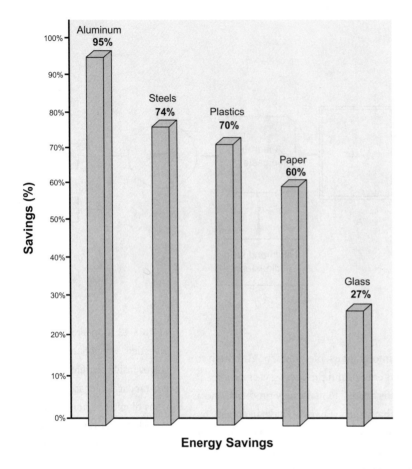

when it reaches the surface of the compost pile and is, therefore, considered negligible (ICF Consulting 2005). Additionally, the diversion of organic materials from landfills to composters will decrease the amount of leachate, greenhouse gases, and odors produced in landfills.

Not only can composting be an inexpensive alternative to landfilling, but it can also foster the growth of more disease-resistant plants that have superior qualities such as better color, flavor, and reproductive capacity. Compostable organic materials include leaves, lawn and garden clippings, fruit and vegetable waste, food scraps, eggshells, coffee grounds with filter papers, tea bags, nut shells, and wood ash from fireplaces and woodstoves.

Composting can be done either individually or communally. Communal composters should be limited to a maximum of six households since the maximum compost pile should be less than 2.0 yards (1.8 m) in height and have a volume that does not exceed 2.6 cubic yards (2

FIGURE 13.5 Examples of energy savings resulting from using recycled rather than virgin source materials in manufacturing.

m³) for aeration purposes. Composting requires minimal maintenance and only three basic requirements: organic materials should be chopped into small pieces, aerated every 3 days, and blended into the existing pile. The pile should be located at ground level for drainage and away from uncontrollable water sources. Additionally, a water supply should be available to prevent the pile from drying out. Composting will generally take 2 weeks to complete, and proper aeration and drainage will prevent the pile from becoming odorous (US EPA 1997).

There are several types of composters to choose from. The most common forms are worm composters, food digesters, and bins or boxes, which are shown in figure 13.6.

Worm composters use earthworms to decompose the organic materials, allowing the composter to operate indoors and outdoors. These composters are very effective for foods, yet they may attract fruit flies and other pests if not properly maintained. Food digesters, also known as green cones, are easy to use outside once installed. Their installation, however, requires digging, and the composter must be moved periodically. While food digesters are able to effectively compost meats, poultry, and fish, they require higher maintenance than bin or worm compos-

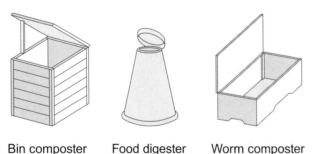

Bin composter   Food digester   Worm composter

FIGURE 13.6 Forms of composters.

ters. The bin or box composters can be built or bought and are particularly effective with yard wastes. Though they are not good choices for meat composting, their appearance, deterrence of animals, ability to hold in heat, and tight lids that keep out rain make them the preferred choice for most dwellings (US EPA 1997).

DIVERSION OF WASTE

As already noted, recycling and composting are the most effective and sustainable methods of waste management. Both processes create materials that can be used again. Additionally, the pollution they produce is far less than what would be emitted by landfilling, incinerating, or anaerobically digesting the same materials. Whenever possible, therefore, waste should be diverted to recycling or composting.

A surprisingly large amount of waste that can be recycled or composted ends up in landfills or incineration plants. In Canada, for example, up to 75 percent of residential waste sent to landfills could have been diverted to recycling, while organic matter that could have been composted makes up 30 to 40 percent of it (Statistics Canada 2005). It is likely that, over the coming years, these numbers will change as households alter their waste management practices. As resources become increasingly rare, recyclable and biodegradable materials will become too vital to simply discard.

Waste diversion can be achieved throughout a dwelling's life cycle. During construction, for example, recycled products can be chosen rather than those made of virgin materials (see chapter 6). During occupancy, residents can be provided with easy ways to recycle and compost. Studies have shown that the most common reason for not recycling is the impression that it is time-consuming (MA DEP 2002). To make waste diversion quick and convenient, curbside pickup of recyclables, now widespread, can be made mandatory in every municipality. Sorting stations like those in figure 13.7 can be provided in multifamily dwelling developments to encourage the inhabitants to recycle. Additionally, composters can be installed so that all organic waste will be composted rather than landfilled. Finally, the demolition stage of a house needs to be considered during the design stages, to ensure easy disassembly and reuse. Waste diversion methods can vary depending on the circumstances, which may change from site to site. Some strategies used to develop solutions will be discussed next.

FIGURE 13.7 Collection stations for recyclables were incorporated in the planning of a neighborhood in Porvoo, Finland.

COMMUNITY-BASED SOCIAL MARKETING

Sustainable dwellings and communities need to encourage proper habits among their inhabitants, making them aware of, and willing to take part in, recycling and composting of waste. *Community-based social marketing* has emerged in several countries as an effective tool to foster behavioral change during occupancy. Four stages comprise such a process: uncovering and selecting barriers, designing a strategy, piloting the program, and finally, evaluating the program, as illustrated in figure 13.8 (McKenzie-Mohr 2000). First, the behavior barriers need to be identified. Three variables will be involved: the potential impact of the desirable behavior, barriers that prevent the residents from engaging in desirable activities, and the resources available to overcome the barriers. The selected behavior should have a large enough potential impact to compensate for the effort it may take to overcome the barriers (MA DEP 2002). Following the selection of a desired behavior, a strategy can be developed to promote it. Before the strategy is broadly executed, it needs to be piloted to ensure that it can obtain the desired level

FIGURE 13.8 Key stages and tasks of a community-based social-marketing program.

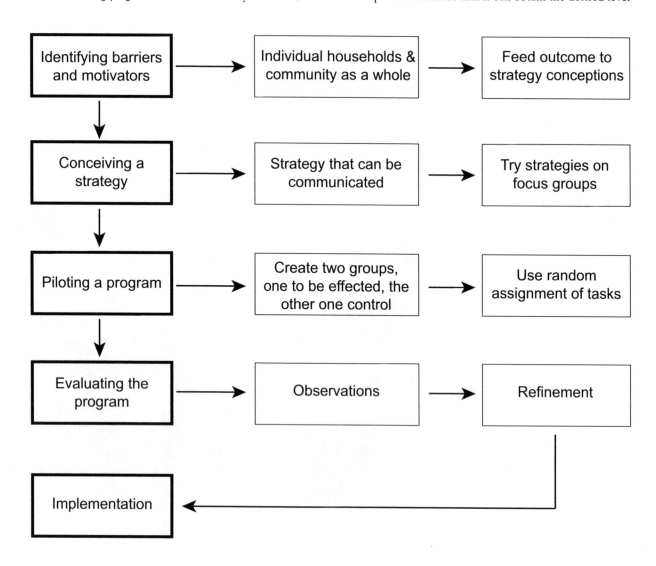

of behavioral change. If the strategy does not reach its objective, it can be reevaluated. This process should be repeated until the desired outcome is attained. Finally, the effectiveness of the implemented strategy should be evaluated and improved through further discussion and implementation elsewhere. The strategies outlined below explain how to achieve sustainability using community-based social marketing.

CHANGING BEHAVIOR

While most North American households participate in a blue-box, or curbside-pickup, recycling program, fewer participate in backyard composting. Many households do not compost because they lack the knowledge to do so or think it is too challenging and time consuming and that they lack space. To determine whether backyard composting behavior was worth promoting, its impact, its barriers, and the resources to overcome those barriers were studied. As noted earlier, 30 to 40 percent of residential waste in Canada is organic material, and it makes up one-third of landfill content. Increasing residential composting has the potential to divert 10 to 13 percent of waste from landfills (McKenzie-Mohr 2000).

Once the residents' behavior that needed improvement was identified, a strategy was developed to change it. Providing the residents with information about composting changed some beliefs that it was inconvenient or unpleasant. Additionally, providing a new dwelling with a composter upon completion of construction can help overcome residents' lack of willingness to purchase one. Moreover, the dwelling can be designed so that it is equipped with a composter and an instruction manual. The strategy can then be piloted to ensure that it is successful at changing backyard composting habits, and once it has met the desired level of behavior change, it can be implemented and evaluated (McKenzie-Mohr 2000).

Researchers also found that there was no community norm to support backyard composting, which was traced to the lack of exposure to the subject. Since recycling occurred in curbside collection, recycling bins had a visual prominence and showed which households were recycling. Backyard composting, on the other hand, was not visible. A strategy to overcome this barrier involved the placement of decals on recycling bins or garbage cans, indicating which households were composting. Additionally, households that did compost were asked to speak to their neighbors about this practice and share their insights on how to do it successfully. Some 80 percent of households who showed interest in composting had begun doing so 7 months later (McKenzie-Mohr 2000).

Since landfill disposal fees are increasing, diverting waste to recycling could reduce municipal taxes per household, and potential for reduced taxes can provide economic incentives for behavior change. However, research has shown that, although monetary incentives can contribute to a willingness to recycle, the amount of effort and time needed to recycle plays a larger role in success (MA DEP 2002). When addressing behavior to increase recycling, it is therefore important to realize that barriers include not only economics but also convenience, and the resources available to overcome various barriers should be considered.

Once the behavior to be promoted is selected, the strategy development can begin to target both neighborhoods and individual dwellings. For instance, in neighborhoods,

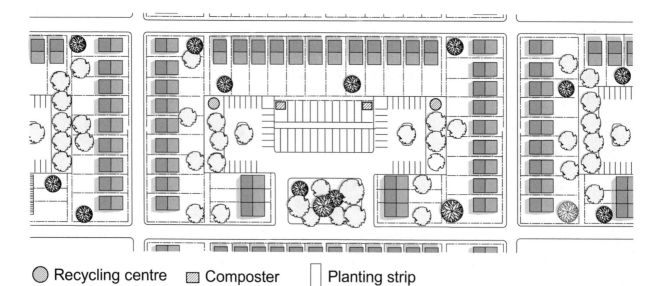

 Recycling centre   Composter   ☐ Planting strip

FIGURE 13.9 Recommended location of recycling centers and composters near clusters of homes.

recycling centers could be located in places easily accessed by all. High-density housing is the most relevant for shared recycling centers since it is often configured in clusters and has common parking lots, as shown in figure 13.9. Rolling bins can also be used in recycling centers. If the neighborhood does not use centers but instead employs curbside recycling, charges could be applied to collected garbage while recycling remains complementary. This would encourage residents to recycle through economic incentives—the more waste diverted to recycling the less the residents would have to pay.

For individual homes, several other strategies can be used. To increase convenience, recycling stations can be made part of each kitchen, where most household waste is generated. A convenient area for a recycling center within the kitchen is under the sink. The recycling center should have separate bins for recyclable plastic, glass, and metal cans in addition to containers for other wastes (fig. 13.10). This makes sorting recyclable materials more efficient and convenient since it avoids a second step.

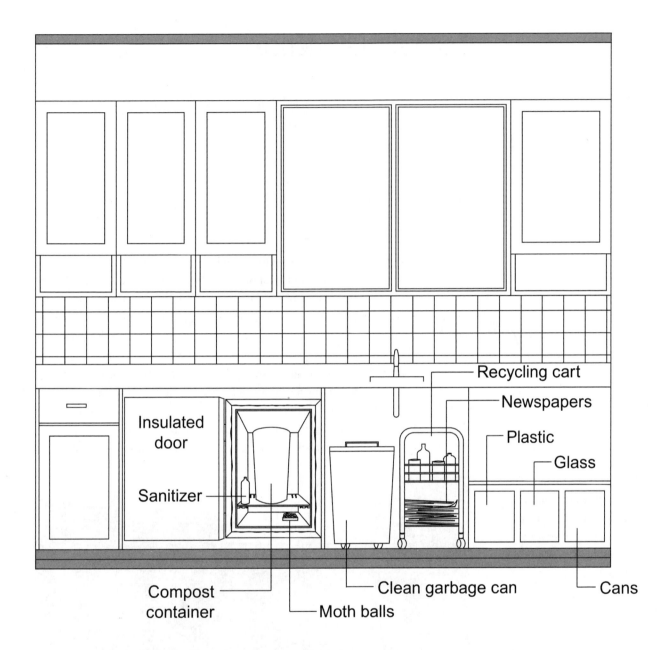

Recycling cart

Newspapers

Plastic

Glass

Insulated door

Sanitizer

Cans

Clean garbage can

Compost container

Moth balls

FIGURE 13.10 A kitchen designed for separation and storage of recyclable items.

Seatrain Residence

Location: Los Angeles, California, USA

Design: Office of Mobile Design

Completion: 2003

Site area: 0.23 acres (0.093 hectares)

Total floor area: 3,000 sq ft (279 m²)

Number of floors: 2

Seatrain Residence was built on a downtown infill site adjacent to the Brewery, a lively community of artists' residences and studios. This urban home achieves a unique identity through its creative application of reused commercial and industrial waste (fig. 13.11). The dwelling's recycled structural elements consist of shipping containers, grain trailers, steel beams and cladding, glass, and wood joists, some of which were salvaged on-site (fig. 13.12). Reusing locally salvaged commercial and industrial waste minimized the use of raw materials and cut down on greenhouse gas emissions by avoiding long transport. Constructing with modular elements further reduced construction waste, time, and labor cost (fig. 13.13). Chosen for their durability, these salvaged materials demonstrate their timeless qualities. Modular construction also allowed a wide range of flexible options in the dwelling's structural and artistic design and an easy future disassembly. The materi-

FIGURE 13.11 Shipping containers contain the master bedroom. The exterior lap pool, made of a grain trailer, extends into the garden. Used with permission.

FIGURE 13.12 Most of the building materials were salvaged on-site to reduce the consumption of raw materials. Used with permission.

als' ability to accommodate the client's needs was demonstrated in the construction process, which involved collaborative work between the client and the material fabricators to make on-site structural and artistic adjustments.

Each space is uniquely distinguished. From the two grain trailers, the designer created an interior koi pond, placed adjacent to the living area, and a lap pool in the exterior, visually continuing from the one inside (figs. 13.14, 13.15). At each side of the north-south axis, two storage containers are stacked one on top of the other and create separate living, working, service, and private areas (fig. 13.16). Recycled carpet was incorporated as well. Because of the modularity of the containers, the rooms could be flexibly arranged and adapted to personalized needs, thereby achieving a pleasant spatial fluidity.

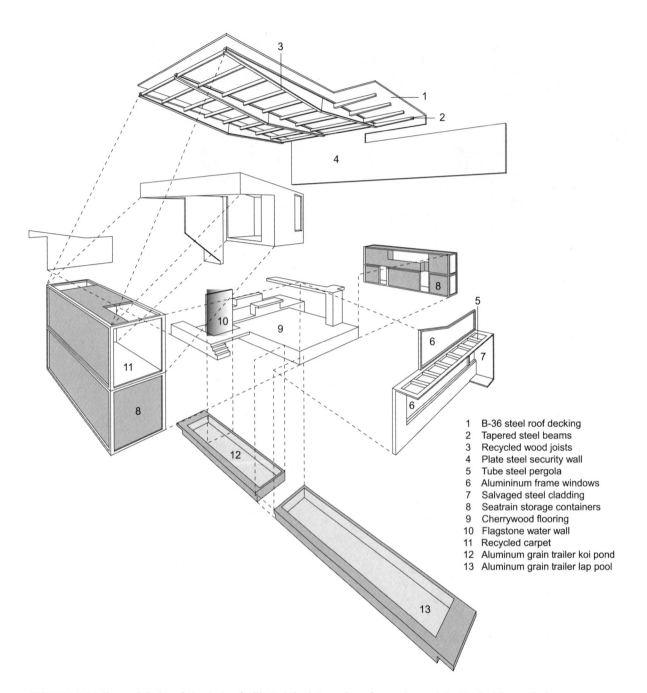

1   B-36 steel roof decking
2   Tapered steel beams
3   Recycled wood joists
4   Plate steel security wall
5   Tube steel pergola
6   Alumininum frame windows
7   Salvaged steel cladding
8   Seatrain storage containers
9   Cherrywood flooring
10   Flagstone water wall
11   Recycled carpet
12   Aluminum grain trailer koi pond
13   Aluminum grain trailer lap pool

FIGURE 13.13 The modularity of the design facilitated the integration of reused materials. Used with permission.

FIGURE 13.14 The main living area features an interior koi pond, built from a grain trailer, and a ceiling supported by recycled wood joists and tapered steel beams. Used with permission.

FIGURE 13.15 The reemergence of recycled materials in modern architecture achieves a powerful gesture that addresses the local industrial context. Used with permission.

FIGURE 13.16 The contrast between different materials, such as industrial container, corrugated metal sheet, and exposed wooden beams, generates a dynamic visual and tactile experience. Used with permission.

BIBLIOGRAPHY

About.com. 2010. *Local Foods: Regional Produce Seasonality Guides. Midwestern and Northeast Seasonal Fruits and Vegetables.* About.com. http://localfoods.about.com/od/searchbyregion /Search_Seasonal_Fruits_Vegetables_By_Region.htm.

ACME DIY.com. 2010. *Carpet, Indoor Air Quality and Your Health.* Flooring. Acme Parts.com. http://www.acmediy.com/flooring/carpet-health.php.

Adams, M. 2004. *Seasonal Affective Disorder Sufferers Need Natural Sunlight, Not Antidepressants or Artificial Light.* Natural News. http://www.naturalnews.com/001541.html.

Adhesives and Sealants Council. 2010. *Work, Health and Environmental Protection When Using Adhesives and Sealants.* Health and Safety. Adhesives.org. http://www.adhesives.org /HealthSafety.aspx.

Allen, E. 2004. *Fundamentals of Building Construction: Materials and Methods.* Hoboken, NJ: John Wiley & Sons.

Aller Air. 2009. *Home and Office Indoor Air Purifiers Featuring Activated Carbon and HEPA.* Aller Air Industries. http://www.allerair.com/.

Anderson, J., and N. Howard. 2000. *The Green Guide to Housing Specification: An Environmental Profiling System for Building Materials and Components Used in Housing.* Watford, UK: BRE Press.

Arieff, A., and B. Burkhart. 2002. *Prefab.* Layton, UT: Gibbs Smith.

ASHRAE (American Society of Heating, Refrigerating, and Air-Conditioning Engineers). 2010. *Indoor Air Quality.* http://www.ashrae.org/.

Baker-Laporte, P., E. Elliot, and J. Banta. 2001. *Prescriptions for a Healthy House: A Practical Guide for Architects, Builders and Homeowners.* Gabriola Island, BC, Canada: New Society Publishers.

Bas, E. 2004. *Indoor Air Quality: A Guide for Facility Managers.* Lilburn, GA: Fairmont Press.

Bauer, D., and S. Siddhaye. 2006. *EBM Roadmap Summary.* http://www.wtec.org/loyola/ebm/usws /ind_summary.htm.

BCIT (British Columbia Institute of Technology). 2009. *The Centre for Architectural Ecology: Collaborations in Green Roofs and Living Walls.* http://commons.bcit.ca/greenroof/.

BRE (Building Research Establishment and Cyril Sweett Sustainability and Cost Consulting Teams). 2005. *Putting a Price on Sustainability.* Watford, UK: BRE Trust Press.

Broadbent, G. 2006. *Eco-Architecture: Harmonisation between Architecture and Nature*, trans. C. A. Brebbia. Boston: WIT Press.

Buchholz, R. A. 1993. *Principles of Environmental Management: The Greening of Business.* Upper Saddle River, NJ: Prentice Hall.

CAC (Cement Association of Canada). 2010. *Cement Manufacturing.* http://www.cement.ca/.

Calkins, M. 2009. *Materials for Sustainable Sites: A Complete Guide to the Evaluation, Selection, and Use of Sustainable Construction Materials.* Hoboken, NJ: Wiley.

Cantor, S. L. 2008. *Green Roofs in Sustainable Landscape Design.* New York: W. W. Norton and Company.

Carpenter, W. J. 2009. *Modern Sustainable Residential Design.* Hoboken, NJ: John Wiley and Sons.

CCOHS (Canadian Centre for Occupational Health and Safety). 2008. *Noise: Auditory Effects.* http://www.ccohs.ca/oshanswers/phys_agents/noise_auditory.html.

CEC (Commission of the European Communities). 1999. *A Green Vitruvius: Principles and Practice of Sustainable Architectural Design*. London: James & James (Science Publishers).

Chan, Y. 2007. *Small Environments*. Gloucester, MA: Rockport Publishers.

Chen, K. 2004. "Housing Design for Elderly People Living with Their Family." Master's thesis, McGill University.

Chueca, P. 2009. *Sustainable Homes—USA*. Barcelona, Spain: Links.

CIMA (Cellulose Insulation Manufacturers Association). 2010. *The Greenest of the Green*. http://www.cellulose.org/CIMA/GreenestOfTheGreen.php.

CMHA (Canadian Mental Health Association). 2010. *Mood Disorders: Seasonal Affective Disorder*. http://www.cmha.ca/BINS/content_page.asp?cid=3-86-93.

CMHC (Canada Mortgage and Housing Corporation). 2000. *Practice for Sustainable Communities*. Ottawa: CMHC.

CMHC (Canada Mortgage and Housing Corporation). 2010. *Breathe Healthier Air in Your Home*. http://www.cmhc.ca/en/.

Craig, B., A. Bourassa, K. Ruest, D. Hill, and S. Marshall. 2004. *Indoor Air Quality in Interior Environments*. Ottawa: Canadian Mortgage and Housing Corporation.

CRI (Carpet and Rug Institute). 2009. *The CRI 2009. Residential Customers*. http://www.carpet-rug.org/.

Crowley, S., V. Patton, and J. Scott. 2008. "Environmental Defense Fund (EDF): Environmental Defense Fund Welcomes EPA Standards for Nonroad Gas Engines." http://www.edf.org/pressrelease.cfm?contentID=8370.

CSSBI (Canadian Sheet Steel Building Institute). 2008. *Environmental Fact Sheet: Steel and the Green Movement*. http://www.cssbi.ca/Eng/features/green.shtml.

De la Salle, J., and M. Holland. 2010. *Agricultural Urbanism: Handbook for Building Sustainable Food and Agriculture Systems in 21st Century Cities*. Winnipeg, Manitoba: Green Frigate Books.

DeBruyn, J., and D. Hilborn. 2010. *Anaerobic Digestion Basics*. Ontario Ministry of Agriculture, Food, and Rural Affairs (OMAFRA). http://www.omafra.gov.on.ca/english/engineer/facts/07-057.htm.

Dietsch, D. K. 2008. *Live/Work: Working at Home, Living at Work*. New York: Abrams.

Dunnett, N., and N. Kingsbury. 2008. *Planting Green Roofs and Living Walls*. Portland, OR: Timber Press.

EAESL. 2011. "Unglazed Solar Collector." In *Encyclopedia of Alternative Energy and Sustainable Living*. The Worlds of David Darling. http://www.daviddarling.info/encyclopedia/U/AE_unglazed_solar_collector.html.

Earth Charter Initiative. 2009. *The Earth Charter*. Earth Charter Initiative. Accessed April 29. http://www.earthcharterinaction.org/content/pages/Read-the-Charter.html.

Ecoworld. 2007. *Landfills vs. Recycling*. http://www.ecoworld.com/technology/landfills-vs-recycling.html.

Efficient Windows Collaborative. 2010. *Improving or Replacing Windows in Existing Homes*. http://www.efficientwindows.org/homesexisting.cfm.

Energy Saving Trust. 2006. *External Insulation for Dwellings*. http://www.servecommunity.ie/download.ashx?f=EST_CE118GPG293_External_insulation_for_dwellings.pdf.

Engineering Edge. 2010. *Air Filter Types and Application*. http://www.engineersedge.com/filtration/air_filter_types.htm.

Environment Canada. 2006. *Canada's 2006 Greenhouse Gas Inventory*. http://www.ec.gc.ca/pdb/GHG/inventory_report/2006/som-sum_eng.cfm.

Environment Canada. 2010. *Wise Water Use*. http://www.ec.gc.ca/eau-water/default.asp?lang=En&n=F25C70EC-1.

Environmental Illness Resource. 2010. *Sick Building Syndrome: Illness Information and Related Conditions*. http://www.ei-resource.org/illness-information/related-conditions/sick-building-syndrome-(sbs)/.

Farley, K., and J. Veitch. 2001. *A Room with a View: A Review of the Effect of Windows on Work and Well-Being*. Ottawa: National Research Council, Canada, IRC-RR-136.

FCM (Federation of Canadian Municipalities). 2004. *Solid Waste as a Resource: Guide for Sustainable Communities*. Ottawa: FCM.

Feng, X. 2000. "The Internet as a Choice and Marketing Tool for Affordable Housing." Unpublished Master's thesis, McGill University.

Fernandez, J. 2006. *Material Architecture: Emergent Materials for Innovative Buildings and Ecological Considerations*. Amsterdam: Elsevier.

Fischer, J. 2009. *Accessible Architecture: Age- and Disability-Friendly Planning and Building in the 21st Century*, trans. P. Meuser. Berlin: DOM.

Fisette, P., and D. Ryan. 2002. *Preserving Trees During Construction*. Amherst, MA: Building Materials and Wood Technology Center.

Foster, R. W., and J. Whitten. 2008. *Rain Screens Help Keep Water Out*. FacilitiesNet. http://www.facilitiesnet.com/windowsexteriorwalls/article/Rain-Screens-Help-Keep-Water -Out--8386.

Friedman, A. 2002. *The Adaptable House: Designing for Choice and Change*. New York: McGraw-Hill.

Friedman, A. 2007. *Sustainable Residential Developments: Design Principles for Green Communities*. New York: McGraw-Hill.

Fuad-Luke, A. 2004. *The Eco-Design Handbook*. London: Thames and Hudson.

Garcia, M. 2009. "Building Products Made of Recycled Materials in the North American Home Building Industry." Unpublished Master's report, McGill University.

GBES (Green Building Education Services). 2009. *LEED Green Associate Study Guide*. Lewisville, TX: Green Building Education Services.

Geotility. 2009. *Geothermal Systems: Cost Savings Advantage*. http://www.geotility.ca/cost_saving.html.

Gerlach, T. 2009. "Backyard Buffet: Your Landscaping Can Both Be Beautiful and Edible." *Flavor Magazine*. April/May 2009.

Gleick, P. 2010. *Turf Wars*. Circle of Blue: Reporting the Global Water Crisis. http://www.circleofblue.org/waternews/2010/world/peter-gleick-turf-wars/.

Gonzalo, R., and K .J. Habermann. 2006. *Energy-Efficient Architecture: Basics for Planning and Construction*. Boston: Birkhauser.

Green Living Tips. 2009. http://www.greenlivingtips.com/articles/185/1/Consumption-statistics.html.

GreenBuilding. 2010. *Indoor Air Quality*. http://www.greenbuilding.com/knowledge-base/ indoor-air-quality.

GreenRoofs. 2010. *Greenroofs 101*. http://www.greenroofs.com/.

Haghighat, F., and H. Huang. 2003. "Integrated IAQ Model for Prediction of VOC Emissions from Building Material." *Building and Environment* 38, no. 8 (August).

Halliday, S. 2008. *Sustainable Construction*. Amsterdam: Elsevier Architectural Press.

Hardwood Floors. 2006. *Linoleum Advantages and Disadvantages*. Buying Flooring. Hardwood Floors. http://www.yourhardwoodfloor.com/buying/linoleum.html.

Harvey, L. D. D. 2006. *A Handbook on Low-Energy Buildings and District-Energy Systems: Fundamentals, Techniques, and Examples*. Sterling, VA: Earthscan.

Hassanain, M., T. Froese, and D. Vanier. 2003. "Framework Model for Asset Maintenance Management." ASCE *Journal of Performance of Constructed Facilities* 17, no. 1: 51–64.

Haworth, D. P. 1975. "The Principles of Life Cycle Costing." *Industrialization Forum* 6, no. 3–4: 13–20.

Headwaters Resources. 2008. *Fly Ash for Concrete*. Resource Library. http://www.flyash.com/data /upimages/press/hwr_brochure_flyash.pdf.

Hegger, M., et al. 2006. *Construction Materials Manual*. Boston: Birkhauser.

HGTVpro. 2010. *Basement Floor Insulation: Installation, Tips and Best Practices.* http://www.hgtvpro.com/hpro/bp_insulation/article/0,,hpro_20150_3463250,00.html.

Hodges, T. 2010. *Public Transportation's Role in Responding to Climate Change.* Federal Transit Administration, US Department of Transportation. http://reconnectingamerica.org/assets /Uploads/publictransportationclimatechange2010.pdf.

House-Energy. 2011. *Baseboard Electric Heaters.* http://www.house-energy.com/Heaters/Electric -Baseboard.htm.

IAI (International Aluminum Institute). 2008. *Fourth Sustainable Bauxite Mining Report.* http://www.world-aluminium.org/cache/fl0000292.pdf.

ICF Consulting. 2005. *Determination of the Impact of Waste Management Activities on Greenhouse Gas Emissions: 2005 Update.* Toronto, Ontario: Environment Canada and Natural Resources Canada.

ICFA (Insulating Concrete Form Association). 2008. *Building with ICFs: About Insulated Concrete Forms.* http://www.forms.org/index.cfm/buildingicf.

International Energy Agency. 2008. *Worldwide Trends in Energy Use and Efficiency: Key Insights from IEA Indicator Analysis.* Paris: International Energy Agency.

Ireland, J. 2007. *Residential Planning and Design.* New York: Fairchild Publications.

Janis, R. R., and W. K. Y. Tao. 2009. *Mechanical and Electrical Systems in Buildings.* 4th ed. Upper Saddle River, NJ: Pearson Prentice Hall.

Johnston, D., and S. Gibson. 2008. *Green from the Ground Up.* Newtown, CT: Taunton Press.

Jones, L. 2008. *Environmentally Responsible Design: Green and Sustainable Design for Interior Designers.* Hoboken, NJ: John Wiley and Sons.

Katsoiyannis, A., P. Leva, and D. Kotzias. 2008. "VOC and Carbonyl Emissions from Carpets: A Comparative Study Using Four Types of Environmental Chambers." *Journal of Hazardous Materials* 152, no. 2: 669–76.

Keeler, M., and B. Burke. 2009. *Fundamentals of Integrated Design for Sustainable Building.* Hoboken, NJ: John Wiley and Sons.

Kennedy, J. F., M. G. Smith, and C. Wanek. 2002. *Natural Building: Design, Construction, Resources.* Gabriola Island, BC: New Society Publishers.

KGS (Kentucky Geological Survey). 2006. *Uses of Coal.* University of Kentucky. http://www.uky.edu/KGS/coal/uses_of_coal.htm.

Khatib, J. 2009. *Sustainability of Construction Materials.* Cambridge, UK: Woodhead Publishing.

Kibert, C. J. 1999. "The Promises and Limits of Sustainability." In *Reshaping the Built Environment: Ecology, Ethics and Economics*, edited by Charles J. Kibert. Washington, DC: Island Press.

Klimchuk, A. 2008. *Xeriscaping: Procedure, Analysis, and Recommendation.* The Living Home. http://www.thelivinghome.ca/index.php?option=com_content&task=view&id=117 &Itemid=159.

Kourik, R. 2004. *Designing and Maintaining Your Edible Landscape Naturally.* Hampshire, UK: Permanent Publications.

Kwok, A. G., and W. T. Grondzik. 2007. *The Green Studio Handbook: Environmental Strategies for Schematic Design.* Amsterdam: Elsevier Architectural Press.

LaMonica, M. 2008. *Revving Up Greener, Cleaner Lawn Mowers.* CNET Green Tech. http://news.cnet.com/8301-11128_3-10034038-54.html.

Lamontagne, J., and D. Brazeau. 1996. *Entretien et taille des jeunes arbres au Québec.* Saint-Laurent, Québec: Edition du Trecarre.

Lawlor, D., and M. A. Thomas. 2008. *Residential Design for Aging in Place.* New Jersey: John Wiley & Sons.

Lawlor, G., B. A. Currie, H. Doshi, and I. Wieditz. 2006. *Green Roofs: A Resource Manual for Municipal Policy Makers.* Ottawa: CMHC.

LiveRoof. 2010. "Prevegetated Hybrid Green Roof Systems." *Green Roof Basics and LEED.* http://www.liveroof.com/?parent=Green_Roof_Basics.

Low, N., et al. 2005. *The Green City: Sustainable Homes, Sustainable Suburbs.* New York: Taylor and Francis.

MA DEP (Massachusetts Department of Environmental Protection). 2002. *Recycling: Why People Participate; Why They Don't: A Barrier/Motivation Inventory: The Basis of Community-Based Social Marketing.* http://www.mass.gov/dep/recycle/reduce/crbdrop.pdf.

Mauritius EcoBuilding. 2008. *Roofs.* alive2green. http://www.ecobuilding.mu/design/1072-roofs.html (site discontinued).

McDonell, G. 2007. *Cooling: Options in Radiant. Modern Hydronics.* http://www.omicronaec.com/resources/options_in_radiant.pdf.

McDonough, W., and M. Braungart. 2002. *Cradle-to-Cradle: Remaking the Way We Make Things.* New York: North Point Press.

McKenzie-Mohr, D. 2000. "Promoting Sustainable Behavior: An Introduction to Community-Based Social Marketing." *Journal of Social Issues* 56, no. 3: 543–44.

Mehta, K. 2001. *Reducing the Environmental Impact of Concrete: Concrete Can Be Durable and Environmentally Friendly.* Farmington Hills, MI: Concrete International.

Meisel, A. 2010. *LEED Materials: A Resource Guide to Green Building.* New York: Princeton Architectural Press.

Mintz, J. 2009. *Building Integrated Photovoltaic Windows and Tiles Generate Electricity.* How to Save Electricity. http://www.howtosaveelectricity.net/building-integrated-photovoltaic/.

Morcos, N. 2009. "Exploring Small Residential Spaces." Unpublished Master's report, McGill University.

Nayab, N. 2010. *Renewable Energy from Landfills.* Bright Hub. http://www.brighthub.com/environment/renewable-energy/articles/75432.aspx.

Nebraska Energy Office. 2006. Fact sheet. http://www.neo.state.ne.us/home_const/factsheets/min_use_lumber.htm (site discontinued).

NFRC (National Fenestration Rating Council). 2005. About NFRC. http://www.nfrc.org/about.aspx.

NJ DEP (New Jersey Department of Environmental Protection). 2008. *Healthy Lawns and Healthy Environmental Initiative.* http://www.nj.gov/dep/healthylawnshealthywater/tech_team_6_12_08.pdf.

Nugon-Baudon, L. 2008. *Ecocitoyen á vous d'agir: énergie, eau, déchets.* Paris: Marabout.

Numbers, M. J. 1995. "Siting a House." *Fine Homebuilding* 93: 40–45.

OECD (Organization for Economic Cooperation and Development). 2004. *OECD Environmental Data Compendium 2004.* Paris: OECD.

OPET (Organisations for the Promotion of [clean and efficient] Energy Technologies). 2011. *Solar Results Purchasing.* Guaranteed Solar Results. http://www.teriin.org/opet/articles/art7.htm.

Optigreen. 2011. *Green Roof "Pitched Roof" Sedum 5–15˚.* Optigrün International. http://www.optigreen-greenroof.com/SystemSolutions/Pitched-Roof-S1a.html.

OR DOE (Oregon Department of Energy). 2008. "Slab Floor Edge Insulation." *Oregon Residential Energy Code.* http://www.oregon.gov/ENERGY/CONS/Codes/docs/ResPub_9.pdf.

Owens, L. B. 2008. "Groundwater: Pollution from Nitrogen Fertilizers." In *Encyclopedia of Water Science.* 2nd ed. doi:10.1081/E-EWS2-120010199.

Pantoja, A. H. 1983. "Site Planning for Low-Rise Housing, with Special Reference to Northern Climates." Unpublished Master's report, McGill University, School of Architecture.

Paschich, E., and J. Zimmerman. 2001. *Mainstreaming Sustainable Architecture.* Corrales, NM: High Desert Press.

PCA (Portland Cement Association). 2009. *Sustainable Development with Concrete.* http://www.concretethinker.com/Benefits.aspx.

Peck, S., and M. Kuhn. 2008. *CMHC Design Guidelines for Green Roofs.* http://www.cmhc.ca/en/inpr/bude/himu/coedar/loader.cfm?url=/commonspot/security/getfile.cfm&PageID=70146.

Perry, L. 2009. *Fuel-Efficient Lawns and Landscapes*. Accessed August 17. http://www.uvm.edu/pss/ppp/articles/fuels.html.

Portland Online. 2006. *Eco Roofs*. http://www.portlandonline.com/bps/index.cfm?a=114728&c=42113.

Prowler, D. 2008. *Sun Control and Shading Devices*. Whole Building Design Guide (WBDG). http://www.wbdg.org/resources/suncontrol.php.

PWGSC (Public Works and Government Services Canada). 2009. *The Environmentally Responsible Construction and Renovation Handbook*. http://www.tpsgc-pwgsc.gc.ca/biens-property/gd -env-cnstrctn/anna-13-eng.html.

Resilient Floor Covering Institute. 2009. *About Resilient Flooring: Technical Information, Standards, Environment*. http://www.rfci.com/.

Roth, E. 2005. *Efficiency of Thermal Power Plants: Why Thermal Power Plants Have Low Efficiency*. http://www.sealnet.org/s/9.pdf.

Sabnis, G. M., et al. 2005. *GreenHouse: The Energy Efficient Home*. Vol. 1. Washington, DC: Drylongso Publications.

Sacramento Hunger Commission. 2005. *The Edible Landscaping Toolkit*. http://www.communitycouncil.org/level-3/shc/EdibleLandscapingGuide.pdf (site discontinued).

Salthammer, T., and E. Uhde. 2009. *Organic Indoor Air Pollutants: Occurrence, Measurement, Evaluation*. Weinheim, Germany: Wiley-VCH.

Sassi, P. 2006. *Strategies for Sustainable Architecture*. New York: Taylor and Francis.

Schaeffer, J. 2005. *The Real Goods Solar Living Sourcebook: Your Complete Guide to Renewable Energy Technologies and Sustainable Living*. 12th ed. Gabriola Island, BC: New Society Publishers.

Scholz-Barth, K. 2001. "From Grey to Green: Environmental Benefits of Green Roofs." In *Planting Green Roofs and Living Walls*, edited by N. Dunnett and N. Kingsbury. 2008. Portland, OR: Timber Press.

SIPA (Structural Insulated Panel Association). 2009. *Green Building with SIPs*. http://www.sips.org/elements/uploads/fckeditor/file/SIPs%20 (site discontinued).

Smith, A. M., and D. A. Rakow. 1992. "Strategies for Reducing Water Input in Woody Landscape Plantings." *Arboricultural Journal* 18, no. 4 (July).

Smith, P. 2005. *Architecture in a Climate of Change: A Guide to Sustainable Design*. Amsterdam: Elsevier.

Smith, P. 2007. *Sustainability at the Cutting Edge: Emerging Technologies for Low-Energy Buildings*. Amsterdam: Elsevier.

Statistics Canada. 2005. *Human Activity and the Environment, Annual Statistics 2005, Solid Waste in Canada*. Ottawa: Minister of Industry.

Statistics Canada. 2010. *Figure 5. Proportion of Households by Housing Tenure and Age Group of Primary Household Maintainer, Canada, 2006*. http://www12.statcan.ca/census-recensement /2006/as-sa/97-554/figures/c5-eng.cfm.

Stein, B., and J. S. Reynolds. 2000. *Mechanical and Electrical Equipment for Buildings*. New York: John Wiley and Sons.

Stirling, C. 2009. *Warm, Cold; Vented, Unvented Roof Construction?* http://www.thenbs.com/topics /constructionproducts/articles/ventedUnventedRoofConstruction.asp.

Strongman, C. 2008. *The Sustainable Home: The Essential Guide to Eco-Building, Renovation and Decoration*. New York: Merrell.

TCEQ (Texas Commission on Environmental Quality). 2010. *The "Take Care of Texas" Guide to Yard Care*. http://www.tceq.state.tx.us/comm_exec/forms_pubs/pubs/gi/gi-028.html.

Texas Groundwater Protection Committee. 2006. *Groundwater Awareness Week*. http://www.tgpc.state.tx.us/Ground Water Awareness Week Mar2006 rev2.pdf (site discontinued).

Thomas, R., ed. 1996. *Environmental Design: An Introduction for Architects and Engineers*. 2nd ed. London: Spon Press.

Thomas, R., ed. 2005. *Sustainable Urban Design: An Environmental Approach*. London: Spon Press.

Trumbore, S. E., and J. B. Gaudinski. 2003. "The Secret Lives of Roots." *Science* 302, no. 21 (November). www.sciencemag.org.

Isover, 2011. "Plane—People—Prosperity: A New and More Global Approach for the Construction Sector.".Our Commitment to Sustainability. Isover. http://www.isover.com/Our-commitment -to-sustainability/Toward-sustainable-buildings/What-is-sustainable-construction.

UNEP/GRID-Arendal. 2002. *Municipal Solid Waste Composition*. United Nations Environment Programme (UNEP)/GRID-Arendal. http://maps.grida.no/go/graphic/municipal_solid_waste_ composition_for_7_oecd_countries_and_7_asian_cities.

UNEP/GRID-Arendal. 2008. "Boosting the 'Green House' Effect—CDM Reform Key to Climate-Friendly Building and Construction Sector." Press release. United Nations Environment Programme (UNEP)/GRID-Arendal. http://www.grida.no/news/press/3350.aspx? p=2 Saint-Gobain Group 2008.

US Census Bureau. 2009. "Americans Spend More Than 100 Hours Commuting to Work Each Year, Census Bureau Reports." Accessed May 1. http://www.census.gov/Press-Release/www/releases /archives/american_community_survey_acs/004489.html (site discontinued).

US Census Bureau. 2010. *Geographical Mobility: 2002–2003*. http://www.census.gov/prod/2004pubs/p20-549.pdf.

US DOE (Department of Energy). 2008. *Energy Efficiency Trends in Residential and Commercial Buildings*. http://apps1.eere.energy.gov/buildings/publications/pdfs/corporate/bt_stateindustry.pdf.

US DOE (Department of Energy). 2009. "Energy Efficiency and Renewable Energy." *Slab-on-Grade Insulation Foundation*. Energy Savers. http://www.energysavers.gov/your_home/insulation _airsealing/index.cfm/mytopic=11490.

US EIA (Energy Information Administration). 2009. *Table 2.2. Residential Sector Energy Consumption*. http://www.eia.doe.gov/emeu/mer/pdf/pages/sec2_5.pdf.

US EPA (Environment Protection Agency). 1997. "Chapter 6: Waste Generation." *Municipal Solid Waste Factbook*. http://www.p2pays.org/ref%5C03/02064/factbook/gen.htm#2.

USGBC (US Green Building Council). 2007. USGBC. http://www.usgbc.org/DisplayPage. aspx?CategoryID=19.

Water Furnace. 2010. *Earth Loops*. Water Furnace International. http://www.waterfurnace.com /earth_loops.aspx.

WaterSense. 2010. *Products*. US EPA. http://www.epa.gov/watersense/products/index.html.

Watson, R. D., and K. S. Chapman. 2002. *Radiant Heating and Cooling Handbook*. New York: McGraw-Hill.

WBCSD (World Business Council for Sustainable Development). 2008. *Osaka Gas: Combined Heat and Power Systems for Large and Small Users: Case Study*. http://www.wbcsd.org/DocRoot /WF8l0QIJsHwnSgc5v7Is/OsakaGasCHP.pdf.

Wenz, P. S. 2008. *Baby, It's Warm Inside, Thanks to Insulated Shutters*. SFGate.com. http://articles.sfgate.com/2008-01-19/home-and-garden/17151090_1_insulation-shutters-foam.

Werthmann, C. 2007. *Green Roof—A Case Study: The American Society of Landscape Architects*. New York: Princeton Architectural Press.

Which? 2010. "Boiler Reviews: Condensing Boilers Explained." *Reviews*. http://www.which.co.uk/reviews/boilers/page/condensing-boilers-explained/.

WHO (World Health Organization). 2010. *Indoor Air Pollution*. Programmes and Projects. http://www.who.int/indoorair/en/.

Wilson, A. 2006. *Your Green Home: A Guide to Planning a Healthy, Environmentally Friendly New Home*. Gabriola, BC: New Society Publishers.

Wilson, A. 2009. *Energy Solutions; Batt Insulation: Fiberglass, Mineral Wool, and Cotton*. Green Building Advisor. http://www.greenbuildingadvisor.com/blogs/dept/energy-solutions /batt-insulation-fiberglass-mineral-wool-and-cotton.

Winchip, S. M. 2007. *Sustainable Design for Interior Environments.* New York: Fairchild Publications.

Wood Energy. 2008. *Wood Gasification Technology.* Wood Energy USA. http://www.woodenergyusa.com/index.php?page=technology.

Woolley, T., and S. Kimmins. 2000. *Green Building Handbook.* Vol. 2. New York: Spon Press.

Yudelson, J. 2007. *Green Building A to Z: Understanding the Language of Green Building.* Gabriola Island, BC: New Society Publishers.

Zero Waste America. 2010. *Landfills: Hazardous to the Environment.* http://www.zerowasteamerica.org/Landfills.htm.

Zhao, J. 2001. "Intergenerational Living and Housing." Unpublished research report, McGill University.

ILLUSTRATION CREDITS

Figures not listed here are in the public domain or have been conceived, drawn, or photographed by the author and members of his research and design teams whose names are listed in the Acknowledgements. Every effort has been made to list all contributors and sources. In case of omission, the author and the publisher will include appropriate acknowledgement or correction in any subsequent edition of this book.

CHAPTER 1
Figure 1.1: Created by the author based on data from the International Energy Agency, 2008.
Figure 1.2: Created by the author based on data from the US Department of Energy, 2009.
Figure 1.3: Created by the author based on data from the International Energy Agency, 2008.
Figure 1.4: Created by the author based on data from the US Department of Energy, 2009.

CHAPTER 2
Figure 2.3: With permission of *Fine Homebuilding* Magazine © 1995, The Taunton Press Inc., Malcolm Wells, illustrator.
Figure 2.4: With permission of *Fine Homebuilding* Magazine © 1995, The Taunton Press Inc., Malcolm Wells, illustrator.
Figure 2.15: Based on a discussion with Jean Lamontagne of La Forêt de Marie Victorin design team.
Figures 2.20–2.24: With permission of Battersby Howat Architects.

CHAPTER 3
Figure 3.4: With permission of Document Bauart, www.bauart.ch.
Figure 3.5: With permission of Brian MacKay-Lyons, Architect; photographer Greg Richardson.

CHAPTER 4
Figures 4.13–4.17: With permission of © Lara Swimmer Photography.

CHAPTER 5
Figures 5.14–5.18: With permission of Bercy Chen Studio.

CHAPTER 6
Figure 6.3: Created by the author after Sassi 2006, Figure 4.3.1, with permission of Taylor and Francis Books, UK.
Figures 6.19–6.22: With permission of Marmol Radziner Prefab.

CHAPTER 7

Figure 7.6: With permission of Ali Tanha.

Figure 7.14: Created by the author based on data from the Commission of the European Communities, 1999.

Figures 7.17–7.21: With permission of Studio 804.

CHAPTER 8

Figure 8.6: With permission of Ali Tanha.

Figure 8.12: Created by the author based on an illustration by Alternate Heating Systems Inc. Published with permission.

Figure 8.17: With permission of Ali Tanha.

Figures 8.19–8.22: With permission of ZeroEnergy Design; photographs by Michael J. Lee Photography.

CHAPTER 9

Figure 9.10: With permission of Darren Petrucci, Architect; photographer Bill Timmerman.

Figure 9.12: Created by the author based on data from the Carpet and Rug Association.

Figures 9.14–9.18: With permission of Dwell Development.

CHAPTER 10

Figure 10.1: Created by the author based on data from Environment Canada, 2010, with permission.

Figures 10.13–10.17: With permission of Pugh + Scarpa Architects; photographer Marvin Rand.

CHAPTER 11

Figure 11.6: Bottom two photos with permission of Ali Tanha.

Figure 11.8: With permission of Ali Tanha.

Figures 11.15–11.19: With permission of Levitt Goodman Architects; photographer Ben Rahn, A Frame.

CHAPTER 12

Figures 12.16–12.19: With permission of Richard Wittschiebe Hand.

CHAPTER 13

Figure 13.5: Created by the author based on data from the Federation of Canadian Municipalities, 2004, with permission.

Figures 13.11–13.16: With permission of the Office of Mobile Design, a Jennifer Siegal Company.

CASE STUDY PROJECTS TEAM

CHAPTER 2. SITING A HOME

Gulf Island Residence
Battersby Howat
230-49 Dunlevy Avenue
Vancouver, British Columbia V6A 3A3
Canada

Principal Architects: David Battersby and
    Heather Howat
Team Member: Kathleen Robertson
Structural Engineer: Fast + Epp

CHAPTER 3. SUSTAINABLE RESIDENTIAL DESIGN CONCEPTS

The Next Home
Avi Friedman, Architect
McGill University, School of Architecture
815 Sherbrooke Street W., Montreal,
Quebec H3A 2K6
Canada

Team Members: Jasmin Fréchette, Cyrus Bilimoria, David
    Krawitz, Doug Raphael, R. Kevin Lee, and Julia Bourke
Builder: Fermco Industries Ltd.
Sponsors: Matériaux Cascades Inc., Canada Mortgage and
    Housing Corporation, Natural Resources Canada, Société
    d'habitation du Québec, IKEA Canada

CHAPTER 4. UNIT-PLANNING PRINCIPLES

Remington Court
HyBrid Architecture
1205 East Pike Street, Suite 2D
Seattle, Washington 98122
USA

Principal Architect: Robert Humble
Team Members: Joel Egan, Barrett Eastwood,
Nick Williams, Melissa Burchett, and Jonathan Lemons
Civil Engineer: Davido Consulting
Structural Engineer: Davido Consulting
Custom Carpentry: Sugar Hill
Builder/General Contractor: Hybrid Assembly

CHAPTER 5. CONSTRUCTING A HOME

Annie Residence
Bercy Chen Studio
1111 East 11th Street, Suite 200
Austin, Texas 78702
USA

Principal Architect: Thomas Bercy
Team Member: Calvin Chen

CHAPTER 6. BUILDING MATERIALS

Palms
Marmol Radziner Prefab
12210 Nebraska Avenue
Los Angeles, California 90025, USA

Principal Architects: Leo Marmol and Ron Radziner
Team Members: Brad Williams and Jared Levy
Structural Engineer: R. S. Tavares
Landscape Designer: Marmol Radziner Prefab

CHAPTER 7. ENERGY-EFFICIENT WINDOWS

Prescott Passive House
Studio 804
1465 Jayhawk Boulevard
Lawrence, Kansas 66044, USA

Team Members: C. J. Armstrong, Elizabeth Beckerle,
    Joshua Brown, William Doran, Colleen Driver, Laura
    Foster, Joel Garcia, Tyler Harrelson, Lauren Hickman,
    Aaron Jensen, Matthew Johnson, Daniel Lipscomb,
    Daniel Matchett, Jennifer Mayfield, Katherine Morell,
    and Tye Zehner

CHAPTER 8. HEATING AND COOLING SYSTEMS

English Residence
ZeroEnergy Design
348 Medford Street, Suite 1
Charlestown, Massachusetts 02129, USA

Principal Architect: Stephanie Horowitz
Team Members: Benjamin Uyeda and Jordan Goldman

Awards:

Finalist, 2010 Excellence in Design Awards by *Environmental Design + Construction* Magazine
LEED for Homes—Gold Certification
Energy Star—39 HERS Index

CHAPTER 9. HEALTHY INDOOR ENVIRONMENTS

18th Avenue South
Dwell Development
3916 South Americus Street
Seattle, Washington 98118
USA

Principal Architect: Julian Weber
Builder/Developer: Anthony Maschmedt
Green Rater: Tom Balderston, Conservation
Services Group

CHAPTER 10. WATER EFFICIENCY

Solar Umbrella
Pugh + Scarpa Architects
2525 Michigan Avenue, Building F1
Santa Monica, California 90404
USA

Principal Architect: Lawrence Scarpa
Team Members: Angela Brooks, Anne Burke, Vanessa
Hardy, Ching Luk, and Gwynne Pugh
Structural Engineer: Gwynne Pugh, Pugh + Scarpa
General Contractor: Above Board Construction

Awards:

AIA National Honor Award, 2007
AIA/COTE Top Ten Green Project, 2006
AIA Los Angeles Decade Award, 2006
AIA National Housing Award, 2006
Residential Architect Design Award, 2006
AIA California Council Award, 2005
AIA Los Angeles Honor Award, 2005
Record House Award, 2005

CHAPTER 11. GREEN ROOFS

Euclid Avenue House
Levitt Goodman Architects
533 College Street, Suite 301
Toronto, Ontario M6G 1A8
Canada

Principal Architect: Dean Goodman
Team Members: Danny Bartman and Janna Levitt
Green Roof Designer: Terry McGlade, Gardens in the Sky
Construction Managers: Boxko and Verity

Award:

OAA Award of Excellence, City of Toronto Green Award

CHAPTER 12. EDIBLE LANDSCAPING AND XERISCAPING

Ross Street House
Richard Wittschiebe Hand
3730 Ross Street
Madison, Wisconsin 53705
USA

Principal Architect: Carol Richard
Landscape Designer: Lisa J. Geer, LJ Geer Design
Mechanical Engineer/LEED Coordinator: Fred Berg
Structural Engineer: Diana Quinn, Diana Quinn Structural
LEED for Homes Provider: Mike Holcomb, Alliance for
Environmental Sustainability
Green Rater: John Viner, GDS Associates
Contractor: John Svenum and Tom Mcdonough

Award:

Future Landmarks Award (Madison Trust for
Historic Preservation)

CHAPTER 13. WASTE MANAGEMENT AND DISPOSAL

Seatrain Residence
Office of Mobile Design
1725 Abbot Kinney Boulevard
Venice, California 90291
USA

Principal Architect: Jennifer Siegal
Senior Designer: Kelly Bair
Team Member: Andrew Todd
Creative Director/General Contractor: Richard Carlson
Interior Designer: David Mocarski, Arkkit Forms
Landscape Designer: James Stone
Waterscape Designer: Jim Thompson
Water Features: Rik Jones, Liquid Works
Steel Fabrication: Don Griggs, Steel Man
Glass Fabrication: Gadie Aharoni, Penguin Construction
Artist: Phillip Slagter

CASE STUDY PROJECTS PHOTOGRAPHERS

CHAPTER 2. SITING A HOME

Gulf Island Residence
Photographer: Tom Arban, Tom Arban Photography

CHAPTER 3. SUSTAINABLE RESIDENTIAL DESIGN CONCEPTS

The Next Home
Photographer: Jack Galsmith

CHAPTER 4. UNIT-PLANNING PRINCIPLES

Remington Court
Photographer: Lara Swimmer, Lara Swimmer Photography

CHAPTER 5. CONSTRUCTING A HOME

Annie Residence
Photographer: Mike Osborne

CHAPTER 6. BUILDING MATERIALS

Palms
Photographer: David Lena, David Lena Photography

CHAPTER 7. ENERGY-EFFICIENT WINDOWS

Prescott Passive House
Photographer: Studio 804

CHAPTER 8. HEATING AND COOLING SYSTEMS

English Residence
Photographer: Micheal J. Lee, Micheal J. Lee Photography

CHAPTER 9. HEALTHY INDOOR ENVIRONMENTS

18th Avenue South
Photographer: Tucker English, Tucker English Photography

CHAPTER 10. WATER EFFICIENCY

Solar Umbrella
Photographer: Marvin Rand, Marvin Rand Photography

CHAPTER 11. GREEN ROOFS

Euclid Avenue House
Photographer: Ben Rahn, A Frame

CHAPTER 12. EDIBLE LANDSCAPING AND XERISCAPING

Ross Street House
Photographer: Zane Williams, Zane Williams Photography

CHAPTER 13. WASTE MANAGEMENT AND DISPOSAL

Seatrain Residence
Photographer: Office of Mobile Design

INDEX

Design principles
    configuration simplification, 51–53,
      51f, 52f
    floor stacking, 53–54, 53f, 54f
    interior space optimization, 58–60,
      58f, 59f, 60f
    joining units, 55–57, 55f, 56f
    modular dimensioning, 57–59, 58f
    Remington Court and, 61–64, 61f,
      62f, 63f, 64f
    size minimization, 51
Dieldrin, 202
Direct control zoning, 13
Disposal. *See* Waste management/disposal
  methods
District heating, 136
Dome-shaped structures, 52
Double glazing, 117, 118f, 119, 119f
Downcycling, 87
Drainage, 26–27, 27f, 188, 193
Drainage layers, 193
Dry cladding EWI systems, 69–70
Dry emissions, 153f, 154
Dual-flush toilets, 173
Dust emissions, 88
Dwell Development, 165

Earth-to-air cooling systems, 139–140
EcoBatt insulation, 165
EcoResidence housing, 6f
Eco-roofs. *See* Green roofs
Edible landscapes
    aesthetics and maintenance of, 202,
      203f
    communal, 209–210, 209f
    dwelling and, 206–209, 207f, 208f
    land form and water in, 206, 206f
    maintenance zones and, 203–204,
      204f
    overview of, 201–202, 201f
    soil and, 204, 205f
    species selection for, 202–203
    wind and, 204–206
Effectiveness, HVAC selection and, 127
Efficiency
    in framing and construction, 72–75,
      73f, 74f, 75f

    HVAC system selection and, 127
    prefabrication and, 76–77, 76f, 77f
18th Avenue South, 165–167, 165f, 166f,
  167f
Elderly, 33–37, 34f, 35f
Electric furnaces, 134, 135f
Electricity-based heating systems, 133f,
  134–139, 134f, 135f, 137f, 138f
Electrochromic windows, 120, 120f
Embodied energy, 85, 85f
Emissions
    aluminum and, 90
    cement and, 88
    incineration and, 220
    indoor air quality and, 153–154, 153f
    landfills and, 218–219
    from lawn maintenance equipment,
      200–201
    steel and, 92–93
Energy and atmosphere section of LEED-
  H, 8
Energy consumption trends, 1–3, 2f, 3f
Energy Star certification, 3, 8–9
Engineered wood, 95, 95f
English Residence, 144–146, 145f, 146f
Envelopes (building), 51, 51f, 65–66, 66f,
  67f
Erosion, prevention of, 26
Euclid Avenue House (Toronto), 194–197,
  194f, 195f, 196f, 197f
Evacuated-tube solar collectors, 129f, 130,
  131f
EWI systems. *See* External wall insulation
  systems
Exfiltration, windows and, 114
Expanded polystyrene (EPS) insulation,
  78, 96–97, 100
Extensive green roofs, 185f, 187–188
External wall insulation (EWI) systems,
  69–70

Faucets, 172, 174, 174f
Fauna
    green roofs and, 187–188, 197, 197f
    siting a home and, 22–25, 23f, 24f,
      25f
Fertilizers, 200

Island Press | Board of Directors

DECKER ANSTROM *(Chair)*
Board of Directors
Comcast Corporation

KATIE DOLAN *(Vice-Chair)*
Conservationist

PAMELA B. MURPHY *(Treasurer)*

CAROLYN PEACHEY *(Secretary)*
President
Campbell, Peachey & Associates

STEPHEN BADGER
Board Member
Mars, Inc.

MARGOT ERNST
New York, New York

RUSSELL B. FAUCETT,
CEO and Chief Investment
Officer, Barrington Wilshire LLC

MERLOYD LUDINGTON LAWRENCE
Merloyd Lawrence, Inc.
  and Perseus Books

WILLIAM H. MEADOWS
President
The Wilderness Society

DRUMMOND PIKE
Founder, Tides
Principal, Equilibrium Capital

ALEXIS G. SANT
Managing Director
Persimmon Tree Capital

CHARLES C. SAVITT
President
Island Press

SUSAN E. SECHLER
President
TransFarm Africa

VICTOR M. SHER, ESQ.
Principal
Sher Leff LLP

SARAH SLUSSER
Executive Vice President
GeoGlobal Energy LLC

DIANA WALL, PH.D.
Director, School of Global
Environmental Sustainability
  and Professor of Biology
Colorado State University

WREN WIRTH
President
Winslow Foundation

Alamance Community College
Library
P.O. Box 8000
Graham,NC 27253